YALE STUDIES IN ENGLISH
RICHARD S. SYLVESTER, EDITOR
VOLUME 165

WILLIAM EDMONDSTOUNE AYTOUN

AND

THE SPASMODIC CONTROVERSY

BY

MARK A. WEINSTEIN

NEW HAVEN AND LONDON
YALE UNIVERSITY PRESS, 1968

To My Dear Wife

PREFACE

Aytoun has not been neglected. His friend and collaborator, Theodore Martin, published a *Memoir of William Edmondstoune Aytoun* in 1867. It is the work to which one must go for the facts of Aytoun's life, but, as Martin emphasized, it does not attempt to evaluate Aytoun's literary significance. In 1898, Rosaline Masson published a long essay on Aytoun which turns out to be little more than a condensation of Martin's book. In 1921, Frederick Page edited the *Poems of William Edmondstoune Aytoun* for the Oxford University Press. Recently, Aytoun has begun to attract attention again. In 1957, Robert Schweik wrote his doctoral dissertation at Notre Dame on *Selected Reviews of William Edmondstoune Aytoun;* he printed ten of Aytoun's literary reviews and wrote an introductory essay for each of them. In 1963, Erik Frykman published a study of Aytoun's literary beliefs and academic career, *W. E. Aytoun, Pioneer Professor of English at Edinburgh,* and, in 1964, W. L. Renwick edited a selection of satirical writings in *W. E. Aytoun: Stories and Verse.* The present study, however, is the first, full-scale attempt to show Aytoun's importance in Victorian literature.

I especially thank the late William C. DeVane for suggesting this subject and helping me along the spasmodic way; the trustees of the National Library of Scotland for allowing me to publish Aytoun's letters; the firm of William Blackwood and Sons Ltd. for the publication and sales records of Aytoun's works; Erik Frykman for permission to quote from *W. E. Aytoun, Pioneer Professor of English at Edinburgh; The New Yorker* for permission to quote from John Updike's "Beerbohm and Others"; and my excellent typist, Frances Weinstein.

M.A.W.

New York, New York
1966

CONTENTS

THE PRE-SPASMODIC YEARS (1813–50)

EARLY LIFE

William Edmondstoune Aytoun was born on the first day of summer in 1813. He had the good fortune to be the youngest of three children, and the only boy, of a prosperous Edinburgh family. His lifelong love of humor and literature developed early:

> As a child he was quick, intelligent, hot in temper, but easily restored to good-humour. He was also very fond of fun, being, as Erasmus says of Sir Thomas More, "from a child so delighted with humour, that he seemed even born for it." A picture of him, when four years old, at his father's side, by John Watson Gordon, shows his little deep-set eyes twinkling with humour, and a well-defined mouth, highly expressive of good-nature. His imagination was, from the first, lively; and the legends current in every Scottish nursery in those days took a strong hold upon him . . . . His love of reading was very early shown, and a book was his constant companion. When about the age of nine or ten he would stretch himself, with a volume of the Scott novels, on the hearthrug, face downwards, for hours, and shout and scream with delight over the humour of the characters.[1]

Later in life, Aytoun claimed that a year never passed without his having reread all of Scott's novels.

His mother's influence underlay much of his personality. She was early left an orphan and spent her youth with her granduncle,

---

1. Theodore Martin, *Memoir of William Edmondstoune Aytoun* (Edinburgh and London, William Blackwood and Sons, 1867) , pp. 6, 11.

Alexander Keith of Ravelstone. He trained her to read him works of a kind and range far beyond the usual studies of a young lady, and she stored up the prose and poetry in her memory. Mrs. Keith was the grandaunt of Walter Scott, who was a constant visitor at Ravelstone;[2] thus, Scotland's most important literary figure, and the most important model for Aytoun's serious literary endeavors, became the friend of Mrs. Aytoun. She and Anne Scott were intimate, and, when Lockhart was compiling his biography, he went to Mrs. Aytoun for anecdotes of Scott's youthful days. It is almost certain that she related the same anecdotes of Scotland's national idol to her own small son.

She herself was a fierce Jacobite, her kindred having supported the Pretender in 1715 and 1745, and a lover of ballad poetry, and her son William inherited her political and literary preferences. In Aytoun's autobiographical novel, *Norman Sinclair,* the hero describes his foster mother, Eppie Osett, as follows:

> So the day went by swiftly, and when evening came, and all were gathered round the fire, many a tale and ballad, not then collected, but familiar through tradition to the peasantry, was recited for our wonder and delight. Eppie Osett, in respect of minstrel learning, would have put Ritson or Leyden to shame. She could not only repeat such fine historical ballads as "The Battle of Otterburn" and "Sir Patrick Spens," but she knew by heart most of the beautiful romantic ditties current on the Border, and she gave them forth with an animation and even pathos that produced the strongest effect upon her simple audience.[3]

Roger Aytoun, the poet's father, was a partner in one of the leading firms of Writers to the Signet in Edinburgh—Youngs, Aytoun, and Rutherford. Successful in business, he could offer his family two homes: Abercromby Place in the north of Edinburgh, and the country estate of Murieston, a property of 200 acres, fourteen miles west of the capital. The latter was far more popular with the future poet; "situated in one of those glens which are so common in that romantic pastoral district" and

2. Ravelstone became the model for Scott's castle of Tullyveolan in *Waverly.*
3. William Edmondstoune Aytoun, *Norman Sinclair* (3 vols. Edinburgh and London, William Blackwood and Sons, 1861), *1,* 16.

untouched as yet by civilization, it appealed to the boy's historical and romantic imagination: "there it was that I first became conscious of the beauty of external nature; where I plucked the gowan, and purple thyme, and yellow crow-foot from the mountain sward." [4]

Roger Aytoun combined his financial advantages with a broad interest in intellectual pursuits. In practical terms, this took the form of a careful consideration and planning of his son's education. From 1821 to 1824, William had a private tutor to prepare him for entrance into the new Edinburgh Academy. The first name on the share list for the projected academy, dated November 28, 1823, is that of Roger Aytoun, W.S. Indeed, in the old records of the school, Roger Aytoun's name always appears second among those of fifteen locally prominent men; first is the name of Walter Scott.

Scott, of course, made the principal address at the opening of the Edinburgh Academy on October 1, 1824. He told his young auditors that there was

> a class in this institution which was not to be found in any similar academy—a class for the study of English literature. It had been justly remarked that the study of classics had sometimes led to the neglect of our own language, and that some scholars could express themselves better in Latin than in English. To avoid this error, a teacher was added to the institution, who was to instruct the boys in the principles of English composition, and to connect with this a knowledge of the history of their own country. He would have the youths taught to venerate the patriots and heroes of our own country, along with those of Greece and Rome; to know the histories of Wallace and Bruce, as well as those of Themistocles and of Caesar; and that the recollection of the fields of Flodden and Bannockburn should not be lost in those of Plataea and Marathon . . . . And when you are come to manhood . . . happy will it be for you if you can say, "I have followed that which I heard." May you do so and live! [5]

4. Ibid., p. 14.

5. Rosaline Masson, *Pollok and Aytoun* (Edinburgh and London, Oliphant Anderson and Ferrier, 1898), p. 98.

Listening were many of the eminent citizens of Edinburgh: the
"Man of Feeling," Henry MacKenzie, Jeffrey, Cockburn, and
Horner. Perhaps the most impressed, however, was one of the
new students, the eleven-year-old William E. Aytoun, who was
later to reestablish "a class for the study of English literature"
at Edinburgh University and whose serious poetry was to deal
with "the fields of Flodden and Bannockburn."

Aytoun soon discovered that the curriculum was still basically
classical. In his first year he studied the *Aeneid*, the Charterhouse
Rudiments of Greek, Sandford's Greek Extracts, the Greek Testa-
ment, the Odes of Anacreon, and Murray's English Reader. He
finished sixth in a class of twenty, but failed to win a prize for
"particular merits." Afterward, his ranking always remained
about the same, but he never again failed to win a special prize.
In his second year he was the "Best Reciter," and in his third
he composed the "Best English Verses"; "Moses bringing water
from the rock" is the earliest specimen we have of Aytoun's
poetic work:

> O Thou! to whom celestial strains belong,
> Divine Urania! fraught with heavenly song,
> Deign, though enshrined above the heavenly sky,
> To view my labour with approving eye.
> For thine the power, by God peculiar given,
> To raise the soul, to lift the thoughts to heaven.
> Assist and guide me from the realms of day,
> And cast around me one propitious ray.

The thirteen-year-old poet was in a class which had just read the
first nine books of *Paradise Lost*. He closed out his final year at
the Academy by taking the special prizes for both "Best English
Verses" and "Best Latin Reciter." The English verses are on
"The Battle of Salamis," and his class was evidently hard at work
at Greek:

> There is a land where spring eternal reigns,
> And sweetest flow'rets deck the verdant plains—
> Where through pure fields of light the zephyrs rove,
> Charged with the fragrance of the spicy grove—

Where smiles the sun with pure attempered ray,
As once he beamed on Eden's earliest day:
That land is Greece—once at that magic sound
Would thousand glorious heroes rise around,
Wave their bright falchions o'er their heads, and cry,
"That is my native land, a Grecian I."

Such prize poems contain echoes of his school reading, not altogether unskillful, but without any individual merits of their own. Unfortunately, this same criticism can be leveled against too much of Aytoun's more mature verse.

The next logical step was Edinburgh University, and Aytoun entered it on a full-time basis in 1828.[6] He himself was later to gain fame as one of its leading professors and, in an address to the graduates of 1863, described in glowing terms his own enthusiastic entrance into the university. In truth, Aytoun the fifteen-year-old student felt far less enthusiasm than Aytoun the fifty-year-old teacher looking back on the student. The truer picture is presented in the fictional *Norman Sinclair:*

For my part, looking back on my early years, I can discern nothing in my school life worthy of being narrated; nor do my first university experiences suggest any important memorabilia. Like most Scottish students of the time, I acquired a good knowledge of Latin, a smattering of Greek, and a considerable stock of general information, increased by private reading of a desultory kind, which was of far more use to me than anything I learned in the schools. My uncle's library was but a poor one; but in it I found the plays of Shakespeare, Anderson's edition of the British Poets, the works of the elder novelists, and the histories of Hume and Gibbon. These I perused with absorbing interest, to the neglect, I must confess, of the mathematical and metaphysical treatises which ought to have engrossed my attention; but on that account I cannot truthfully say that I have any tears to shed. I never took kindly to mathematics; partly because the practical use of that study was not explained to me, and partly because I could see nothing in it to interest the imagination.

6. He matriculated in 1827 and took one class that year, at the age of fourteen.

Metaphysics I detested. The science appeared to me an
elaborate diabolical invention for mystifying what was clear,
and confounding what was intelligible.[7]

These likes and dislikes never changed during his later life.

Aytoun at the university was repeating his performance at the
academy: while going about his assigned tasks in rather un-
spectacular fashion, he was devoting himself to the cultivation of
his voice and his poetry. He became a member of the Speculative
Society, where he learned the art of public speaking. He learned
the art well, for he was later to return to this same university
as professor of rhetoric and also was to become one of the most
popular lecturers in Scotland. His chief concern, however, was
already with poetry.

POLAND, HOMER, AND OTHER POEMS

Amid normal school activities, the Speculative Society, and long
holiday rambles throughout Scotland, Aytoun found time to
write a small volume of poetry. He finished the poems in 1830,
at the age of seventeen, but they were not published until 1832.
The costs of publication were apparently assumed by Roger
Aytoun, for in a later letter to his father concerning the possible
publication of his translation of *Faust,* the young author writes,
"I should by no means like to publish it at my own risk, as
Blackie has somewhat confidently done—but perhaps Longman
would *go half,* or make some other arrangement, which has not
only the effect of preventing, but makes them take a real
interest in the tale, which I know by experience to be indispen-
sable." [1] The 117-page volume, entitled *Poland, Homer, and
Other Poems* and published anonymously, contains six poems:
"Poland," the major work, which takes up one-half of the book;
"Homer," which forms one-quarter of the volume; two short
poems, "A Lament for Percy Bysshe Shelley" and "Ode to the
Past"; and two sonnets, "Shadows of Recollection" and "The
Mausoleum."

7. Aytoun, *Norman Sinclair, 1,* 49.
1. Letter of Feb. 24, 1834. Footnotes in this form indicate that I am quoting
from my own microfilms of Aytoun's letters, the great majority of which are unpublished.

In the liberal thirties in Britain, considerable public sympathy was aroused by the Poles' struggle to regain their independence from autocratic Russia. The poet Campbell founded an association in London which for many years was the chief support of the exiles who sought shelter in Britain. Many of the exiles, including their leader Prince Czartoryski, took refuge in Edinburgh, and some were frequent visitors at 21 Abercromby Place. Young Aytoun, who met them there, dedicated his first published work to Prince Czartoryski and made a major poetic effort in "Poland."

This poem remains the chief anomaly in Aytoun's literary and political careers, which are otherwise remarkable for their consistency. In form, "Poland" shows the influence of the eighteenth-century poets. It is written in heroic couplets of the Popean kind. The young Aytoun explodes monosyllabic rhymes and emphasizes the effect still further by continual end-stopping. His inability to handle the form is most obvious in the many scenes of violence and excitement where he is unable to produce a sense of movement and continuity. Other less essential faults also reveal the young poet's incapacity. The reader grows weary of such repetitions as "Alas! Alas!" "Back-back," "for shame! for shame!" "awake! awake" and tautological repetitions such as, "How can a brother e'er forget a brother?/You were the children of the self-same mother." [2] There is also too much use of expletives and too little variety in the handling of the iambic pentameter line, all combining to give the impression of a mechanical production of ten-syllable verses.

In later years, Aytoun was to scorn the eighteenth century as artificial and turn to the more congenial ballad measure. When he reluctantly gave Theodore Martin a copy of this early volume in 1844, he inscribed on it: "To Theodore Martin, with tears and penitence. William E. Aytoun. O mihi praeteritos referet si Jupiter annos!" [3] Otherwise, he never mentioned this work but occasionally dropped revealing innuendos in his prose articles in *Blackwood's*. For example, without apparent provocation, in

2. Anonymous [Aytoun], *Poland, Homer, and Other Poems* (London, Longman, Rees, Orme, Brown, Green, and Longman; and Edinburgh, Black, 1832) , p. 29.
3. Martin, *Memoir,* pp. 33–34.

1857 he writes, "Some men shrink with horror from the sight of their early manuscripts, and would proffer a larger ransom than the Sibyl demanded of Tarquin, so that they could see them burning." [4] The chief reason for Aytoun's violent reaction against "Poland," however, lies not in its form, but in its content.

Aytoun had committed what he was later to call "the original sin of radicalism." [5] Structurally, "Poland" is composed of three sections. In the first, the poet addresses the "Spirit of Freedom" and then various European countries; he begs the latter to foster Liberty. In the second, he presents the guilty dreams of the Czar of Russia, the oppressor of the Poles. Finally, there is a depiction of the ultimate reign of the Spirit of Freedom. The whole production appears rather mechanical. For instance, the first section is little more than a series of vocatives: "Spirit of Freedom" and then twenty lines of poetry, "O thou poor country" and thirty lines, "O Europe! Europe!" then O France, Britain, and so on. Within this framework is found a textbook of radicalism, somewhat reminiscent of *Queen Mab*. The present world is unjust and miserable; the coming world will be perfect. The great events of the past were the American and French Revolutions; the great heroes were Brutus, Cato, Attila the Hun, and Tyrtaeus. Conversely, titles such as "king" and "aristocracy" are, somewhat contradictorily, evil and meaningless formulas. It is all too obvious that the young Aytoun became intoxicated with the revolutionary ideas of the exiled Poles during the exciting days of the English Reform Bill and must have presented a disgusting spectacle to the mature Aytoun, champion of the Conservative party during its most difficult years.

In order to emphasize Aytoun's change in political thought, it is revealing to glance at a prose article which is typical of what he later wrote for *Blackwood's:*

> With the old partition of Poland we have nothing now to do, any more than with the junction of the Slavonic provinces with Austria. Right or wrong, these have long become acknowledged facts in European history, and the boundary

4. *Blackwood's, 81* (1857), 363.
5. Ibid., *70* (1851), 220.

divisions have been acquiesced in by a congress of the as-
sembled nations. We cannot go back upon matters of ancient
right and occupation; were we to do so, the peace of every
nation in Europe must necessarily be disturbed, and no alternative would remain, save the Utopian one of parcelling
out territory according to the language of the inhabitants.
Boundaries must be settled somehow. They were so settled,
by the consent of all the nations, at the treaty of Vienna; and
our duty, as well as our interest, is to adhere to that arrangement.[6]

The chief models for the seventeen-year-old author of "Poland"
were Byron and Shelley, or, more specifically, the serious freedom-
fighter Byron and the radical visionary Shelley, in ascending order
of importance. Of the several passages in the poem which call
Byron to mind, here is one of the less embarrassing:

> Seest thou that dying soldier on the ground,
> Whose life is ebbing from a ghastly wound?
> He hath no bed except the frozen snow,
> No friend to wipe the death-damp from his brow;
> His eye is struggling through the mist afar
> To catch the glimmer of that feeble star;
> Why doth he seek its light so faint and dim?
> It is no star of hope, alas, to him!
> Ay—but it shineth on his quiet home,
> That nest of peace, where war hath never come;
> Within his fancy, even now he sees
> The old thatch'd roof beneath the linden trees,
> The cradle, where his youngest infant sleeps,
> Rock'd by his widow'd wife, who bends and weeps;
> He sees his children that around her kneel,
> And try to calm the grief they cannot feel. (pp. 38–39)

This certainly seems to have been suggested by the famous
Gladiator passage in the fourth canto of *Childe Harold*.[7] It is
Shelley, however, whose influence is continually felt, both in
the general movement of the poem from misery and wrong to

6. *Ibid.*, *66* (1849), 591–92.
7. Lines 1252–68.

redemption on earth and in various expressions and turns of
thought.

> Peace shall descend from Heaven, and banish'd love
> Shall haunt again the mountain and the grove;
> Again at shut of eve, and dawn of morn,
> The low sweet notes of blessing shall be borne,
> Like rich and fuming incense shall they rise,
> Earth's grateful tribute to the smiling skies:
> The serpent, Hate, shall find some cavern deep,
> And coil itself to everlasting sleep:
> And Fear shall die, and Death itself grow mild. (p. 58)

"Poland" is thus Aytoun's one radical poem, a poem which
postulates perfect bliss in a utopian future; in all of his other
poetry he will look to the past for greatness and consolation. Yet,
even in "Poland," there are scattered indications of Aytoun's
essential bias. When the youthful poet calls on the nations of
Europe to aid Poland, he bids them remember battles long ago.
He asks the English to recall the famous landmarks in their
history. The past represents for him a tradition of nobility and
virtue:

> Another Alfred, come to lead us back
> Unto our ancient and deserted track;
> To bring again those unforgotten days,
> When virtue only won the meed of praise. (p. 15)

This emphasis on the past becomes more preponderant in the
other poems of the volume.

Still experimenting with verse forms, Aytoun tried ottava rima
in "Homer." Unfortunately for the young poet, this form requires
considerable dexterity in the handling of rhymes, and it forced
him into several awkward situations. Again, there are too many
expletives and exclamations of "alas." A new difficulty develops
from the large number of inversions which unnecessarily compli-
cate the author's meaning, a difficulty that may be due to the
desperate search for rhyme words.

The structure of the poem is circular: Homer grows up on a
sequestered isle in the Aegean sea where he has magnificent

poetic visions, travels to the Greek mainland where he gains
fame through his stirring lays, and returns to the isle to die.
Throughout the poem, Homer is played off against his brother,
who leads an ordinary domestic existence; this allows the author
to rhapsodize over the superiority of a life dedicated to poetry,
which alone lives forever and can give immortal fame to its
creator. In addition, in the digressions, which take up as much
space as the narrative, the glorious life of the Greek poet is contrasted with present-day lives of pride and triviality. The author
complains about the current age and praises the past:

> O happy days! when there were none to mar
>   The gush of feeling in its sunny morn;
> When no invidious lips waged rancorous war,
>   Or struck down genius with the blow of scorn;
> On every forehead now some graven scar,
>   Cut in by secret jealousy, is borne;
> No heart can open but 'tis chilled or crost,
> As buds are smitten by the nightly frost.
>
>   .   .   .
>
> Or is it, that because the world is old,
>   The hearts of men are waxing older too;
> So that each lay, however sweetly told,
>   Dies in its birth, because it is not new?
> Why then to them the very sun is cold,
>   And the mere sky has lost its glorious hue—
> Ay, and their dull philosophy can see
> No wonder in the strangest mystery!
>
> In the dark oven of their minds they parch
>   All nature's brilliant colours into one;
> They marvel nothing at the seasons' march,
>   They speak not of the rise or set of sun;
> They can dissolve the rainbow's glorious arch,
>   They count the stars within their garrison;
> They drag to day the secrets of the tomb,
> And call it light where it is deepest gloom! (pp. 82–83)

Some of the fundamental beliefs of the mature Aytoun are beginning to emerge clearly. He turns to the "happy days" of the
past with their "gush of feeling." Now, very unlike Shelley, he has
little use for modern science; instead, more in the manner of
Keats, he distrusts metaphysics, astronomy, geology—whatever
has a tendency to explain the glories of the universe. This distrust
will find its final expression in *Firmilian*.

The next two poems restate the themes of "Homer" and show
that "Poland" is the exception in this volume. "A Lament for
Percy Bysshe Shelley" employs the Spenserian stanza, perhaps because Shelley himself used this form for his elegy on Keats. The
poem is not, however, about Shelley; it is a restatement of Aytoun's
ideas about life and fame. Throughout the poem, Shelley is identified with the bright ages of Greece and Rome; like Homer, he
wrote poetry to merit eternal renown, while most people waste
themselves for gain and gold:

> Fame is the sole elixir, that can give
> Life and eternity! It is the part,
> Poet, that thou didst choose; within the mart
> Of this wide world that precious merchandise
> Is rarely sought or found. (p. 103)

Shelley was unfortunate in not having lived in the glorious past:

> Thine eye was like thy heart—thou could'st not view
> The burdens under which we struggle on,
> And not lament; men blindly come and strew
> Thorns for our naked feet, and for their own;
> The earth sends up a universal groan
> Beneath its own oppression;—thou wert made
> For those bright ages that have long since gone,
> When love was virtue, virtue had no shade—
> Alas! that man's faint heart hath let those ages fade! (p. 104)

The "Ode to the Past," as the title indicates, states most explicitly the basic theme of the entire volume. The virtue and
nobility of the "bright ages" are contrasted with the vice and
sordidness of the present.

The reviews of this thin, anonymous volume were not numerous but were uniformly favorable. Such praise, surprising at first sight, is perhaps attributable more to fervor over the Polish cause than to the intrinsic merits of the poetry. The *Eclectic Review* begins:

> The word Poland falls upon the imagination like a knell, but that knell has awaked the slumbering spirit of poetry, which, in these beautiful and soul-stirring numbers, seems to have started up with the vigour conferred by sleep.[8] So thrilling an air has not for a long time been heard from the Spartan fife; and though the time is gone by, when swords leaped from their scabbards at the voice of either bard or orator, all that poetry can do, by kindling a passionate sympathy, in these days of sober reason and political calculation, this new system may hope to achieve.[9]

And the *New Monthly Magazine* writes:

> There is a great deal of true and beautiful poetry, and much enthusiasm in the cause of freedom in this little volume: but alas for Poland! What signify our songs and sayings if we only incite her sons to combat in order to look tamely on while they perish in the death struggle? Far better had it been to have left them in their old repose than rouse them to an impotent effort, which, unaided, could only end in riveting their chains more firmly.[1]

Even more surprising to the modern reader are the comparisons which are drawn between Shelley and Aytoun, with all of the advantage going to the seventeen-year-old:

> A "Lament for Percy Bysshe Shelley" betrays the school from which our poet has sprung, but which he already so far transcends, that we hope he will shake off its fatal trammels. The most extraordinary attribute of Shelley's mind, though unquestionably a man of high and original genius, was the fascination he seems to have exerted over minds superior to

8. This rather dubious metaphor probably derives from Aytoun's repeated call to the nations of Europe to awake.

9. *The Eclectic Review*, 7 (1832), 444–45.

1. *The New Monthly Magazine* (1832), Pt. 3, p. 302.

his own, and the passionate admiration with which he inspired his votaries, rather than his companions. The "Ode
to the Past," in the present volume, is a finer poem, in our
humble judgement, than any of Shelley's compositions that
we have seen; and we have only to regret that it is slightly
tinctured with his melancholy and cheerless philosophy.[2]

The *Monthly Review* also regrets the damaging influence of Shelley: "The stanzas on Homer are also respectable, but with respect
to those on poor Shelley, we fear that, like his own productions,
they are too mystic, too etherialized to be generally understood." [3]
Obviously, Shelley was yet to attain his great reputation with the
Victorians.[4]

Despite the favorable critical reception, *Poland, Homer, and
Other Poems* did not sell, partially because the publishers had no
financial stake in the volume and consequently did nothing to
push it. Corresponding with his sister Margaret a year after publication, Aytoun, not at all depressed by public apathy, wrote, "I
forgot in my last to tell my mother what to do with my immortal
work—I leave it entirely to her discretion—She may get as many
boarded copies as she can, from Black [5] and you may distribute
them right and left to any one who will take them." [6]

SEEKING A LIVELIHOOD

After his studies at Edinburgh University had been completed,
Aytoun became an articled clerk in his father's firm. The firm of
Youngs, Aytoun, and Rutherford was the solicitor and political
agent of the Duke of Hamilton, a prominent Whig, and thus
Aytoun became engaged in the Lanarkshire election which immediately preceded the passing of the Reform Bill. He worked
for his father's firm only because it was the sole respectable opportunity open to him. He complains in a letter to his father that
each man encounters one science which he can never master, and

2. *The Eclectic Review,* 7 (1832), 450–51.
3. *The Monthly Review,* 2 (1832), 302.
4. For other favorable notices of *Poland, Homer, and Other Poems,* see *The
Gentleman's Magazine, 102* (1832), 537, and *The Metropolitan, 4* (1832), 11.
5. Adam Black, the Edinburgh publisher.
6. Letter of June 22, 1833.

that his "stumbling-block is most unfortunately the profession which is just at my feet," the law.[1] In 1832, no alternative seemed available, but soon Aytoun was to make strenuous efforts to enter a more compatible profession. In the meantime, he had little difficulty in reconciling his conscience to his small efforts on behalf of the Reform Bill, for even in his mature days of unbending Conservatism, he admitted the Tories had been unjust and unwise in delaying such needed change.

The men who knew Aytoun well are unanimous in their testimony as to the strength of his Conservatism, a Conservatism so deep that it seemed constitutional.[2] Professor Lorimer, a colleague at Edinburgh University, writes of him:

If any man forgot his position, whether that position was acquired or inherited, whether it was above his own position or below it, his endurance was at an end. Other faults of conduct he viewed like other honest men,—but faults of this class,—impudence, insolence, want of self-respect and respect for others, were faults which subtended, so to speak, a larger angle of moral vision with him than with other people. It was not so much that disorderly conduct of this kind displeased him and made him angry, as that it disgusted him; it seemed to offend his very bodily organs, and far from reciprocating it, or responding to it in mind, he fled from it or thrust it from him as if it had been an outrage on his person. The feelings I have described, as the feelings of all of us do, modified Professor Aytoun's opinions, both social and political; and they even account, if I mistake not, for some important occurrences of his personal history. Once aware of their strength, so far from wondering that he became a Conservative, or doubting the reality or distrusting the motives of his conversion, I have always felt that it would have been impossible for him throughout life to have avoided going in the direction in which his sympathies from the first must have impelled him so decidedly. From his abhorrence for rudeness and all that was disorderly and anarchic in social

1. Letter of Dec. 28, 1833.
2. See Martin, *Memoir*, p. 77 and passim.

intercourse, it naturally followed that he attached a very high value to social organization, to the existence, I mean, of the various classes into which society is arranged in old historical countries, and to the traditional rules by which these distinctions are maintained.[3]

This conservatism was already well on its way to final crystallization in the early 1830s. It must have been a strong feeling which made him tell his loved and respected Whig father in 1833 that the Edinburgh Whigs "collectively and individually are altogether impotent and contemptible." [4] In the following year, he complained of Lord Gray and praised the King to his father, whom he accused of having written "treasonable" articles against the House of Lords.[5] In 1836, Aytoun was to begin his connection with *Blackwood's Edinburgh Magazine,* the outspoken champion of Conservatism.

After a few months in London in the offices of Mr. McDougall, learning the procedure in Scottish appeals and the rudiments of Parliamentary business, Aytoun obtained permission from his father to go to Aschaffenburg on the Main to study the German language and literature. Caught, like Scott, between the conflicting claims of law and literature, Aytoun was gradually deciding to devote himself to the Muse. His letters and those of his teacher, Professor Merkel, indicate that he remained a dedicated student throughout his seven months in Germany, although the temptations to relax his diligence, often strong with a young man in a foreign land, must have been especially powerful in Aytoun's case. This twenty-year-old was exceptionally good-looking: a well-knit body, clear complexion, light brown hair, and, according to Theodore Martin, "what most claimed observation was the play of humour about a full and good-natured mouth, and the merry inward light that danced in his small but expressive eyes." [6] Most observers, however, would focus on the massive curve of that lower jaw—jaw of determination! [7] In addition, he grew "a very

3. James Lorimer, *Studies—National and International* (Edinburgh, William Green and Sons, 1890) , pp. 19–20.

4. Letter of Nov. 7, 1833.

5. Letter of Feb. 24, 1834.

6. Martin, *Memoir,* p. 31.

7. A bust of Aytoun by Patrick Park is reproduced opposite the title page of Martin's *Memoir.*

fierce pair of mustachios . . . though a little of the Dixie dialect still cleaves to my tongue." [8] Yet, despite the lures which his youth, attractiveness, and ready wit might have been expected to call into being, Aytoun continued to "lead a lonely and philosophic life, doing little else than reading German." [9] His only references to women are facetious remarks on the enormous mouths and feet of the German ladies.

His letters from Germany deal with his growing interest in German literature and his impatience with the thought of law. He writes to his mother that "I have been chiefly occupied with translating Goethe's Faust into English verse, which is a difficult task but Merkel vows the translation to be excellent . . . . I have had more time here than perhaps at any former period of my life to cultivate my mind by reflection and by study." [1] Two months later, he tells his father that he would like to have the translation published, for, although his immediate concern must unfortunately be the law, his ultimate objective is a literary career. Furthermore, he feels that publication will support his "push" in the future for the chair of belles lettres in Edinburgh University. [2] The translation of *Faust* was never published because four others were already available before Aytoun returned to London, but, eleven years after this letter to his father, he did become professor of rhetoric and belles lettres in the University of Edinburgh.

Aytoun thought that this period of intensive study and reflection in Germany formed one of the turning points of his life, and this opinion is echoed by his old school friend, George Makgill:

> After being with Merkel some time, Aytoun came to visit me at Frankfurt, and I remember being much struck with the change a few months had produced in the vigour and development of a tone of thought which then plainly showed itself as genius. I remember, too, his enthusiasm about Tieck, whose works he had just read, and which seem to have opened to him, as I suppose they do to every one, a new state of existence. [3]

8. Letter of July 13, 1833.
9. Letter of Dec. 15, 1833.
1. Ibid.
2. Letter of Feb. 24, 1834.
3. Martin, *Memoir*, pp. 48–49.

Returning to Scotland in April 1834, Aytoun submitted to the desires of his father and the dictates of practicality and resumed work with Youngs, Aytoun, and Rutherford. Having passed the necessary examinations, he became a Writer to the Signet in 1835, in which capacity he remained until 1840, when, his father's business declining, he became a member of the Scottish Bar. Successful here, as in every one of his multifarious undertakings, Aytoun had one of the largest criminal practices in Scotland by 1852.[4]

Simultaneously, he began to struggle to establish a literary reputation. In February 1836, he writes a guarded letter to *Blackwood's:*

> Gentlemen,
>   I take the liberty of enclosing you an article, which I hope you may find suitable for the Magazine, and am,
>
> > Your most obed. Sert.,
> > William E. Aytoun [5]

The contribution was accepted, and the changed address and tone of Aytoun's next letter indicate that the future "No. 1" writer for *Blackwood's* was already on friendly terms with his employers:

> My Dear Blackwood,
>   I enclose you a very beautiful touching and classical ballad of my own manufacture, fit to be sung under the influence of the moon by all lovesick and deserted maidens, but as the gods have not made your Magazine poetical of late, I suppose this goes to the Balaam box like other soul searching ditties,
>
> > Yours fraternally,
> > William E. Aytoun [6]

These early efforts were original poems and ballads and translations of the German ballads of Uhland, Romaic ballads, and the twenty-second book of *The Iliad*. The latter, done in dashing trochaics, gains a certain interest because of the praise it evoked

4. Letter of Feb. 28, 1852.
5. Letter of Feb. 5, 1836.
6. Letter of Mar. 16, 1836.

from a careful student of the classics, Aytoun's future political enemy, William Gladstone.[7]

In addition, three independent prose works by Aytoun were published in the early 1840s—two pamphlets on topical religious controversies and a full-length historical biography. In *Our Zion: or Presbyterian Popery*, by Ane of that Ilk (1840), Aytoun, although an Episcopalian, predicts and fights against the disruption of the Scottish National Church. The other pamphlet, *The Drummond Schism Examined and Exposed* (1842), is the only explicit record of Aytoun's religious beliefs and serves as an index of his general trend of thought. As in politics, Aytoun's primary concern in religion is the maintenance of order; he always argues for discipline and belittles talk of individual insight and consequent independence. Speaking of Drummond, he says:

> Is he not clearly a contemner of the Canons, of Church authority, and of discipline—an Independent, in short, who having entered the Church, will submit to no curb whatever? Vows of obedience, to those who entertain such lax views, are no stronger than bonds of straw—they are no better than fuel, at all times ready to be sacrificed at the altar of that darling idol, "private judgment." These are not harsh words. Either the discipline of a Church is to be maintained, or it is to be broken. If every one is to be allowed to follow out his own whims and crotchets in defiance of constituted authority and written law there is an end of the Church. I am almost weary of this theme, for the proposition is so self-evident, that I cannot conceive how any person endowed with the ordinary faculty of reasoning can question it, or evade it, except by side winds and high-flown phrases, which sound well but signify nothing.[8]

Just as in a well-regulated country there must be a gradation of ranks up to king, so in the Church there must be a bishop to whom the officiating child of the Church is responsible.[9] Aytoun's general trend of thought is consistent throughout the particular

7. Letter of Jan. 16, 1862, from Gladstone to Aytoun.
8. A Layman of the Church, *The Drummond Schism Examined and Exposed* (Edinburgh, R. Grant and Son, 1842), p. 17.
9. Ibid., pp. 24–25.

areas—politics, religion, society, literature—to which he devotes himself. He struggles for the time-honored, that which rests upon a broad empirical basis; he distrusts the new, the individual.

The Life and Times of Richard the First (1840) has a twofold purpose: "to keep Richard personally in view throughout" and "to give as clear and distinct, and, at the same time, as particular a narrative, of the principal events which occurred at home and abroad during the reign of the Lion-hearted monarch." [1] Not an important biography, it does help us to understand Aytoun's tenor of thought. Richard is an ideal subject for Aytoun. First, he is a king, and this allows the biographer to include some of his own cherished beliefs, such as the belief that the doctrine of divine right has been sanctioned by "the tacit consent of ages." [2] Second, Richard is a "fertile subject of romance and song," [3] the kind of subject Aytoun loved to read about and which he himself later attempted to create. Finally, Richard is the hero in history, a figure who dominates circumstances; Aytoun uses such a belief in the hero in his own *Lays of the Scottish Cavaliers*.

The complementary purpose of depicting the age also offered quite a congenial subject to the author. In all of Aytoun's serious writing from this point on, he turns to the past, usually to a past of violent action. Here violence abounds in plenty, but the moralist is always present to warn the people of his own time that revolution cannot be tolerated:

> All internal changes in the administration of a country should be approached with extreme caution; for though it is easy to launch a stone from the top of a precipice by the mere exertion of a finger, it may baffle human strength to arrest its progress when once set in motion . . . . No one but a fool will deny that change is sometimes necessary; but it is only in peaceful seasons and prosperous times that such a task can be attempted with safety, or brought to conclusion without the chance of disastrous failure. [4]

1. William Edmondstoune Aytoun, *The Life and Times of Richard the First* (London, T. Tegg, 1840) , p. vii.
2. Ibid., p. 262.
3. Ibid., p. 106.
4. Ibid., p. 348.

The well-written volume was ignored by the reviewers and attained no popularity; it merely remained No. 72 in John Murray's *Family Library* series. Aytoun had not yet established his literary reputation, but he was soon to become coauthor of one of the most popular books in early Victorian literature.

EARLY CAREER

THE BON GAULTIER BALLADS

The Victorian age is the first great period of English parody and
burlesque [1]—and understandably so. Being derivative, parody depends for its success upon the nature of belles lettres. The poets
of the first half of the nineteenth century provided the raw materials for the parodists; Romanticism called into being the Conservative no, the exposé, the snicker. The centrifugal nature of
the poetic movement in the first half of the nineteenth century
precludes any simple classification, but the period is certainly
marked by experimentation with poetic forms, the cult of the
individual, a new emphasis on subjectivity and analysis, and the
emergence of exceptionally individual voices and personalities.
To several classically trained and conservative critics, retaliation
lay in parody.[2] Parody became criticism in motion.

Two of these critics, William Edmondstoune Aytoun and Theodore Martin, published a *Book of Ballads* in 1845 under the
pseudonym, Bon Gaultier.[3] Martin deceptively declares in 1867
that "It was precisely the poets whom we most admired that we
imitated the most frequently. This was not certainly from any
want of reverence, but rather out of the fulness of our admiration,

1. Burlesque imitates the style of an original for purposes of topical humor.
Parody concentrates on both the style and thought of the original. In practice, the
distinction between the two is often fine indeed.

2. It is no coincidence that so many Victorian parodists were classical scholars
living at Oxford and Cambridge.

3. The name comes from the prologue of the first book of Rabelais: "A moy
n'est que honneur et gloire d'estre dict et repute Bon Gaultier et bon compaignon;
en ce nom, suis bien venu en toutes bonnes compaignies de Pantagruelistes."

just as the excess of a lover's fondness often runs over into raillery of the very qualities that are dearest to his heart." [4] On the other hand, George Kitchin, the author of the authoritative work on English parody and burlesque, begins his discussion of these ballads with the assertion, "Never have parodists more consciously striven to correct the bad taste of their day." [5] He ends by speaking of "the deliberate crusade its authors intended against inferior literary manners." [6] The contradictory claims of Martin and Kitchin can, in some cases, be reconciled. Aytoun and Martin, for instance, did admire Tennyson and Elizabeth Barrett but disliked the exaggerated romantic sensibility of "The May Queen" and the pretty romance tricks of "The Rhyme of the Duchess May" and so held these individual performances up to ridicule. Still, Martin's statement is indefensible when applied to most of the parodies. In the social sphere, for example, the brutal depiction of America is motivated by a serious desire to censure the moral standards of that supposedly violent country. In the literary sphere, Aytoun's whole career was a battle against the elements parodied in *The Book of Ballads:* the obscurity and impiety of Robert Montgomery, the spasmodic exclamations and egotism of the hero of "Locksley Hall," the softness of Leigh Hunt. Aytoun, at least, was the serious moralist in this book—but so was Martin. Dropping his earlier disguise, he writes in the preface to the 1903 edition, "Like most of the papers on which we subsequently worked together, the object was not merely to amuse, but also to strike at some prevailing literary craze or vitiation of taste. I have lived to see many such crazes since. Every decade seems to produce one." [7] He then describes, for ten pages, the duty parodists must perform in guarding public taste and morality.

Although *The Book of Ballads* failed to prevent successive literary "crazes," it did make an impression on the nineteenth century. Saintsbury characterized it as "that admirable book of light verse, the equal of anything earlier and certainly not surpassed

4. Martin, *Memoir,* p. 63.

5. George Kitchin, *A Survey of Burlesque and Parody in English* (Edinburgh and London, Oliver and Boyd, 1931), p. 290.

6. Ibid., p. 295.

7. *The Book of Ballads,* ed. Bon Gaultier (16th ed. Edinburgh and London, William Blackwood and Sons, 1903), p. vii.

since," [8] and other Victorian critics were almost as enthusiastic.[9] Today, in an age of close parody, Bon Gaultier's humor seems too broad; he is didactic rather than aesthetically sensitive. Still, it is difficult to overrate the historical importance of the book.[1] *The Book of Ballads* marks the beginning of the popularity of parody and burlesque in Victorian England. Because of its enormous scope, it served as a sort of textbook for later parodists; Bon Gaultier showed what subjects could be legitimately and successfully exposed to laughter. *The Book of Ballads* includes imitations of national ballads, the Eastern tale, the philosophical poem, the reflective poem, the "poetical puff," the epigram, thieves' literature, young ladies' literature, and, of course, the leading stylists of the day. Kitchin calls the collection "a mannequin's parade of Victorian modes." [2]

Furthermore, the very success of the volume must have encouraged subsequent parodists to continue in the genre. Bon Gaultier proved the existence of a large public with enough understanding of serious poetry to snicker a little at it. Nothing of the kind had been known in the literary world since the *Rejected Addresses* of James and Horace Smith, published a generation before.[3] *The Book of Ballads* ran through thirteen editions from 1845 to 1877 in England alone; the number of pirated editions in America, despite the vicious satire leveled against this country, was at least as large.[4] The firm of William Blackwood and Sons, after it had finally gained control of *The Book of Ballads* from W. S. Orr and Company, sold over 32,000 copies from 1857 to 1909. This total includes neither the popular first four editions

8. Masson, *Pollok and Aytoun,* p. 153.

9. See J. H. Millar, *A Literary History of Scotland* (New York, Charles Scribner's Sons, 1903), pp. 593–95; Hugh Walker, *The Literature of the Victorian Era* (Cambridge, Cambridge University Press, 1910), pp. 332–33; and James Hannay, "Recent Humorists: Aytoun, Peacock, Prout," *The North British Review, 45* (1866), 82.

1. See Saintsbury, *The Cambridge History of English Literature* (Cambridge, Cambridge University Press, 1953), *13,* 161–62.

2. Kitchin, p. 295.

3. The Bon Gaultier performance is greater—in conception, in quantity, and in quality. Cf. the Smiths' "Living Lustres" and Bon Gaultier's "Bard of Erin's Lament," both parodies of Tom Moore.

4. Three of the piratical American publishers were J. S. Redfield, W. J. Wittleton, and Worthington Co.

nor the numerous pirated ones. The first edition of 1845 contained 39 ballads. Because of their popularity, the second edition in 1849 had 51, and the third edition, also published in 1849, contained 53. The fourth contained 54, and this number remained standard until the sixteenth, the last edition published during Martin's lifetime, which had 56 ballads and an illuminating preface by Martin.[5] Five different American editions all have the same 52 ballads.

These ballads represent, however, only a small remnant of an enormous comic scheme. In the pages of *Tait's* and *Fraser's* magazines from 1841 to 1845, there were many Bon Gaultier articles, in which appeared prose parody and burlesque, social criticism, serious literary discussion, coarse jokes, and the many ballads and songs from which the eventual *Book of Ballads* was composed. These articles had a unity of their own. One, for instance, was a review, with extracts, of the *Topaz,* "the quintessence of all possible Annuals," and it attempted to demolish "those periodical visitants of our drawing rooms and boudoirs." Another was entitled "Lays of the Would-Be Laureates" and contained poetic applications for the post left vacant by the death of Southey. Naturally, when selections were made for book publication, the original design was largely effaced, and *The Book of Ballads* lost most semblance of unity. Aytoun and Martin, however, did their best to relate various groups. One section contains three Spanish ballads, another five American; seven examples of the "puff poetical" appear together, and the central section on "The Laureate's Tourney," containing six poems, is taken over from "Lays of the Would-Be Laureates." No prose parodies appear.

Even more detrimental to the final unity of the book is the considerable difference in talent between the coauthors. Martin had a plodding assiduity which made him one of the most prolific translators and biographers of the Victorian age,[6] but which also prevented his verse from acquiring much bite. His individual venture in parody and burlesque, "Flowers of Hemp; or, The Newgate Garland," a thieves' anthology, is a terribly heavy affair.

---

5. All of my quotations will be from *The Book of Ballads,* ed. Bon Gaultier, (5th ed. Edinburgh and London, William Blackwood and Sons, 1857).
6. Victoria knighted him for his five-volume biography of Albert.

Aytoun, who balances his seriousness and critical insight with humor and mimetic ability, carries *The Book of Ballads*. Of the six parodies from the volume which have been frequently anthologized, five are known to be definitely his.[7]

The most frequently employed tactic in the volume is the familiar one of surprise through incongruity. A well-known style is used casually, and then, suddenly, a vulgarization produces a ludicrous effect. Here, the man of common sense exposes the romantic whiner, a favorite target, taking Tennyson's "May Queen" as the example:

The Biter Bit

The sun is in the sky, mother, the flowers
    are springing fair,
And the melody of woodland birds is stirring
    in the air;
The river, smiling to the sky, glides onward to
    the sea,
And happiness is everywhere, oh mother, but with me!

They are going to the church, mother,—I hear
    the marriage bell;
It booms along the upland,—oh, it haunts me
    like a knell;
He leads her on his arm, mother, he cheers
    her faltering step,
And closely to his side she clings,—she does,
    the demirep!

They are crossing by the stile, mother, where we
    so oft have stood,
The stile beside the shady thorn, at the corner
    of the wood;
And the boughs, that wont to murmur back the
    words that won my ear,

7. "The Broken Pitcher," "The Queen in France," "The Massacre of the Mac-Pherson," "La Mort D'Arthur," and "The Lay of the Lovelorn." The authorship of "The Biter Bit" is unknown.

Wave their silver blossoms o'er him, as he
    leads his bridal fere.[8]

He will pass beside the stream, mother, where first
    my hand he pressed,
By the meadow where, with quivering lip, his
    passion he confessed;
And down the hedgerows where we've strayed
    again and yet again;
But he will not think of me, mother, his broken-
    hearted Jane!

He said that I was proud, mother,—that I
    looked for rank and gold;
He said I did not love him,—he said my
    words were cold;
He said I kept him off and on, in hope of
    higher game,
And it may be that I did, mother; but who
    hasn't done the same?

I did not know my heart, mother,—I know
    it now too late;
I thought that I without a pang could
    wed some nobler mate;
But no nobler suitor sought me,—and he
    has taken wing,
And my heart is gone, and I am left a lone
    and blighted thing.

You may lay me in my bed, mother,—my
    head is throbbing sore;
And, mother, prithee let the sheets be duly
    aired before;
And, if you'd do a kindness to your poor
    desponding child,

8. The first edition reads: "Now bend their blossoms o'er him as he leads his
bridal fere."

> Draw me a pot of beer, mother, and, mother,
>   draw it mild!

Certainly it has always been the function of the parodist to bring
the Romantic down from the stratosphere, but characteristically
Bon Gaultier smashes the young lady to earth with a terribly
violent thud. According to Kitchin, this parody "became the jest
of the day." [9]

Next, Bon Gaultier favored the parody of greater verisimili-
tude. He imitates with some exactness the style of an individual
author or of a school of writing, but pushes the peculiarities of
that style just beyond the edge of acceptability. Here is the beginning of "Francesca Da Rimini," a parody of Leigh Hunt and,
by association, the early John Keats:

> Didst thou not praise me, Gaultier, at the ball,
> Ripe lips, trim bodice, and a waist so small,
> With clipsome lightness, dwindling ever less,
> Beneath the robe of pea-y greeniness?
> Dost thou remember, when with stately prance,
> Our heads went crosswise in the country dance;
> How soft, warm fingers, tipp'd like buds of balm,
> Trembled within the squeezing of thy palm;
> And how a cheek grew flush'd and peachy-wise
> At the frank lifting of thy cordial eyes?
> Ah me! that night there was one gentle thing,
> Who, like a dove, with its scarce feather'd wing,
> Fluttered at the approach of thy quaint swaggering.

The general critical favorite in *The Book of Ballads* was "The
Queen in France," a burlesque of the ancient Scottish ballad as
applied to Queen Victoria's recent visit to France. Aytoun had
known and mastered the ballad technique early,[1] and, in this
labor of love, he picks off one familiar device after another:

> The Queen was sitting at the cards,
>   The King ahint her back;

9. Kitchin, *A Survey of Burlesque and Parody in English,* p. 294.
1. In the same year (1843) in which this imitation first appeared, Aytoun's own
ballads, "The Burial March of Dundee" and "Charles Edward at Versailles," caught
the public fancy.

> And aye she dealed the red honours,
> And aye she dealed the black.

In fact, in his desire to include all of the familiar ballad devices, Aytoun imitates the form in everything but length, "The Queen in France" being inordinately long for the ancient type. Still, it has been called "the best parody ever made upon the style of the old Ballads." [2]

Most popular with the public was another parody of a literary genre. "The Massacre of the MacPherson," in imitation of the Celtic lyric, has that spirited exuberance and emphatic rhythm which, once the poem catches on, assure continued popularity:

> Fhairshon swore a feud
>> Against the clan McTavish;
> Marched into their land
>> To murder and to rafish;

> For he did resolve
>> To extirpate the vipers,
> With four-and-twenty men
>> And five-and-thirty pipers.

Furthermore, the whole is relatively short and lends itself to memorization. Millar, writing sixty years later, claimed it was still widely known, and Whyte, at about the same time, predicted it would be a joy forever. [3]

Aytoun wrote the above two parodies with what Martin called "the excess of a lover's fondness." Generally, however, when he mimicked a literary genre, he acted as a public guardian against what he considered degraded taste. Few of these parodies retain much relevance today, although those directed against the debased offspring of the Byron-Moore Eastern school still read well. [4]

Since Aytoun was to become the author of *Firmilian* in another ten years, it is pertinent to ask whether *The Book of Ballads*

2. Millar, *A Literary History of Scotland*, p. 595. See also *The Westminster Review*, 62, (1854), 111, and Whyte, *Poets and Poetry of the Century*, 9, 390.

3. Millar, *A Literary History of Scotland*, p. 594, Walter Whyte, *The Poets and the Poetry of the Century*, ed. A. H. Miles (10 vols. London, Hutchinson and Co., 1898), 9, 390. See also Hannay, "Recent Humorists," p. 79.

4. See "Eastern Serenade" and "The Cadi's Daughter."

foreshadows the role Aytoun was to play in the Spasmodic controversy. In other words, are there any resemblances between Bon
Gaultier and T. Percy Jones? "The Lay of the Lovelorn" does
mimic the rhythm of "Locksley Hall" with consummate skill,
from the roll of the grand trochaics down to the unexpected
caesuras. In addition, the parody *almost* copies stanzas from the
original:

> Fool! again the dream, the fancy! But I know
> 　　my words are mad,
> For I hold the grey barbarian lower than
> 　　the Christian cad.

Bon Gaultier occasionally departs from the original, however, in
order to employ his favorite tactic of attributing his hero's
romantic rhetoric to a rather undistinguished cause:

> Whether 'twas the sauce at dinner, or that
> 　　glass of gingerbeer,
> Or these strong cheroots, I know not, but I
> 　　feel a little queer.

Bon Gaultier's triumph here, like T. Percy Jones' in *Firmilian*,
is in setting his hero loose on his own strain of passionate rhetoric,
leading inevitably to Spasmodic nonsense:

> There the passions, cramped no longer, shall
> 　　have space to breathe, my cousin!
> I will wed some savage woman—nay,
> 　　I'll wed at least a dozen.[5]
>
> There I'll rear my young mulattoes, as
> 　　no Bond Street brats are reared:
> They shall dive for alligators, catch the
> 　　wild goats by the beard—
>
> Whistle to the cockatoos, and mock the
> 　　hairy-faced baboon,
> Worship mighty Mumbo-Jumbo in the
> 　　Mountains of the Moon.

5. An anticipation of sec. xiv in *Firmilian*, which parodies *Festus*.

I myself, in far Timbuctoo, leopard's blood
     will daily quaff,
Ride a tiger-hunting, mounted on a
     thorough-bred giraffe.

Fiercely shall I shout the war-whoop, as
     some sullen stream he crosses,
Startling from their noonday slumbers
     iron-bound rhinoceroses.

In his preface of 1903, Martin proudly claims that he had heard
Aytoun's parody "quoted through the years up till now almost
as often as the original poem." [6] On the other hand, Dwight
Macdonald, in a recent book on parody, complains that the shafts
in "The Lay of the Lovelorn" "miss the vital spot." [7] Expressing
the modern ideal in parody, he desires a close artistic imitation of
the particular poem "Locksley Hall." Aytoun, however, was more
concerned with stifling, in the interests of society, the tendencies
of a particular literary type, the antisocial young man who raves
about injustice on a cosmic plane. This young man of "Locksley
Hall" anticipates in important respects that other nameless hero
of *Maud*, about whom the Spasmodic controversy was to rage.

    Aytoun abhorred the obscurity, the implied impiety, and the
unpoetic quality of Philip James Bailey's *Festus* and attacked
them in critical articles and in *Firmilian*. Bailey, however, attained his enormous popularity after 1845, so Bon Gaultier's
victim had to be Robert Montgomery, who was a dominant
figure in the early 1840s in a way almost incomprehensible today; [8]
the familiar excuse of a lack of good poets at the time seems
irrelevant in his case. He combined in his poetry all of Bailey's
weaknesses without any of his compensating strengths: he had a
poor ear and could not sustain poetic passages; he was often
unintelligible; his Satan seems riduculous; and he himself often

----

6. Martin, in *The Book of Ballads* (16th ed.) , p. xxi.

7. Dwight Macdonald, ed., *Parodies: An Anthology from Chaucer to Beerbohm—
and After* (New York, Random House, 1960), p. xii.

8. See Douglas Bush, *Mythology and the Romantic Tradition in English Poetry*
(New York, Pageant Book Co., 1957) , p. 265.

appears too egotistical. Consequently, it is not surprising to find that lines from Bon Gaultier's "Montgomery" anticipate Aytoun's later parody of Bailey and the Spasmodics:

> There are who move so far above the great,
> Their very look disarms the glance of hate;
> Their thoughts, more rich than emerald or gold,
> Enwrap them like the prophet's mantle's fold.

After the first edition of *The Book of Ballads,* Bon Gaultier added another parody of Montgomery in an attempt to expose his Spasmodic qualities to ridicule.[9]

Several types of prose parody appear in the original magazine articles by Bon Gaultier. The parodies of novelists are most frequent, and they resemble the verse parodies in their rather broad hits. They, too, come right at the beginning of the Victorian tradition of humor, antedating Thackeray's *Novels by Eminent Hands.* Aytoun again makes the more significant contributions, the best being "David Hagart, a Romance in Three Epochs, by the author of Jack Sheppard"[1] and *Endymion; or a Family Party of Olympus,* an imitation of Disraeli's early manner. In the latter, Aytoun accomplishes the seemingly impossible: he burlesques burlesque, and it was thought good enough to be reprinted by Eric Partridge in 1927.[2] More important, however, as anticipations of the Spasmodic controversy are the prose parodies of the literary critic. David Twaddles, for example, the "author" of *Reminiscences of Grub Street,* spouts forth the most ridiculously eulogistic praise of Jonas Smifzer's *The Blind Old Milkman.*[3] No particular critic seems to be the object of attack here, but the parody resembles in principle the later parodies that Aytoun was to write against the eulogizer of the Spasmodics, George Gilfillan.

Finally, in the serious literary discussions of these articles, one can already see the two positions forming which were to divide the Victorian world of letters into two antagonistic camps in

9. "The Death of Space."

1. Ainsworth, not DeFoe.

2. Eric Partridge, ed., *Ixion in Heaven and Endymion,* Disraeli's Skit and Aytoun's Burlesque (London, Scholartis Press, 1927).

3. *Tait's,* 9 (1842), 241.

the 1850s. Bon Gaultier here represents Martin, and Young Scotland Aytoun:

> Bon Gaultier: Come, come, you are too hard upon Milnes. I grant you, that his principle in poetry is a bad one. He makes reflection predominate over passion, and there lies the grand mistake. Passion is the all in all in poetry. We do not go to it either for our facts or our metaphysics: we want to hear the voice of the heart speaking out in the language of universal truth, and interfusing the inanimate objects of nature with its own stirring life-blood.
> Young Scotland: Right, old fellow! Give me the poet who makes your heart burn within you, who sends your blood dancing along your veins in a stronger current, who makes you lose yourself in the joys and sorrows of himself or his heroes. What heresy is this of Monckton Milnes? "To interest or benefit *us,* poetry must be reflective, sentimental, subjective; it must accord with the conscious, analytical spirit of present men." [4]

In the one camp, with more classical sympathies, there is an advocacy of action, strong passion, and objectivity in poetry, represented ideally by the epics of Homer, the Greek tragedies, and the ancient ballads and appealing to the great mass of humanity. In the other camp, the emphasis falls upon reflection, sentimentality, subjectivity, and concern with contemporary subjects. Aytoun's critical position never changes; the man writing here is the same critic who leads his camp to victory ten years later. Bon Gaultier not only marks an important beginning in the tradition of Victorian light verse but also speaks the prologue to the "tragedy" of *Firmilian.* [5]

A BLACKWOOD'S *MAN*

In 1845, Aytoun realized his youthful ambition and became professor of rhetoric and belles lettres at the University of Edin-

4. Ibid., *11* (1844), 344.

5. For contemporary comment on Bon Gaultier, see *Fraser's, 31* (1845), 415–21; *The Westminster Review,* N.S. *6* (1854), 95–115; *The Westminster and Foreign Quarterly Review, 51* (1849), 246–47; *The Athenaeum* (1849), p. 13; *The Dublin University Magazine, 33* (1849), 216–17; and *The Literary Gazette* (1845), p. 420.

burgh, receiving the appointment chiefly because of a lack of
serious competition. The duties of the professorship involved
four lectures a week, plus the usual incidental chores, for six
months of the year; the emolument was 100 pounds plus student
fees. Since only about 30 students a year took the course, which
was not required for a degree, at best another 130 pounds could
be expected. Aytoun, however, became one of those lecturers
who draw crowds: his ingratiating blend of serious scholarship
and gentle humor, his growing literary reputation, and his sincere concern for his students [1] soon raised the annual number
of students to 150. The University Commission of 1826 had
recommended the abolishment of the professorship; the University Commission of 1858–62 doubled its base salary and made
the course a requisite for the arts degree. It is little wonder that
Sir Alexander Grant, the historian of Edinburgh University,
called Aytoun "far the most brilliant and at the same time the
most efficient of former occupants of the Chair of Rhetoric." [2]

Aytoun's life was assuming the pattern it was to retain throughout the 1840s. After his father's death in 1843, he had moved
with his mother and two unmarried sisters to 11 Fettes Row, a
neighboring and smaller house. In addition to his academic duties,
he continued to practice at the Scottish Bar, his growing criminal
practice being supplemented by appearances before Parliamentary
committees convened to legislate on railroad bills and to judge
the claims of competing lines. In 1844, in the most important act
of his business career, Aytoun formally joined the staff of *Blackwood's Edinburgh Magazine*.

Begun in 1817 as a rival to the liberal *Edinburgh Review*,
Blackwood's began to achieve celebrity when put under the joint
editorship of John "Christopher North" Wilson, James Hogg,
and J. G. Lockhart. The great contribution of *Maga* to the
evolving standard of periodical literature was its emphasis on
original criticism,[3] and it achieved its earliest notoriety from

1. He himself always marked the written exercises.
2. Sir Alexander Grant, *The Story of the University of Edinburgh During Its
First Three Hundred Years* (2 vols. London, Longmans, Green, and Co., 1884), 2,
360.
3. Walter Graham, *English Literary Periodicals* (New York, T. Nelson and Sons,
1930), p. 276.

vicious literary attacks. Most famous among its early articles were Lockhart's "On the Cockney School of Poetry. Leigh Hunt," Wilson's brutal assault against Coleridge, and an unidentified condemnation of Byron's *Don Juan*. Sweetening the acerbity of these early days were the discerning critiques of Wordsworth and the unique early championship of Shelley. Still, in literature as in politics, *Maga* was basically conservative.

Aytoun found in *Blackwood's* the objective correlative for his innermost feelings and beliefs. In politics, society, and literature, he looked back to the past with an admiration approaching reverence. He distrusted the new and unusual because he ultimately disliked change; he tended to identify the status quo with order. His recurrent introduction to his articles in *Blackwood's*—"the spirit of innovation, which so peculiarly marks the present age, and which, if persevered in, must . . ."—always sounded like a trumpet blast for attack.

Aytoun soon became *Maga's* most prolific writer and, after the death of "Christopher North" in 1854, was acknowledged to be its best. His writings covered a thirty-year period from 1836 to 1865, with 1850 marking a high point of 1,000 columns in the magazine. These writings were of almost every possible form and content—prose, poetry, translation, politics, literature, railways, magic, boxing, art, wines and so on. In May–June 1850, for example, he had a prose article on the Protectionists' meeting in London, reviews of Carlyle's *Latter-Day Pamphlets* and Alison's political essays, four poems on political subjects, and a translation from Ovid's *Tristia*.

Aytoun became identified with *Blackwood's* in the public imagination to such an extent that a popular misconception arose as to his editorship of the magazine. Even his friend Thackeray seems to have had this false impression, for he writes to Aytoun saying that if he "had the command of 'Blackwood,' " he would give Titmarsh a hand.[4] Soon afterward, he withdrew the request, admitting that a writer "ought to stand as the public chooses to put him." [5] Yet, despite repeated disclaimers by *Blackwood's* and by

4. Letter of Jan. 2, 1847, from Thackeray to Aytoun.
5. Letter of Jan. 13, 1847, from Thackeray to Aytoun.

Aytoun himself, the notion of Aytoun's editorship has been perpetuated down to the present day.[6]

Perhaps the most impressive testimony to Aytoun's success as a periodical writer comes from a confidential letter to him from an expert in the field and a political opponent, the editor of the London *Times:* "I venture to put to you a somewhat delicate question . . . . Would you like . . . to become 'one of us.' "[7] Although the *Times* represented the apex of periodical literature and the editor promised a significant remuneration, Aytoun could not become a writer for the leading organ of the Whig Ministry and remained a *Blackwood's* man to the end.

In the mid-forties, Aytoun dealt most extensively with the railway mania then sweeping Great Britain. His approach here anticipates all of his later magazine writing: he rejects innovation. In this particular case, he was justified, as later events were to prove, in his warnings against unscrupulous railway companies, lax governmental guidance, and gullible speculators. His articles, however, frequently indicate that he feared not merely corrupt speculations but the railroads themselves. Something fundamental to his character is involved here:

> Was nature made in vain, in order that men might hasten from town to town, at the tail of a shrieking engine, regardless of all the glorious scenery which intervenes? To our taste, the old mode of travelling—nay, the oldest—was infinitely superior to the present sickening system . . . . You moved through merry England as a man ought to do, who is both content with his own lot and can enjoy the happiness of others . . . you felt that you were the richer by a day spent in the fresh air and gladsome sunshine, and made happy by all the sounds and sights which are dear to the heart of man.
>
> . . . . Can you associate the story of Palamon and Arcite— can you connect anything which is noble, lofty, inspiriting, humane, or gentle, with a journey made in an express train? If not, so much the worse for the present time. Doubtless you

6. See, for example, Jerome Thale, "Sidney Dobell: A Spasmodic Poet" (Unpublished Doctoral Dissertation, Northwestern University, 1953).

7. Letter of Feb. 20, 1850.

may hear something about Thompson or Bright, but we may be excused if we prefer the mention of the earlier heroes.[8]

Aytoun could honestly say of the railways that "a question more important can hardly be conceived." [9]

A more important question, however, soon developed and demanded much of Aytoun's political and economic ingenuity from 1847 to 1852—the question of free trade. He continually associates the free trade "gamble" with the railway "gamble" and, once again, personally feels that the new method is helping to destroy the glorious old life of Britain. In *Blackwood's*, Aytoun's main strategy was to claim that, theoretically, it was unfair to sacrifice the interests of the agriculturalists to those of the manufacturers, and that, in fact, the expected profits of the manufacturers after the repeal of the Corn Laws had turned out to be losses. His most impressive article, "British Agriculture and Foreign Competition," [1] in which he summarized evidence from all over Scotland and presented the Protectionist cause in all of its strength, made him famous above the Tweed as the most articulate of the pleaders for that cause. *Blackwood's* next issue contained a 112-page appendix of "Opinions of the Press" with regard to Aytoun's article. Protection, however, was a lost cause in that heyday of British liberalism, and, when in 1852 the Conservatives under Derby and Disraeli were forced to resign and were replaced by the Aberdeen Coalition, Aytoun gave up the fight. For his efforts, Disraeli and Lord Eglinton personally thanked him on various occasions, and the Derby Administration rewarded him with the Sheriffship and Lord Admiralty of Orkney and Zetland in 1852. From that year to his death, Aytoun spent August and September in those Western Islands, administering justice and conducting business, fishing, and grouse hunting.

More interesting, however, in a study of Aytoun's literary significance are his short stories in *Blackwood's*. Critics acquainted with them have lavished high praise upon these works, considering them among the best short stories written during the Victorian period. Millar claims that

8. *Blackwood's 70* (1851) , 742.
9. Ibid., *58* (1845) , 648.
1. Ibid., *67* (1850) , 94–136.

while Aytoun's glory as a writer of parodies is shared by others, his distinction as a writer of humorous short stories is unique . . . no more difficulty in "placing" Aytoun's personages, so to speak, than in "placing" those of Maupassant . . . in these perpetually refreshing stories is to be found not merely the pleasure of hearty and good-natured laughter, but the more subtle and exquisite gratification which springs from the contemplation of adroit and finished literary workmanship.[2]

He goes even further in a later evaluation: "they approach as closely to perfection in their own kind as it is possible for human performances to do."[3] Walter Whyte believes "His stories are irresistibly amusing. Few recent writers have evoked heartier laughter than he."[4] James Hannay concurs in this latter view:

He owed his chief distinction all along to what he did in literature; and popular as his "Bon Gaultier Ballads," and his "Lays of the Scottish Cavaliers" were, they were neither of them more relished than some of his prose articles in *Blackwood,* such as "How we got up the Glenmutchkin Railway," and "How I stood for the Dreepdailie Burghs." These are fair representatives of his comic talent, and comic talent, we repeat, was his *forte.*[5]

A record nine of Aytoun's ten short stories were reprinted in *Tales from Blackwood,* but, though they outstrip the other works in that series, it is difficult to help feeling that the praise of the Victorian critics is somewhat overenthusiastic.

Although some of them exist simply as humorous short stories,[6] the best and most famous deal, in a serio-comic manner, with social, literary, and political problems.[7] They are closely related to

2. J. H. Millar, "William Edmondstoune Aytoun," *The New Review, 14* (1896), pp. 111–12.

3. Millar, *A Literary History of Scotland,* p. 590.

4. Whyte, *Poets and Poetry of the Century, 9,* 388.

5. Hannay, "Recent Humorists," pp. 82–83.

6. "How I Became a Yeoman," "The Emerald Studs," "The Raid of Arnaboll."

7. Social Problems: "The Glenmutchkin Railway," "The Congress and the Agapedome," "Rapping the Question," "My First Spec in the Biggleswades." Literary: "The Surveyor's Tale." Political: "How I stood for the Dreepdaily burghs," "How we got possession of the Tuileries."

Aytoun's prose articles, exposing Whig knavery and such modern crazes as the railways, peace congresses, magic, and literary romance. One of the reasons for the "adroit and finished literary workmanship" of these tales is the repeated use of the same basic situation. In the political short stories, for example, the protagonist is always a Whig. He enthusiastically propounds to strangers the principles of Whiggery but secretly confides to his cohorts that he knows those principles are a sham. He attempts to pull off an illegal operation, which usually bears a telling resemblance to some actual Whig scheme, is thwarted, and ends as a repentant Tory. In the less politically oriented stories, Aytoun's Whigs become railway directors or magicians or vegetarians, but their careers are remarkably the same. All serve ultimately as amusing spokesmen for the serious beliefs of their author.

The masterpiece is "How we got up the Glenmutchkin Railway, and how we got out of it," an exposé of the railway mania, indicting both unscrupulous directors and gullible buyers and intermingling the drollest humor with the "deep moral." The story gave *Maga* "one of those thrilling sensations of triumph and success familiar to her younger days"; [8] the *Times* reprinted it at full length; and "Glenmutchkin" became a byword for many outrageous projects. This story was naturally placed first in the first volume of *Tales from Blackwood,* and Aytoun had to add an introductory note disclaiming that he had intended any direct satire against particular individuals or projects.[9] This is one of the highest compliments that can be paid to this type of fiction— to be mistaken for and discussed as reality.

Aytoun's *annus mirabilis* was 1894. On April 11, at the age of thirty-six, he married Jane Emily Wilson, the youngest daughter of "Christopher North," his colleague both on the staff of *Blackwood's* and at Edinburgh University. After obtaining the young lady's consent, he was too diffident to speak to Christopher about the marriage, so Jane undertook the task. Christopher favored his

8. Mrs. Oliphant, *William Blackwood and His Sons* (3 vols. New York, Charles Scribner's Sons, 1897), 2, 408.

9. *Tales from Blackwood* (Edinburgh and London, William Blackwood and Sons, 1860), p. 1.

successful colleague but said to his daughter, "If your suitor is so shamefaced, I had better write my reply and pin it to your back." On her return, the lover read, "With the author's compliments!" [1]

The couple resided at Inverleith Terrace in a northern suburb of Edinburgh until 1853 when they moved to a palatial house in Great Stuart Street, close to the university. This symbol of success remained Aytoun's home until his death. His activities became habitual. He arose at ten and proceeded to his study, where he passed the day until it was time to start for his lecture at four o'clock. If he had no social engagement for the evening, he would return to the study for more reading and writing. Later, he was to attribute his painful dyspepsia to the sedentary habits acquired during these years. According to the friends who have written about him, his ten-year marriage was one of great contentedness.

In 1849 Edinburgh University also conferred the honorary degree of A.M. upon Aytoun; four years later, Oxford was to make him a D.C.L. And, finally, 1849 was the publication date of *Lays of the Scottish Cavaliers, and Other Poems*,[2] Aytoun's most famous work and a Victorian best seller.

1. Edith Swann, *Christopher North* (Edinburgh, Oliver and Boyd, 1934) , p. 214.
2. Actually, 750 copies were printed in December 1848.

LAYS OF THE SCOTTISH CAVALIERS

Lays of the Scottish Cavaliers reached its fifteenth British edition in fifteen years and its thirty-second in thirty-two years. The firm of William Blackwood and Sons sold over 60,000 copies during the Victorian period alone, and, with foreign editions, the final total approaches the 100,000 mark. The book attained considerable popularity in America, Australia, and Germany.[1] Its greatest vogue was, of course, in Scotland, where selections were included in students' reading books. Aytoun's ultimate model was Scott, whose poetry, ballads, and historical romances had early pervaded his whole being. But which writer of ballads in the nineteenth century, particularly in Scotland, did Scott not influence? He had gratified and simultaneously stimulated the public hunger "For old, unhappy, far-off things, And battles long ago." He had changed the nature of the old ballad, extending it into a lay, stripping it of its coarseness, and throwing over ancient manners the gorgeous splendors of fancy. He had accomplished a revolution, and his greatest tribute, after his public popularity, was his legion of followers.

Aytoun's immediate model, however, as his title suggests, was Thomas Babington Macaulay,[2] who was himself influenced signi-

1. The first complete German translation, by Dr. Alexander Smith, appeared in 1866, but earlier translations had been made of "Edinburgh after Flodden," "The Burial March of Dundee," and "Charles Edward at Versailles."

2. Theodore Martin claimed that Wilhelm Müller, the German balladist, had an important influence upon Aytoun's work. He asserts that the "Marco Bozzaris" in particular determined the measure of "The Burial March of Dundee." Since, however, this measure is a common one, appearing even in "Edinburgh after Flodden" and "Charles Edward at Versailles," and no other evidence of specific influence can be discovered, Martin's claim, other than in a general sense, seems unfounded.

ficantly by Scott. An early essay on "History" praises Sir Walter for his imaginative treatment of the past.[3] In Macaulay's juvenile ballad, "The Battle of Bosworth Field," it is only too obvious who supplied the model:

> It is an eve in summer-time, as fair as fair can be:
> It is a lordly castle high upon the banks of Dee:
> A lady from the lattice looks: she there hath looked
>   since morn:
> A squire before the outer gate winds long and loud
>   his horn:
> And up the huge portcullis flies, and down the
>   drawbridge falls;
> And fast the gallant spurs his steed within the
>   castle walls;
> And rustling in her gorgeous robes of satin
>   and of vair
> That lofty dame, with anxious eye, sweeps down
>   the winding stair:
> On either side her train falls back and leaves
>   a passage free,
> And the young horseman vaults to earth, and
>   drops on bended knee.[4]

Fortunately, Macaulay soon came to perceive that he could not join Scott in this world of chivalry, and he turned instead to a world which had greater reality for him, the world of ancient Rome. Even in the preface to the *Lays of Ancient Rome,* however, he acknowledges his famous predecessor: "It would have been obviously improper to mimic the manner of any particular age or country. Something has been borrowed, however, from our own old ballads, and more from Sir Walter Scott, the great restorer of our ballad poetry. To the Iliad still greater obligations are

It is true, however, that Aytoun did translate Müller's "Epitaph of Constantine Kanaris."

3. Thomas Babington Macaulay, *Critical, Historical and Miscellaneous Essays* (6 vols. Boston, Houghton, Mifflin and Co., 1886) , *1,* 428–29.

4. Thomas Babington Macaulay, *Lays of Ancient Rome and Other Historical Poems,* ed. G. M. Trevelyan (London, Longmans, Green, and Co. Ltd., 1928) , p. 176.

due." [5] Within the lays themselves, reminders of Scott appear, down even to close verbal parallels, as, for example, between Horatius' swim and William of Deloraine's midnight ride.[6] Indeed, the popular tradition of the British historical ballad in the early nineteenth century starts with Scott, continues with Macaulay, and, as shall be shown, ends with Aytoun.

Among the many descendants of Sir Walter, however, why should Macaulay and Aytoun have caught the public ear? What happened to the others—Monckton Milnes, whose "Death of Sarsfield" anticipates Aytoun's "Island of the Scots"; the anonymous author of *Lays and Legends of Cromwell and the Noncomformist Heroes* who is imitating Aytoun; [7] George Sydney Smythe, whose "Death of Mary of Scots" shows considerable skill? All were soon forgotten, but the *Lays of Ancient Rome,* which first appeared in 1842, the year of Tennyson's *Poems* and Browning's *Dramatic Lyrics,* left all competitors behind and reached the 100,000 mark by 1875.[8] Why should only the lays of Macaulay and Aytoun have kept coming out in edition after edition?

To begin with, both Macaulay and Aytoun understood the nature of the genre. Admittedly, the historical ballad cannot reach the highest poetic levels. Macaulay himself wrote to Napier, "Without the smallest affectation of modesty, I confess that the success of my little book has far exceeded its just claims. I shall be in no hurry to repeat the experiment; for I am well aware that a second attempt would be made under much less favorable circumstances. A far more severe test would now be applied to my verses." [9] But, despite Arnold's sneers at "pinchbeck," such ballads form a legitimate, and not unimportant, literary genre and serve a literary need based on a broader popular appeal than many works of higher poetic merit. At their best, such ballads offer blood and fire in a "cut-and-thrust style"; they have a movement and nervous energy that appeal immediately to the heart. They lie on that razor-sharp line between admirable rhetoric and true poetry, neither too low nor too high for the great mass of educated

5. Ibid., p. 29.

6. Cf. Macaulay, *Lays,* p. 56, and Scott, *Lay of the Last Minstrel,* stanza xxix.

7. See *The Eclectric Review,* N.S. *1* (1861), 84–104.

8. George Otto Trevelyan, *The Life and Letters of Lord Macaulay* (New York, Harper and Brothers, 1877), p. 111.

9. Ibid., pp. 111–12.

readers, and they come off better on first or second reading than on fifth or sixth. They are, to use the words in their common significance, "simple, sensuous, and passionate."

Macaulay and Aytoun not only understood the nature of the genre but also were able to meet its requirements because of the sense of immediacy with which they approached the historical ballad. The worlds they wrote about were just as real to them as the worlds in which they moved. Just as Scott felt at home with the damsels and squires on bended knee, these two scholars lived, in an important sense, in the days of ancient Rome and Stuart Scotland. For them, the past was not merely a thing apart, not merely a series of facts to be studied as history, but a living reality. Their ballads alone, among the many descendants of Sir Walter, do not merely reproduce or imitate the ancient; instead, they are animated by a highly personal, modern spirit. With Macaulay and Aytoun this spirit is largely of a propagandistic nature, unique in successful ballad literature, and requiring examination.

Macaulay, the arch-Whig, wisely chose those events in Roman history about which he could write with most intensity. "Horatius" and "The Battle of the Lake Regillus" both depict the struggles of a liberated people to prevent the reimposition of tyrannic rule:

> "Hear, Senator and people
>   Of the good town of Rome,
> The Thirty Cities charge you
>   To bring the Tarquins home:
> And if ye still be stubborn,
>   To work the Tarquins wrong,
> The Thirty Cities warn you,
>   Look that your walls be strong." (p. 74)

When the gods Castor and Pollux announce "And for the right we come to fight/Before the ranks of Rome" (p. 94), they are referring to the right of a state to throw off despotic rule.

Macaulay's partisan fervor is visible just as clearly, though from a different angle, in the deceptively entitled "Virginia." In the preface to this poem, Macaulay reminds the reader that the heroic warriors of the two preceding lays were all members of the dominant order, and a poet singing their praises, "whatever his own political opinions might be," would abstain from insulting their class. "Viriginia" however is one of a group of compositions that did attack the privileged families by relating the bitter contest between the great houses and the commonalty, whose position "bore some resemblance to that of the Irish Catholics during the intervals between the year 1792 and the year 1829." Macaulay's partisanship is evident throughout the preface:

> During more than a century after the institution of the Tribuneship, the Commons struggled manfully for the removal of the grievances under which they laboured; and, in spite of many checks and reverses, succeeded in wringing concession after concession from the stubborn aristocracy . . . the good cause triumphed. The Licinian Laws were carried. Lucius Sextus was the first Plebeian Consul, Caius Licinius the third.
>
> The results of this great change were singularly happy and glorious. Two centuries of prosperity, harmony, and victory followed the reconciliation of the orders.

It all sounds just like another popular work that Macaulay was soon to write.

An awareness of Macaulay's position here explains the apparent artistic failure of the lay itself. Appius Claudius, representing unbridled governmental authority, is the villain of the piece:

> He stalked along the Forum like King Tarquin
>   in his pride:
>
> .   .   .
>
> For never was there Claudius yet but
>   wished the Commons ill. (p. 113)

The plebeians cannot oppose his wanton seizure of the beautiful Virginia:

> For then there was no Tribune to speak
>   the word of might,
> Which makes the rich man tremble, and guards
>   the poor man's right.

> There was no brave Licinius, no honest Sextius
>   then;
> But all the city, in great fear, obeyed the
>   wicked ten. (p. 117)

They can, however, express among themselves their disgust with
a society which allows such outrages. Right before the merciful
killing of Virginia by her father, Icilius shouts forth fifty-two lines
on freedom in the best revolutionary manner. Critics have
blamed Macaulay for this "digression" right at the crucial moment
of the narrative:

> All must have felt, for example, the absurdity of Icilius's ad-
> dressing the Roman populace in a speech of some fifty lines,
> when the outrage is threatened to his betrothed Virginia.
> Men's words are few and terrible at such a crisis. Two lines
> could have done the work far better than fifty, and they
> *would* have done it in the verses of a true poet.[1]

This misses the point. The lines on freedom are not intrusive,
but the subject of the poem. Virginia, who neither says nor does
anything, gains significance only as the focal point of the publi-
can—plebeian opposition. Such an interpretation of the *Lays of
Ancient Rome* makes clear E. E. Kellett's generalization:

> Their moving impulse was perhaps political rather than
> ethereal. Proud Tarquin was to him a sort of James the
> Second; Valerius an earlier Schomberg; Titus was the Duke
> of Berwick; Julius was Sarsfield, and Regillus a luckier
> Steinkirk: nay, the Sublican Bridge was the bridge over the
> Gette, which William, retreating before Luxemburg, crossed
> so willingly. Had there been no British significance in these
> old Roman stories, nay, had they not possessed a specially
> Whig significance, Macaulay would never have retold them
> with such spirit. But though his inspiration thus came as
> much from Constitution Hill as from Helicon it is a high
> and genuine inspiration nevertheless.[2]

1. *The Dublin University Magazine, 33* (1849), 216.
2. E. E. Kellett, *Suggestions* (Cambridge, Cambridge University Press, 1923), pp.
164–65.

Aytoun's *Lays of the Scottish Cavaliers* represents the Tory equivalent of Macaulay's *Lays of Ancient Rome*. The first two lays, "The Burial March of Dundee" and "Charles Edward at Versailles," appeared in *Blackwood's* in early 1843, soon after the publication of Macaulay's ballads, and the political opposition is explicitly dramatized in the appendix to the second edition of Aytoun's *Lays*, "Examination of the Statements in Mr. Macaulay's History of England, regarding John Grahame of Claverhouse, Viscount of Dundee." Of the eight lays, six deal with the fortunes of the Stuarts and their loyal followers.[3] Much of Aytoun's emotional and intellectual being had become concentrated on that unhappy family. His religious faith, the Episcopalian, and his political party, the Tory, had been the firmest and last defenders of the Stuarts; defeat for that royal house meant triumph for Whiggery in England and Presbyterianism in Scotland.[4] Perhaps most importantly, all of Aytoun's cherished notions about the past, about chivalry, and about loyalty to the sovereign found their focal point in his devotion to the Stuarts:

> His attachment to the Stuarts was as genuine a passion as ever stirred the heart of a Cavalier. Of course it was a thing of his imagination: all devotion is so more or less. But for him it was so real that it coloured his views of the history of that dynasty and its followers to a degree which surprised those who knew how critical was his observation and how practical his judgment in all other matters. Touch this theme at any time, even when his flow of mirthful spirits was at its fullest, and his tremulous voice and quivering lip told how deeply seated were his feelings in all that related to it. On any other point he would bear to be rallied, but not upon this. His historical faith was to him only less sacred than his religious creed. It was a part of his very self, imbibed, doubtless, at his mother's knee, in the tales with which she charmed his childish ears, and riveted to his heart by the songs and ballads on which his youthful passion for romance and chivalry had

3. The exceptions are "Edinburgh after Flodden" and "The Heart of the Bruce," both of which are nationalistic in theme.

4. The best treatment of this knotty problem is in Agnes Mure Mackenzie, *The Passing of the Stuarts* (New York, Macmillan Co., 1937), pp. 299–360.

been fed. The men and women of that race were substantial
realities, around which not "merely his pastime and his happiness had grown," but to whom the worship of his imagination and the devotion of his loyalty had been given. He believed in them, lived with them, and could no more brook a
slight or wrong to their names, than to the honour of a living
friend. What he wrote about them was written, therefore,
with the force of an almost personal devotion . . . . he
selected the subjects of his "Lays of the Cavaliers" . . . because he felt on no other subjects so strongly, and knew that
they would certainly bring out whatever of the poet was in
him.[5]

It is no wonder that Aytoun included elaborate notes defending
the historical validity of his lays, and that, in contrast to the rapid-
ity with which he turned out light verse, he devoted great effort
and care to this poetic expression of his deepest self.

After five of his lays had been published and before the final
three were begun, Aytoun wrote an article, "Ancient and Modern
Ballad Poetry," [6] which is most valuable for an understanding of
his general thoughts about literature and his particular principles
in the construction of his own ballads. He begins by recalling
Christopher North's "merited tribute to the genius of Mr. Macaulay, commenting upon the thews and sinews of his verse, and
the manly vigour of his Lays of Ancient Rome" and later adds
that "few men have written with more fire and energy than Mr.
Macaulay." With regard to the ballad as a literary genre, he has
only the highest praise:

The truth is, that instead of being the easiest, the ballad is
incomparably the most difficult kind of all poetical composition. Many men, who were not poets in the highest sense of
the word, because they wanted the inventive faculty, have
nevertheless, by dint of perseverance, great accomplishment,
and dexterous use of those materials which are ready to the
hand of every artificer, gained a respectable name in the roll
of British literature—but never, in any single instance, by at-

5. Martin, *Memoir,* pp. 72–74.
6. *Blackwood's, 61* (1847) , 622–44.

tempting the construction of a ballad. That is the Shibboleth, by which you can at once distinguish the true minstrel from mere imposter or pretender. It is the simplest, and at the same time the sublimest form of poetry, nor can it be written except under the influence of that strong and absorbing emotion, which bears the poet away from the present time, makes him an actor and a participator in the vivid scenes which he describes, and which is, in fact, inspiration of the very loftiest kind.

The future author of *Firmilian* approves of these true minstrels because

> they take no thought of ornament, or of any rhetorical arti-
> fice, but throw themselves headlong into their subject, trust-
> ing to nature for that language which is at once the shortest
> and the most appropriate to the occasion; spurning all far-
> fetched metaphors aside, and ringing out their verse as the
> iron rings upon the anvil!

In sharp contrast, the allegorist treats ideal rather than real subjects, is highly intellectual and artificial rather than simple and direct, slow-paced rather than energetic. Aytoun includes in this unfavorable category allegories of the poet's mind, works such as the forthcoming *Life-Drama* and *Balder*. Finally, apropos of the biased Tory viewpoint of his own ballads, Aytoun advances the following justification:

> Unless the poet is imbued with a deep sympathy for his sub-
> ject, we would not give sixpence for his chance of producing
> a tolerable ballad. Nay, we go further, and aver that he ought
> when possible to write in the unscrupulous character of a
> partisan. In historical and martial ballads, there always must
> be two sides; and it is the business of the poet to adopt one of
> these with as much enthusiasm and prejudice as if his life and
> fortunes depended upon the issue of the cause. For the ballad
> is the reflex of keen and rapid sensation, and has nothing to
> do with judgment or with calm deliberative justice. It should
> embody, from beginning to end, one fiery absorbing passion,

such as men feel when their blood is up, and their souls
thoroughly roused within them.

Thus, Macaulay was correct in writing Whig ballads, while
Aytoun could not have chosen a more appropriate subject than
the Stuarts and their followers.

The Scottish cavalier as hero conditions Aytoun's use of the
ballad. This romantic figure has been defeated in earthly terms:
he has either been killed, like James IV, Montrose, Sir James
Douglas, Dundee, and the Old Scottish Cavalier; or lost loved
ones, like the Widow of Glencoe; or been exiled, like Charles
Edward and Dundee's Scottish regiment.[7] He must, if he is to
triumph at all, triumph spiritually; therefore, the movement of
Aytoun's ballads is frequently toward the calm of Heaven after
earth's fitful fever:

> "God, our father, will not fail us
>   In that last tremendous hour,—
> If all other bulwarks crumble,
>   He will be our strength and tower:
> Though the ramparts rock beneath us,
>   And the walls go crashing down,
> Though the roar of conflagration
>   Bellow o'er the sinking town;
> There is yet one place of shelter,
>   Where the foeman cannot come
> Where the summons never sounded
>   Of the trumpet or the drum.
> There again we'll meet our children,
>   Who, on Flodden's trampled sod,
> For their king and for their country
>   Rendered up their souls to God.
> There shall we find rest and refuge,
>   With our dear departed brave;

7. This last figure, the exiled, romantic hero, is the dominant figure in Aytoun's
serious poetry. He appears first in "Poland," in the passage reminiscent of Byron's
dying gladiator, occurs frequently in the lays and incidental poetry, and receives
his most complete treatment in Aytoun's most serious endeavor, *Bothwell*.

> And the ashes of the city
>   Be our universal grave!" [8]

Such an ending was impossible in Macaulay's *Lays of Ancient Rome* and is alien to the ballad tradition, which tends to remain on the earthly level.

Aytoun again departs from standard ballad practice by making the narrator an active participant in half of the lays. By such a change, he tends to make the ballad a more partisan vehicle, as he establishes a more sympathetic point of view for the cavaliers. He is usually successful, as in "The Burial March of Dundee," where the immediate effect of Dundee's conduct and death on the soldier-narrator emphasizes the greatness of Claverhouse. In "The Execution of Montrose," however, the subjective element detracts unnecessarily from the movement of the narrative.

Finally, Aytoun likes to include classical allusions in the ballad. Macaulay set the example here; his allusions are either inevitable, "The Battle of Lake Regillus" being modeled on a situation in *The Iliad*, or quite natural, his Roman minstrels having been trained in the epic literature of Greece. Aytoun's allusions, however, seem inorganic. Prince Charles exclaims: "Woman's love is writ in water!/Woman's faith is traced on sand!" (p. 198). It is an exclamation reminiscent of song seventy in Catullus, but certainly Aytoun does not want to relate Prince Charles to one of Catullus' young lovers. He uses the expression for its own sake, not for its allusiveness.

"The Island of the Scots" (pp. 137–48), though the least known of Aytoun's lays,[9] provides a good example of his general technique and the quality of his verse. It describes the heroic capture of a strategic island from the Germans by the remnants of the dead Dundee's Scottish force, a force now fighting for France because it is the home of their exiled King James. The situation is presented immediately, abruptly, in the opening lines; the French mareschal speaks:

8. William Edmondstoune Aytoun, *Lays of the Scottish Cavaliers and Other Poems* (Edinburgh and London, William Blackwood and Sons, 1849), pp. 26–27. All quotations will be from the first edition of the *Lays*.

9. It was the only one which did not appear in *Blackwood's* before publication in book form.

The Rhine is running red and deep,
    The island lies before—
"Now is there one of all the host
    Will dare to venture o'er?
For not alone the river's sweep
    Might make a brave man quail:
The foe are on the further side,
    Their shot comes fast as hail.
God help us, if the middle isle
    We may not hope to win!
Now, is there any of the host
    Will dare to venture in?"

After a brief description of the difficulties of such a feat, attention focuses on "The relics of the bravest force/That ever fought in fray." Their past glories are quickly recounted, and then their leader cries out rousingly:

"But we have hearts, and we have arms
    As strong to will and dare
As when our ancient banners flew
    Within the northern air.
Come, brothers! let me name a spell
    Shall rouse your souls again,
And send the old blood bounding free
    Through pulse, and heart, and vein!
Call back the days of bygone years—
    Be young and strong once more;
Think yonder stream, so stark and red,
    Is one we've crossed before.
Rise, hill and glen! rise, crag and wood!
    Rise up on either hand—
Again upon the Garry's banks,
    On Scottish soil we stand!
Again I see the tartans wave,
    Again the trumpets ring,
Again I hear our leader's call—
    'Upon them, for the King!' "

This level of heroic excitement is maintained throughout the
dangerous crossing to the isle and the eventual victory. Then
comes the switch! Since the ballad does not deal in subleties, the
poet often achieves his effects by the use of strong contrasts. Scott
does this repeatedly in *The Lay of the Last Minstrel,* Macaulay
quite effectively in the famous conclusion to "Horatius," and
Aytoun most movingly here. Right at the moment of victory,
when the flush of exultation should be highest, the narrator asks:

> And did they twine the laurel-wreath
> For those who fought so well?
> And did they honour those who lived,
> And weep for those who fell?
> What meed of thanks was given to them
> Let aged annals tell.
> Why should they twine the laurel-wreath—
> Why crown the cup with wine?
> It was not Frenchmen's blood that flowed
> So freely on the Rhine—
> A stranger band of beggared men
> Had done the venturous deed:
> The glory was to France alone,
> The danger was their meed.
> And what cared they for idle thanks
> From foreign prince and peer?
> What virtue had such honied words
> The exiles' hearts to cheer?
> What mattered it that men should vaunt
> And loud and fondly swear,
> That higher feat of chivalry
> Was never wrought elsewhere?
> They bore within their breasts the grief
> That fame can never heal—
> The deep, unutterable woe
> Which none save exiles feel.
> Their hearts were yearning for the land
> They ne'er might see again—
> For Scotland's high and heathered hills,

> For mountain, loch, and glen—
> For those who haply lay at rest
> Beyond the distant sea,
> Beneath the green and daisied turf
> Where they would gladly be!

This passage indicates the critical problem of evaluating these lays. The stanza is a little diffuse and not entirely free of vain epithets and flat lines; yet, it is difficult for most people to read it, in the context of the whole, without being moved and feeling that here is something fine. Such poetry finds its sanction in the heart of the multitude rather than in the head of the analyst. The popularity of the *Lays of the Scottish Cavaliers* reveals the nature of its appeal, and so do the many letters that the author received, letters that speak much of gratitude, tears, the spirit, and immortality.

Most satisfying of all to Aytoun, however, must have been the letter from Charles Kean, the famous actor and public reciter. In his London and Edinburgh poetry lectures of 1853, Aytoun was to emphasize the distinction between the minstrel and the poet, the man whose works are to be read aloud to a group and the man whose works are to be studied by the individual. Aytoun awarded the palm to the former on the basis of universality of appeal; he preferred Scott to Wordsworth. Kean wrote:

> I hope I may be gratified by making your personal acquaintance on passing through Edinburgh . . . . Allow me to add that I feel myself under very great obligations to you in the matter of "Lays of the Scottish Cavaliers." The execution of Montrose has been one of my most successful recitations in the few public readings I have given, for the beauty of the poem inspires me—Not very long since I repeated it at the Vice Regal Lodge, Dublin, and Lord Carlisle, a poet himself, expressed himself in the warmest manner.
>
> I am now studying Charles Stuart at Versailles and after that shall commence with that exquisite and grand poem "Edinburgh after Flodden." [1]

Aytoun must have felt that he had reached the minstrel class.

1. Letter of Mar. 9, 1863, from Kean to Aytoun.

By writing ballads and exalting them in his prose article, Aytoun was entering into a controversy that had begun to split a significant segment of the Victorian world of letters. The Romantic Revolution, in its own enormous, contradictory manner, brought into English literature of the nineteenth century the most objective and the most subjective forms of poetry: it reintroduced the ballad and introduced the secular confessional. Right beside the *Prelude* (1805), the growth of a poet's mind, stands *The Lay of the Last Minstrel*. Wordsworth's poem, however, still deals recognizably with that common world "wherein we find our happiness or not at all." By mid-century, the split had become more marked. Critics were beginning to resent the increasing withdrawal of young poets from the common field of action and the young poets, like Indian fakirs, continued to look into their own navels for the solution of the incomprehensible mystery of all things.

Even incidental criticism of books like Aytoun's often revealed the growing controversy. In "Modern Ballad Writers," purportedly a review of Aytoun's and Tennyson's poems but, in the tradition of Victorian reviewing, actually a lengthy discussion of contemporary poetry in general, the *Westminster* reviewer offers his solution for the modern dichotomy. Recognizing a need for both the objective and the subjective in poetry, both action and intellect, he pleads for a union in individual works:

But whatever the attention given to each new metaphysical theory or alleged fact, life and its incidents claim and gain a yet greater and more enduring attention. Not that we regret, or would vainly seek to repress the unconquerable desire to search into the depths of our nature; a search in which the tendency and the ever-baffling result mutually balance each other, and to which we owe some of the grandest and most original outpourings of modern poetry, the fittest vehicle, perhaps, and certainly the most attractive, for displaying the results of metaphysical inquiry, as in Wordsworth generally, and in much of Tennyson. The poetic faculty has been directed into this channel with increased force by the writers of the late generation, but as its tendency,

if purely in this direction, is to generate or to extend a
dreamy and unhealthy tone in literature, it is the more necessary to vindicate from the neglect into which it has been
suffered to fall, that other and visible domain of poetry in
which there is more of satisfaction attainable; where the
perplexities are less grave, the disturbances more easily
resolvable, than those which meet us in that dark mental
region where there is so much that is chaotic to baffle our
inquiry. The tendency of the poetic faculty appears to point
to the union of these two great sources of inspiration, the
subjective and the objective, neither all Epic nor all Meta-
physic.[2]

Rare indeed was such a spirit of eclecticism. To most reviewers,
as later to Aytoun, Arnold, Clough, and Gilfillan, it became an
either-or question. The typical reviewer used his article about a
particular work as a stalking-horse for an attack against the
school he opposed. Thus, in a favorable evaluation of Aytoun's
lays:

> Professor Aytoun has appreciated the wealth of his country's
> history in themes for the historical ballad. He has done well
> to forego the easier praise of adding to the already too
> numerous band of poets of mere personal emotion, or what
> is worse, of versified reflections. He has spared the public
> pocket handkerchief the tears of sympathetic woe, wisely
> agreeing with Shakespeare—
>
> > "That now 'tis stale to sigh, to weep and groan,
> > So woe hath wearied woe, moan tired moan." [3]

Little did this reviewer suspect that the Scottish professor who
thus joined one side in the contemporary controversy would
eventually lead his side to victory. The struggle is, of course,

---

2. *The Westminster Review, 55* (1851), 18–19.

3. *The Dublin University Magazine, 33* (1849), 217–18. For other reviews, see
The Times (May 31, 1849), p. 6; *The Spectator, 21* (1848), 1258–59; *The Literary
Gazette* (1849), pp. 187–88; *The British Quarterly Review, 11* (1850), 80–101; *John
Bull* (1849), p. 71; *Fraser's, 39* (1849), 489–98; *The Dublin Review, 27* (1849), 74–
91; and *The Christian Examiner, 52* (1852), 226–34, written by Edward Everett
Hale.

an eternal one, but Aytoun's *Firmilian* determined its outcome in the particular form it assumed in the 1850s. He cleared the critical atmosphere for the reception of the objective and traditional, as opposed to the subjective and Spasmodic. In order to understand his achievement, it is necessary to understand the Spasmodic movement, whose history shall now be traced.

THE SPASMODIC YEARS (1850–56)

THE SPASMODIC SCHOOL

GOETHE AND BYRON

Being a diffuse movement which included writers of various interests, the Spasmodic school was subject to multiple influences. As might be expected, these early Victorians worked most frequently under the influence of their immediate predecessors, the Romantics. Wordsworth, who legitimatized the secular confessional in English poetry, Shelley, with his visionary hopes of a regenerate world and his subtle, difficult imagery, and Keats, with his color, sensuousness, and piling up of images, all affected Spasmodic writings in varying degrees. Dobell, for instance, was the poet most influenced by Shelley, while Smith was accused of being a mere plagiarizer of Keats. Still, viewing the tradition as a whole, the grandfathers of the Spasmodic school were those two poets of greatest European renown, Byron and Goethe.

Goethe's *Faust* remained an important model for young poets throughout the nineteenth century, Aytoun, as we have seen, became so intoxicated with this work when in Germany that he spent long hours translating it into English. By the time he was an established *Blackwood's* critic, however, his attitude toward the work had changed. In his first direct attack against Spasmodic poetry,[1] he censured his former idol because he now viewed *Faust* as a model for the dangerous literary practices of young English poets. He begins by mentioning "the numerous efforts which have been made to produce imitations" of *Faust:* "From Byron to Festus Bailey—a sad declension, we admit." Then he discusses

---

1. *Blackwood's, 71* (1852), 212–25.

the reasons why Goethe's celebrated drama should not serve as a
model. Although "there are, unquestionably, isolated scenes of
singular power and magnificence," yet

> much matter still remains of inferior merit. The scenes in
> the witch's apartment, and in Auerbach's cellar—the conver-
> sations of Wagner, and even some of the more recondite
> dialogue between Faust and Mephistopheles—are clearly
> unworthy of Goethe. Notwithstanding an occasional affected
> mysticism, as if they conveyed, or were intended to convey,
> some occult or allegorical significance to the reader, these
> latter passages are, take them all in all, dull and monotonous.

(It is significant that T. Percy Jones defends himself in his
preface to *Firmilian* by reference to these very scenes in *Faust*.)
Aytoun continues: "Sometimes, according to our view, Goethe
is too metaphysical—at other times he condescends to a style
beneath the dignity of a poet. Humour was by no means his
forte." His final criticism is that

> if we look to the relation which the represented characters
> bear to the world without, it is impossible to deny that
> Goethe has failed in giving extrinsic interest to his drama.
> There is nothing in it to indicate time, which, as much as
> locality, is an implied requisite in a poem, especially if it
> be cast in the dramatic form. The reason of this is obvious.
> Unless time and locality be distinctly marked, there is no
> room for that interest which is created by our willing sur-
> render of belief to the poet. What we require from him is,
> that he shall establish that degree of probability which gives
> life and animation to the poem, by identifying it to a certain
> extent, with human action and character.

Because of all these negative qualities, Aytoun's final judgment
on *Faust* is that "we cannot regard it, on the whole, either as a
perfect poem, or as one which, from its form, should recommend
itself to later poets as a model."

Here, two years before the publication of *Firmilian*, Aytoun
has enumerated several of the important characteristics that he
found so reprehensible in the Spasmodics: isolated scenes of

varying quality rather than a unified whole, the alternation between styles too metaphysical and too low, the prevalence of
mysticism and the absence of humor, and the extreme insulation
of the characters. Just as T. S. Eliot in a later day was to attack
Milton largely because of the unfortunate influence he wielded
over lesser poets, so Aytoun turned against *Faust* because he now
saw Goethe as one of the progenitors of the Spasmodics.

Aytoun maintained the same attitude toward Byron. It was
Byron, he thought, to whom "in a great measure the declension
in our literature is owing. I admit his genius, his versatility and
power, but I have no sympathy either with the man or with his
taste." A host of misguided imitators had sprung up, "each of
them attempting, after the vein of their great original, to convince
us that he was a sort of persecuted Prometheus with singular
notions of religious subjects." [2] It was this persecuted Prometheus,
the descendant of Byron's Manfred and Cain and Harold, who
became the chief identifying feature in the Spasmodic tradition,
the Spasmodic hero.

It is perhaps impossible to name a significant poet of the mid-
nineteenth century whom Byron did not influence, but his impact
upon the Spasmodics was especially powerful. Bailey memorized
Childe Harold, and Dobell memorized *Manfred;* [3] they were
fascinated by these extreme examples of the Byronic hero.[4] Fused
out of individual protagonists into a vague general conception in
the public mind, the Byronic hero has an air of mysteriousness
and concentrated passion; he dwells apart from other human
beings and often hates them; he strives to discover the secrets of
the universe and undergoes spiritual sufferings which drive him
to the threshold of insanity. Unlike Faust, the Byronic hero is
a passionate, aspiring, disillusioned youth. On the other hand,
the Spasmodic hero is a more extreme individual and is addi-
tionally, uniquely, a Byronic poet.

2. Erik Frykman, *W. E. Aytoun, Pioneer Professor of English at Edinburgh*
(Goteborg, Almquist and Wiksell, 1963), p. 43.

3. John C. Francis, *Notes and Queries,* Ninth Series, *10* (1902), p. 243; E. Jolly,
The Life and Letters of Sydney Dobell (2 vols. London, Smith, Elder, and Co.,
1878), *1,* 37.

4. The best discussion that I know of the genealogy and nature of the Byronic
hero is in Eino Railo, *The Haunted Castle* (London, G. Routledge and Sons, Ltd.,
1927), esp. pt. vi.

PHILIP JAMES BAILEY

Philip James Bailey (1816–1902) was accused by Aytoun of fathering the Spasmodics, and, despite his own violent protests, this paternity has been confirmed by the testimony of almost all commentators. Although afflicted with a wild, diffuse romanticism, his one significant achievement, *Festus,* still shows the individual influences of Byron and Goethe. Bailey's poem, like *Faust* and in contradistinction to the old Faustus tradition, does not depict the struggle between the forces of good and evil, but is rather a quest poem. The superior and disillusioned hero makes a compact with Lucifer, who thereupon unveils new realms of experience to the mortal. After little action but interminable speculation, Festus, who has retained his faith in the midst of the most sinful experience, achieves salvation—and so does everyone else, including Lucifer, in the comforting doctrine of universal redemption.[1]

What mattered most to the author and his large Victorian audience was not the movement of the poem, but the speculation itself. *Festus* is a sententious, didactic, comforting work. Bailey explains, in his typical prose, that the poem deals with

> Humanity generally, under its twofold aspect, primarily, spiritual, exemplified in two instances; one recently released from bodily bonds, and passing through the process of probational purification; another, rejoicing in assured beatitude; secondarily, as outlined in the person and career of the hero and his companion characters, with such peculiarities and qualifications of gift and temperament as pertain to their chief, and the various members of the poetical circle alluded to, as suffice to vitalize the framework of the pageant, and demark it from the range of allegory.[2]

If the reader charts the movement of the poem over its 40,000 lines, however, he will find that it follows the general pattern of *Faust:*

1. In the rare first edition of *Festus* (1839) , Lucifer is not saved.
2. P. J. Bailey, *Festus* (London, George Routledge and Sons, 1903) , p. 5.

Of the terrestrial scenes, more numerous, as might be expected, than those of any other class, devoted to the earthly
experiences of the hero, his loves, his friends, his companions,
his adventures, the temptations and trials by which he is
tested, and the offences of pride and passion by which he is
temporarily overcome, his aspirations and shortcomings, his
penitences and griefs, his voluntary self-demission of the
surpassing and so to speak miraculous gifts and privileges
with which he has been endowed, and his gradual advance
morally and spiritually from the world chaos of conflicting
partialist and imperfect beliefs to the sufficing system of
simple and philosophic truth to which he at last attains, it
is at this time unnecessary to speak.[3]

Besides the overall scheme, many particular elements in
Festus reveal the influence of *Faust*. Bailey has followed the
advice of Goethe's stage manager to "show the whole circle of
creation, and travel with reasonable speed from Heaven through
the world to Hell." [4] The original version of *Festus* opens dramatically in Heaven. Just as in *Faust*, the choral singing of the
angels alternates with God's discussion with the Devil, in which
they agree to a test of the hero's soul. No dramatic suspense is
raised, however, for it is immediately asserted that the hero is
secure:

> That though he plunge his soul in sin like a sword
> In water, it shall nowise cling to him.
> He is of Heaven.[5]

Thus, Bailey makes clear at the start that *Festus* does not deal
with the struggle between good and evil, but with the increasing
experience and understanding of the protagonist.

The poem soon drops from the heavenly sphere and introduces
the hero. Although a young man, Festus resembles Faust in his
feeling of disillusioned satiety and his need for new experience.
Thus, upon Lucifer's appearance, he overcomes his initial fear,

3. Ibid., p. 2.
4. Goethe, *Faust* (New York, New Directions, 1949), Pt. 1, p. 180.
5. P. J. Bailey, *Festus* (New York, T. R. Knox and Co., 1885), p. 20. All subsequent references to *Festus* will be to this edition, unless otherwise specified.

asserts his mastery, and expresses his willingness to accept the Devil as his instructor. Seeking to exhaust experience in order to find some sort of personal salvation, Festus follows closely the progress of his German predecessor. Even Lucifer, in his function of useful mediator between God and man, "the friendly fiend" [6] rather than the Miltonic or Byronic destroyer, is closest to Goethe's Mephistopheles. The finest episode in *Festus*, Lucifer's ironic sermon to the people, gained its inspiration from Mephistopheles' ironic advice to the student.[7]

Because of these similarities, several men of letters criticized Bailey for his dependence upon Goethe. Carlyle refused to read *Festus* because it was "a new garment, a sort of lunar shadow of Faust. Having eaten his pudding he was content, and felt no inclination to eat it again réchauffé." [8] Emerson complained that "Bailey is a brilliant young man who has got his head brimful of *Faust*, and then pours away a gallon of ink. But no secondary inspiration, as on Milton, or Shakespeare, or on Goethe is permitted; only an inspiration direct from the Almighty." [9] And Edmund Gosse, who admired Bailey, granted that *Festus* "was founded, almost too closely on that [conception] of Goethe's 'Faust.' " [1] Gosse also asserted that "the attack of the utilitarians had been chiefly directed against the disciples of Byron, and the new poet evaded the censure of the critics by ignoring in the main the influence of that daemonic enchanter." [2]

It would be unwise, however, to discount too soon the influence of that demonic enchanter upon the young poet. Bailey was born and bred in Nottingham, near Newstead Abbey, whose lord he saw lying in state; he knew by heart *Childe Harold*, a poem of over 4,500 lines. Indeed, a reading of *Festus* makes clear that Byron is at least as important an influence as Goethe. Dominating

6. Ibid., p. 256.

7. Ibid., pp. 80–86; Goethe, *Faust*, pp. 58–64.

8. Sir Charles Gavan Duffy, *Conversations with Carlyle* (New York, Charles Scribner's Sons, 1892) , p. 101.

9. Ralph Waldo Emerson, *Journals*, eds. E. W. Emerson and W. E. Forbes (10 vols. Boston and New York, Houghton Mifflin Co., 1909–14) , 7, 285.

1. Edmund Gosse, "Philip James Bailey," *Portraits and Sketches* (New York, Charles Scribner's Sons, 1912) , p. 73.

2. Ibid., p. 72.

the poem, the hero Festus falls clearly into the Byronic tradition. Unlike Faust, he is the superior, solitary, passionate, disillusioned youth. In his moments of ecstasy he feels he can become portion of that around him:

> Hail beauteous Earth! Gazing o'er thee, I all
> Forget the bonds of being; and I long
> To fill thee, as a lover pines to blend
> Soul, passion, yea existence, with the fair
> Creature he calls his own. (p. 50)

More frequently, however, he appears as the malcontent. Although a young man, he has suffered incalculable woes; his soul "as a sudden star . . . /Passes for ever, not eclipsed, consumed" (p. 71).

> Whose woes are like to my woes? What is madness?
> The mind, exalted to a sense of ill,
> Soon sinks beyond it into utter sadness,
> And sees its grief before it like a hill.
> Oh! I have suffered till my brain became
> Distinct with woe, as is the skeleton leaf
> Whose green hath fretted off its fibrous frame,
> And bare to our immortality of grief. (p. 181)

> .   .   .

> My bosom, like the grave, holds all quenched passions.
> It is not that I have not found what I sought—
> But, that the world—tush! I shall see it die. (p. 354).

Such outbursts, like Childe Harold's, are generally not the result of any external stimulus, but proceed from the action of the mind upon itself; the motivation is temperamental rather than logical. Consequently, such outbursts can and do occur at any point in the poem; the three quotations above come from the beginning, middle, and end of *Festus*.

Festus not only remains apart from other men, but generally despises them. He is like "Planets and suns, that set themselves on fire" (p. 47); they are "Not suns—not planets—darkness organized" (p. 57). One of his thoughts "is clearly worth a thousand lives/Like many men's" (p. 76). It follows naturally that "I live but for myself—/The whole world but for me" (p. 351). The Byronic hero, now developing into the more extreme Spasmodic hero under the hand of Bailey, turns away from people and seeks solace in nature:

> Come, let us to the hills! where none but God
> Can overlook us; for I hate to breathe
> The breaths and think the thoughts of other men,
> In close and crowded cities, where the sky
> Frowns like an angry father mournfully.
> I love the hills and I love loneliness. (p. 95)

The natural man and the natural world can never go wrong by themselves:

> Nature does
> Never wrong: 'tis society which sins.
> Look on the bee. (p. 114)

No need to spell out that familiar analogy here. It is society which sins, and as for the hero, well, "Yes! if I have sinned, I have sinned sublimely" (p. 205).

Festus goes to the extremes of experience in love, just as in everything else. He swears eternal fidelity to Angela, and Clara, and Marian, and Helen, and Elissa, stealing the last away from Lucifer himself. Making love at a party to another woman, he assures the dead Angela (in an aside) that "If on her breast I lay my head,/My heart on thine is fixed" (p. 190). Generally, however, he does not play the hypocrite with himself:

> Oh! Why was woman made so fair? or man
> So weak as to see that more than one had beauty?
> It is impossible to love but one. (p. 71)

And, after all, if such promiscuity was a fault in him, "Twas one which made him do the sweetest wrongs/Man ever did" (p. 239).

Bailey is adding a new characteristic to the Byronic hero, what Aytoun was to call "pruriency." Figures like Harold and Manfred are characterized by fidelity to an ideal woman, lost in some mysterious manner and causing the hero bitter remorse. The

influence of Byron on Bailey is so strong, however, that, despite
Festus' blasé attitude toward women, he occasionally speaks of a
lost love and uses the Byronic language of penitence. Where such
an emotion forms a consistent and essential part of the characters
of Harold and Manfred, it is merely an excrescence in Festus.

Bailey adds still one more element to the Byronic hero: he now
becomes an extremely Romantic, or Spasmodic, poet. Festus did
not appear as such in the original volume of 1839. To clear up
the obscurity of that version, however, Bailey added an Additional
Scene in the second edition, in which Festus gives Helen and the
Student a detailed account of a young poet. The poet turns out
to be the speaker, and his poem is *Festus*. This remains a favorite
Spasmodic device: a poet-hero talking about himself and about
the very poem in which he has his being.

It is important for an understanding of the Spasmodic tradition
to examine Festus' description of the poet-hero, for many of
these ideas are applied by Gilfillan, Smith, and Dobell to real
poets. The Spamodic poet-hero remains a solitary and communi-
cates only with the happy few:

> Yet the true bard doth make himself ghost-like;
> He lives apart from men; he waits and walks
> By nights; he puts himself into the world
> Above him; and he is but what few see.
> He knows, too, of the old hid treasure, truth:
> And the world wonders, shortly, how some one
> Hath come so rich of soul; it little dreams
> Of the poor ghost that made him. Yet he comes
> To none save of his own blood, and lets pass
> Many a generation till his like
> Turns up; moreover, this same genius
> Comes, ghost-like, to those only who are lonely
> In life and in desire; never to crowds. (p. 266)

(How Aytoun, the lover of popular ballad poetry, must have
shuddered.)

Festus, speaking about himself with an unmistakable Byronic
echo, describes how the poet-hero writes about his own misery:

He was no sooner made than marred. Though young,
He wrote amid the ruins of his heart;
They were his throne and theme;—like some lone king,
Who tells the story of the land he lost,
And how he lost it. (p. 237)

This central Spasmodic theme, however, does not exclude others;
anything is allowed:

But once
Begun, work thou all things into thy work;
And set thyself about it, as the sea
About earth, lashing at it day and night,
And leave the stamp of thine own soul in it. (p. 270)

The 40,000-line *Festus* itself stands as a practical example of
all things being worked in.

The poet-hero is always inspired, never a craftsman; he con-
cerns himself with great thoughts, not their effective communication:

There is no style is good but nature's style.
And the great ancients' writings, beside ours,
Look like illuminated manuscripts
Before plain press print; all had different minds,
And followed only their own bents: for this
Nor copied that, nor that the other; each
Is finished in his writing, each is best
For his own mind, and that it was upon.

.   .   .

Write to the mind and heart, and let the ear
Glean after what it can. The voice of great
Or graceful thoughts is sweeter far than all
Word-music; and great thoughts, like great deeds, need
No trumpet. Never be in haste in writing.
Let that thou utterest be of nature's flow,
Not art's; a fountain's, not a pump's. (pp. 269, 270)

Certainly *Festus* itself exemplifies a lack of concern with the "artificial" aspects of poetry; unfortunately, there often seems to have

been a lack of inspiration. Bailey has little control over blank verse and frequently loses the rhythm:

> It is time that something should be done for the poor.
> (p. 95)

Sometimes his lines sound silly:

> Forefated, fore-atoned for from the first. (p. 27)

Sometimes his meaning seems silly:

> But it is not more true that what is, is,
> Than that what is not, is not. (p. 265)

Sometimes confused:

> I would ruin sight
> To give its virtue to thy lips, whereon
> I would die now, or ever live (pp. 407–08) [3]

Sometimes obscure:

> God seeketh us, illuminating life;
> Not that it is our earth rise into Heaven,
> Forced by orbitual reason towards the Truth
> Even when retrogressive. (p. 356)

Nor does Bailey show much sense of propriety: he dresses prosaic details in the most lavish ornaments and spoils passages of imaginative intensity with colloquial expressions.

> Sometimes we feel the wish across the mind
> Rush, like a rocket tearing up the sky,
> That we should join with God and give the world the
> slip. (p. 30)

His more ambitious rhetorical passages almost always fail to maintain a high level. I think we must agree with Swinburne that "Bailey had no ear and no metrical power at all." [4]

Yet *Festus* enjoyed unbelievable popularity for about fifty years. It is uncertain just how many editions there have been, but the

3. This and the following quotation are taken from a different, expanded edition of *Festus:* P. J. Bailey, *Festus* (New York, Worthington Co., 1889).

4. Edmund Gosse, "The Life of Algernon Charles Swinburne," *Works of Algernon Charles Swinburne* (20 vols. London, William Heinemann Ltd., 1927), *19,* 268.

number goes over 100.[5] "No English poem, it was said, ever sold through so many American editions as 'Festus.' " [6] Undoubtedly, the majority of readers can be explained away as a nonliterary group who read the book for its didacticism and comforting religious doctrine. Still, many literary men and intelligent readers gave high praise to *Festus*. Thackeray called Bailey "an author of much merit and genius"; Ainsworth said, "His place will be among the first, if not the first, of our native poets." [7]

Two factors combine to explain this popularity among the literati. In the first place, the original *Festus* of 1839 is a finer poem than the editions more readily available today. It contained 8,000 lines of Bailey's best work and made some pretense to form, while later editions have up to 40,000 lines of the most incongruous matter. Bailey not only kept adding to *Festus* itself but also included in it large portions of his later unsuccessful poems, *The Angel World* (1850), *The Mystic* (1855), and the *Universal Hymn* (1867). He was indeed working into it all that he could. As early as 1876, W. M. Rossetti suggested that *Festus* should be made available again in its earliest version.[8]

Richard Hengist Horne's article, "Henry Taylor and the Author of 'Festus,' " [9] to which both Robert Browning and Elizabeth Barrett contributed,[1] indicates the second and chief reason for the effect of *Festus* upon young writers. Horne contrasts the sound-sense poetry practiced by Taylor in *Philip van Artevelde* unfavorably with the passionate and imaginative work of Bailey. The critical field had been dominated recently by utilitarians and rationalists; highly passionate and personal poetry existed under-

5. Jerome Thale, "Browning's 'Popularity' and the Spasmodic Poets," *JEGP*, 54 (1955), 351.

6. T. W. Higginson, *Studies in History and Letters* (Boston, Houghton Mifflin and Co., 1900), p. 262.

7. Bailey's publisher, Pickering, printed all the favorable notices he could in the back of the second edition (1845). See also A. D. McKillop, "A Victorian Faust," *PMLA, 40* (1925), 758–62.

8. W. M. Rossetti, "William Bell Scott and Modern British Poetry," *MacMillan's Magazine, 33* (1876), 425.

9. R. H. Horne, *A New Spirit of the Age* (New York, Harper and Brothers, 1844) pp. 349–65.

1. W. C. DeVane and K. L. Knickerbocker, eds., *New Letters of Robert Browning* (New Haven, Yale University Press, 1950), p. 31; Gardner B. Taplin, *The Life of Elizabeth Barrett Browning* (New Haven, Yale University Press, 1957), p. 117.

ground: Robert Browning was unread, and Robert Montgomery was unreadable. Then came *Festus,* and ardent young spirits, feeling a sense of liberation, tended to confuse its merit with its intent.

Whereas Taylor desired that poetry be limited to the objects of sense, Bailey soared and sunk into Heaven, Hell, Everywhere, and Nowhere. He spoke of "feeling stars" and "moons and planets . . . gibbous-faced." [2] He employed violent and grandiloquent imagery, which may have occasionally recalled that of Byron. Elizabeth Barrett perceived just how terrible Bailey was at times, but she could still shout out, like many another young reader, "what poet-stuff remains! what power! what fire of imagination!" [3]

Among the young poets who were influenced emotionally by Bailey, the Spasmodics most clearly exhibit poetic discipleship. Indeed, *Festus* contains all of the elements to be found in that school. The attitude toward literature which Aytoun had attacked in *Faust* had now become established in English poetry. The *Festus* of the 1850s, containing heterogenous matter from different poems written at various times, makes no pretense to unity; it is composed of isolated, often unconnected, scenes. It is an insulated drama, completely withdrawn from the world of men; it is even questionable, as Bailey was the first to point out, "if that may be termed dramatic which boasts no plot, no action; and only a few characters." [4] Bailey's alternations between styles too metaphysical and too low become more uncontrolled than Goethe's, his attempts at humor are no more successful, and he makes even freer use of the Satanic character.

The Byronic hero has become Spasmodic. With the elimination of plot and action, attention focuses on this dominant individual and his attempt to establish a relationship with his universe.[5] This new hero has become even more passionate, aspiring, superior, and disillusioned than his great prototype. He appears

2. Bailey, *Festus,* pp. 79, 218.
3. Elizabeth Barrett Browning, *Letters to Richard Hengist Horne* (New York, James Miller, 1877) pp. 223–24.
4. McKillop, "A Victorian Faust," p. 744.
5. See Bailey, *Festus* (New York, Worthington Co., 1889), p. 385.

capable of any and all experience and exhibits a new interest in women and poetry.

Finally, as to the question of the poet's manner, Bailey both advocates the use of and sets the example for the spontaneous, natural style, the grandiloquent, colorful image, and the extended poetic digression. It is no wonder that almost all commentators on the Spasmodic school, from Aytoun, its first important assailant, to Buchanan, its last significant defender, have acknowledged Philip James Bailey to be the father.[6]

GERALD

Aytoun's *Firmilian* (1854) labeled as Spasmodic poems Bailey's *Festus*, Alexander Smith's *A Life-Drama* (1852, but dated 1853), and Sydney Dobell's *Balder* (1853). It was, however, attacking an entire attitude toward literature, and the size of membership in the contemporary school of poetry will depend upon the breadth of our definition of Spasmodic. Keeping to a narrow definition and requiring a Spasmodic poem to contain the major features enumerated in *Festus* and found later in *A Life-Drama* and *Balder,* we may include as full-fledged members John Westland Marston's *Gerald* (1842), John Stanyan Bigg's *Night and the Soul* (1854), and the anonymous *Arnold* (1855). None of them has the historical importance of *Festus* or the literary quality of *A Life-Drama* and *Balder,* but *Gerald* provides an interesting link between *Festus* and the later poems. Contemporary works with significant Spasmodic tendencies, cognate members of the school, include Bigg's *Sea-King* (1848), Longfellow's *Golden Legend* (1851), Tennyson's *Maud* (1855), and Mrs. Browning's *Aurora Leigh* (1856); the latter two will be discussed later.

John Westland Marston (1819–90) knew Philip James Bailey well and became one of the first fervent admirers of *Festus*. A member of the mystical group which gathered around James Pierrepont Greaves, he contributed to John Abraham Heraud's

---

6. Robert Buchanan, "Sidney Dobell and the Spasmodic School," *A Look Round Literature* (London, Ward and Downey, 1887), p. 188; Rossetti, "William Bell Scott and Modern British Poetry," 418–29; *The North British Review, 28* (1858), 132; *The Saturday Review, 1* (1855), 34; *Athenaeum, 66* (1876), 465. The dissenting voice is Hugh Walker's in *The Literature of the Victorian Era,* p. 349.

Sunbeam and later became editor of his own mystical magazine, *Psyche*.[1] It was this English coterie which made its fellow Concord transcendentalists aware of Bailey and thus precipitated *Festus* on its successful American career. Bailey himself, the year after *Festus* was published, received an invitation to one of these transcendental soirees. The question discussed that evening was on what authority two and two are affirmed to be four, and Bailey afterward told his father that this sort of meeting "beats everything."[2] In this same year, 1840—the date is important because it precludes the possibility that Browning influenced Bailey, despite the use of the name Festus—Marston gave Bailey his first copy of *Paracelsus,* thus introducing him to a poet with whom he is frequently associated.[3] Marston, in turn, received considerable guidance from Bailey, one critic accusing the author of *Gerald* of "betraying much less influence from the muse than from his friend the author of 'Festus.' "[4]

In his preface to *Gerald,* Marston reveals "my intention was, from such materials—whether dignified or humble—as the times presented, to construct a Poem of Dramatic—perhaps of Tragic—interest."[5] Yet "I have not thought it necessary to adhere to the canons of the Drama, so strictly, as if the Poem had been intended for Theatrical representation" (p. vii). The reader is not to expect a traditional drama built upon a great action; instead, Marston, like all the Spasmodics, has chosen "the struggles and experiences of *Genius* as a subject." He adds, "the delineation of a great mind, subject to infirmities and swayed by passions, is not without peculiar advantages," advantages "too obvious to need specification" (p. vi). His method is exactly the same as that used later by Smith, Dobell, and Tennyson; his concern is not with plot development or logical continuity, but with "the illumination of *certain points* in Gerald's mental history—to show the *crises* of his

1. *DNB,* "Marston, John Westland."
2. *The Christian Science Monitor* (Apr. 9, 1919), p. 3; McKillop, "A Victorian Faust," p. 762.
3. See, for example, Walker, *The Literature of the Victorian Era,* p. 343, and Horne, *A New Spirit of the Age,* p. 278.
4. *DNB,* "Marston."
5. John Westland Marston, *Gerald; a Dramatic Poem: and Other Poems* (London, C. Mitchell, 1842), p. v.

developments, not their *progress*" (p. vi). This illumination comes through reveries rather than soliloquies, an important distinction for Spasmodic practice which Marston makes in a footnote to the second act. The hero's lines "are intended to represent thoughts which one would scarcely express in language to oneself —far less to another—involuntary thoughts by which the mind is borne along without any conscious effort of its own" (p. 23).

Gerald is a Spasmodic hero, although a tamer version than Dobell's Balder or Smith's Walter. He is the Great Man:

> The omens of my life have been too clear—
> Too noble to delude! No common end
> My past points out. Believe 'twas not in vain
> My young inclinings, spurning common lore,
> And saws of village Solons, led my feet
> Up mountain heights ere dawn to cheer the Sun
> On his great march, and feel that we were born
> To kindred destinies. (p. 11)

Marston uses another favorite analogy for the Spasmodic hero: Gerald is identified with "the kingly Eagle" who dwells "On the rock's peak in solitude" (p. 14). He feels he can accomplish anything; external forces are contemptible, "ourselves the bound/ To our own fate" (p. 13). To succeed, the individual must act extravagantly:

> the right
> Lies ever in extremes. Of all the saws
> That ever duped the world, that "mediate" saw
> Hath wrought most bane to man. If truth be truth,
> It may not be compounded without sin. (p. 44)

It is also significant that Gerald is "A lad that can't laugh" (p. 12).

Gerald is a Great Poet of the Festus school, but whereas Festus was such incidentally, poetry is Gerald's occupation. He emphasizes the importance of divine inspiration rather than human thought:

> The truly great are *fashioned* so, and shed
> Their affluent beauty round—as planets shine,

Birds sing, and rivers roll from laws within,
From native impulse, elemental life!
Their origin, their motive—is above;
And nought below compels them—or restrains. (p. 96)

The true bard writes about his own life, more particularly, his inner life:

Fiction! Poetry
Lives but by truth. Truth is its heart. Bards write
The life of soul—the only life. Each line
Breathes life—or *nothing*. Fiction! Who narrates
The stature of a man, his gait, his dress,
The colour of his hair, what meats he loved,
Where he abode, what haunts he frequented,
His place and time of birth, his age at death,
And how much cape and cambric mourned his end—
Writes a *biography!* But who records
The yearnings of the heart, its joys, and pangs,
Its alternating apathy, and hope,
Its stores of memory which the richer grow
The longer they are hived, its faith that stands
Upon the grave, and counts it as a beach
Whence souls embark for home, its prayers for man,
Its trust in Heaven, despite of man—writes fiction!
Get a new lexicon. (p. 47)

The desired effect of such poetry is a quivering delight (p. 11). And, finally, like all the Spasmodic poet-heroes, Gerald expresses a vague wish to win enduring good for mankind through his own solitary poetizing (p. 47).

Gerald marks an important development in the career of the Spasmodic hero. Although immoderate, he remains a recognizable human being. Essentially a poet, he moves on earth, not in Heaven, Hell, the circumambient air, or Anywhere. Along with Bailey's illimitable physical universe, the metaphysical speculation and religious seriousness of *Festus* have dwindled. It is true that Gerald spouts religiosity at the end, but the fine closing sentiments do not cancel out the hero's egotism throughout the bulk of the drama. Marston, like Smith and Dobell, has his hero follow the

familiar pattern of sin, hubris, fall, understanding, and regenera-
tion, but because he concentrates so preponderantly on the opening stages, he lays himself open to the charge of moral irresponsi-
bility that Aytoun was to level against the entire school. Richard
Hengist Horne, for example, complains that

> Gerald leaves his home feeling a strong impulse to do *some-
> thing* great in the world. Here at once we see the old sad error
> —a vague aspiration or ambition mistaken for an object and
> a power. A man of genius rushes out of his solitude, or takes
> some extreme step, because he is possessed with a ruling pas-
> sion—a predominating idea—a conviction that he can accom-
> plish a particular thing, and so relieve his breast of the
> ever-smouldering image—his imagination of the ever-haunt-
> ing thought. He does not rush forth with expanded arms to
> grasp at whatever presents itself to his inflamed desires. . . .
> We think that towards the close of his work Mr. Marston dis-
> covered this; in fact, we see signs that he did; but it was too
> late, and all he could do was to make his hero accuse himself
> of a selfish ambition as an excuse for his want of success.[6]

Smith and Dobell will offer even more striking illustrations of
poets, perfectly moral in intention, who draw upon themselves
the charge of immorality, a charge justified by their poetry itself.

Other important elements from *Festus* are developed or modified in *Gerald* and later reappear in *A Life-Drama* and *Balder*.
Festus contains so many digressions that it becomes difficult to
speak of digression in connection with that work, for the concept
implies a central subject. Despite their number, however, these
digressions usually deal with topics related to the nature of the
drama—metaphysics, religion, epistemology, the poet Festus.
Gerald, on the other hand, contains pure digressions, completely
unrelated to the immediate context. The hero is a poet, and so the
reader gets isolated examples of his work. It is as though the author had some extra poetry lying around and decided to pad his
drama with purple passages—in fact, such was the technique of
Smith.

Attacks on study and science, begun in the opening scene of

6. Horne, *A New Spirit of the Age,* p. 288.

Faust and continuing throughout the Spasmodic tradition, reappear here. So does a portion of the imprecise imagery of *Festus:* especially anticipative is the metaphor of the "overloaded heart," which appears frequently in Dobell and reaches its amazing culmination in Smith. Gerald, for example, is asked:

> Would not the portals of thy heart unfold?
> It is *my home* they guard, and I should find
> Its chambers in the darkness. Though the cold
> Hath chill'd them, and for buried hopes, the wind
> Chaunts mournful requiems; though the dusky walls
> Be draped with the dim 'scutcheons of the dead;
> Yet would I cry—"Dearer than festal halls,
> The sacred, shrouded, solitudes I tread!" (p. 58)

In the final analysis, Marston is not as Spasmodic as Smith and Dobell. He cannot soar to their heights, nor does he ever fall as low; he generally maintains a level mediocrity. He shows more interest in plot, and his hero moves more in the world of men. Otherwise, all of the important Spasmodic features are evident, and he seems to form a curious link between Bailey and Smith-Dobell. It is interesting to speculate whether his handling of the *Festus* elements influenced the similar treatment by the later poets. Dobell knew Marston, having contributed articles to his *National Magazine*,[7] and, in the three-character *Balder*, an artist named Gerald, an "old friend," makes an unexplained appearance. A few passages also bear a close resemblance, but to assert direct verbal influences in a tradition in which the various authors were all using the same themes and techniques is dangerous. It is especially difficult to believe that the egotistical Dobell or Smith would pay much attention to an inferior, unpopular predecessor. It seems safest to assume that they found independently a similar manner of treating the same basic material.

THE SPASMODIC CRITIC: GEORGE GILFILLAN

George Gilfillan (1813–78) was the critical advocate of the Spasmodics, the opponent of Aytoun, and, from 1849 to 1854,

7. *DNB*, "Marston."

probably the greatest critical influence upon young Victorian poets.[1] He was seeking a vatic poet of Shelley's type, "in his earnestness, his *possession*, his manner of communication—[one] of Israel's prophets."[2] Unlike the atheistic Romantic, however, the Victorian bard must reconcile the Christian religion with the realities of nineteenth-century life and thought. The critic and dissenting minister awaited "a new teacher, who, by uniting the spirit of Christianity to that of philosophy, shall present us with a satisfactory whole—with nothing less than which our eager inquirers will rest contented. May all the quick and cunning forces of nature combine in forming such an august spirit."[3]

Such an august spirit was not apparent among the ranking poets of the time. Gilfillan refused to acquiesce in the popular admiration for Tennyson, frequently criticizing the new laureate for not expressing "the spirit of the age": "has he written any great work, or has he even said any great things in his little works—has he done aught like *Festus?* or has he produced any such noble dramatic hymn as *The Roman?*"[4] (His remarks were telling enough to sting the established king. George Meredith describes a walk with Tennyson, in which "every now and then the irate bard paused, drew himself up, and said: 'But Apollodorus [Gilfillan's pen name] says I am not a poet.' "[5]) Instead, Gilfillan turned eagerly to the young poets for his august spirit. In his typical, excited prose he cries out:

> "The young mind of the age!" What a multitude of thoughts crowd on us when we utter these simple words! What mingled hope and fear—what tremulous anticipations rush in, as we think of what it is, and of what it may become—of the work it has to do, and the sufferings it has to endure. Never was there an age where there were so many young, ardent, and

1. Only Carlyle could compete with him. See George Gilfillan, *A Gallery of Literary Portraits*, ed. W. R. Nicoll (London, Dutton and Dent, 1909), p. vii.

2. R. A. and E. S. Watson, *George Gilfillan: Letters and Journals, with Memoir* (London, Hodder and Stoughton, 1892), p. 93. Gilfillan was one of the first to insist upon Shelley's greatness.

3. George Gilfillan, "Philip James Bailey," *A Second Gallery of Literary Portraits* (Edinburgh, James Hogg, 1850), p. 393.

4. *The Critic, II* (1852), 68. See also *The Eclectric Review*, N.S. *I* (1851), 410.

5. Gilfillan, *A Gallery of Portraits*, p. xviii.

gifted spirits—never was there an age when they more required wise guidance. The desideratum may be thus expressed, "Wanted a tutor to the rising age; he must be a creedless Christian—full of faith, but full of charity—wise in head and large in heart—a poet and a priest—an 'eternal child,' as well as a thoroughly furnished man." [6]

Many "young, ardent, and gifted spirits" accepted this enthusiast as their tutor and sent him their books and their manuscripts.

Gilfillan thought he had found his prophet in Bailey and wrote notice after notice on the new poet.[7] It is amusing to watch enthusiasm increase with each successive article. He moved from "a shock of surprise, mixed with pain, and not free from a shade of disgust," to an advocacy of *Festus* as "the poem of the age's hope," to a belief that it stood second only to Dobell's *Roman,* to an assurance that it was "the richest volume" of poetry in the Victorian age. *Festus* had the qualities Gilfillan looked for in a poem —high seriousness, broad scope, and spectacular imagery. Only the doctrine of universal salvation seemed noxious to the critic, but, even here, Bailey had at least made the attempt to reconcile religion and philosophy. Gilfillan's panegyrics, however, were not responsible for the growing popularity of *Festus;* he merely became the loudest member of a large chorus.

Gilfillan's strongest influence was upon the later Spasmodics: he gave Dobell his poetic start in the world by having an extract from the manuscript of *The Roman* published in *Tait's Magazine* in 1849.[8] In the same year he whetted the public appetite by a glowing eulogy of the forthcoming author.[9] As Dobell's biographer expresses it,

It is not, therefore, difficult . . . to enter to some extent into the feelings of the ambitious young writer receiving for the first time, from one to whose judgment he attached value and

6. Gilfillan, "Philip James Bailey," p. 393.

7. See *Hogg's Instructor, 6* (1847), 37, and N.S. 6 (1851), 173, and N.S. 7 (1851), 102; *Tait's, 14* (1847), 234, and *15* (1848), 728; *The Eclectic Review,* N.S. *1* (1851), 410; Gilfillan, "Philip James Bailey," pp. 387–94; and George Gilfillan, *A Third Gallery of Portraits* (New York, Sheldon, Lamport, and Blakeman, 1855), p. 116.

8. See Gilfillan, *A Gallery of Portraits,* p. xi.

9. *Hogg's Instructor,* N.S. *3* (1849), 337–41.

importance, the kind of eulogy freely bestowed by Mr. Gilfillan: who pronounced his work to have the royal stamp—of genius—upon the whole of it; and prophesied that its author was to be "another Shelley, of a manlier, Christian type." [1]

The young poet sent grateful letters to the famous critic for his encouragement: "If in after years I should ever be called 'Poet' you will know that my success is, in some sort, your work." In addition, he submitted the entire poem to Gilfillan and amended all but one of the passages that the critic condemned. [2]

The first edition of *The Roman* was published in April 1850 and instantaneously achieved a remarkable success. "Since Byron 'woke one morning to find himself famous' no young poet of this century had achieved so great and so unexpected a success." [3] Gilfillan, of course, was among the enthusiastic reviewers. [4] He devotes the first half of his article to denying the thesis of Macaulay that poetry becomes inferior as civilization progresses and to affirming the Spasmodic belief in the contemporary subject. It is true, he admits, that as yet no poet answers fully to his ideal:

Macaulay and Aytoun are content with being brilliant ballad singers—they never seek to touch the deeper spiritual chords of our being. Tennyson's exquisite genius is neutralized, whether by fastidiousness of taste or by morbidity of temperament—neutralized, we mean, so far as great future achievements are concerned. Emerson's undisguised Pantheism casts a cool shade over his genius and his poetry. There is something odd, mystical, and shall we say affected, about both the Brownings, which mars their general effect—the wine is good, but the shape of the cyathus is deliberately *queer*. Samuel Brown is devoted to other pursuits. Marston's very elegant, refined, and accomplished mind, lacks, perhaps, enough of the manly, the forceful, and the profound. Bailey of "Festus," and Yendys [Sydney Dobell's pen name] of the poem before us, are the most likely candidates for the vacant laurel. [5]

1. Jolly, *Sydney Dobell*, *1*, 103.
2. Ibid., pp. 104, 106.
3. Ibid., p. 117.
4. *The Eclectic Review*, 91 (1850), 672–84.
5. Ibid., pp. 678–79.

Gilfillan then rhapsodizes over this "extraordinary production." He levels only one criticism against *The Roman:* it is too unconnected. "He must give us next, not scattered scenes, but a whole epic, the middle of which shall be as obvious as the beginning or the end." But Dobell, who had written a fairly objective, coherent work in *The Roman,* was next to give them *Balder.*

Gilfillan himself was partially responsible for the increased Spasmodic quality of the poet's next work. He apparently had encouraged Dobell to read *Festus,* for the latter writes to him in 1849, "I am going to read Bailey's 'Festus,' of which I, as yet, know nothing but by report. Envy me." [6] He read it sometime between the completion of *The Roman* and the commencement of *Balder,* for a friend describes how "Dobell in completing 'Balder' planned to act in harmony with the advice given to all young poets by the author of 'Festus,' 'to work all things into their work.' " [7]

After the success of *The Roman,* Dobell exhibited greater self-confidence; he made no changes in what Gilfillan considered the "faults" of *Balder.* Gilfillan never seems to have felt comfortable about the poem and tells Dobell that "had I seen Balder as a whole, ere it appeared, I should have demurred to its publication, since as a piece of poetical power it is wondrous, but as an act in the great drama of your genius it rather hinders than helps the catastrophe." [8] Nevertheless, he still gave *Balder* a glowing review in public: despite its monotony and obscurity, the poem is "a 'wilderness' of thought—a sea of towering imagery and surging passion"; it stands as "the richest volume of recent poetry next to Festus." [9] Later, however, Gilfillan added an apologetic note to this review:

> Our paper was written immediately after reading the poem for the first time. Were we re-writing it now, our language would require considerable alteration. . . . Balder, with all its power and brilliance, has certainly a degree of disease in it. It is a great organ cracked. Its selection of a subject was an

6. Jolly, *Sydney Dobell, 1,* 108.
7. Ibid., p. 389.
8. Watson, *George Gilfillan,* pp. 170–71.
9. Gilfillan, *A Third Gallery,* pp. 116–29.

error, and its treatment of it is disfigured with obscurities and affectations.[1]

His final opinion places him in the Aytoun camp; Gilfillan was eventually to sum up *Balder* as "that hideous spasm of a true poet." [2]

Gilfillan exercised greater authority over Alexander Smith. A designer of sewed muslims who wrote poetry on the side, Smith had long admired the well-known critic:

> Everything from the pen of that gifted minister of Dundee was hailed and diligently perused by him; and on every occasion of his visiting Glasgow as a preacher or lecturer, Smith was certain to be one of his hearers. No mind in Scotland wielded at that time so great an influence over young aspiring minds intent on self-culture as Mr. Gilfillan; and among others, Smith was attracted to him by his hearty, impartial appreciation of genius, and the bold utterance of his convictions. By his writings in "Hogg's Instructor," "The Eclectic," "The Critic," etc., Smith's mind was in no slight degree stimulated.[3]

Eventually, in April 1851, "emboldened by Mr. Gilfillan's commendations of the 'Roman' by Sidney Yendys, or Dobell, Smith . . . resolved to submit a selection of his poems to him whom he had so long admired, and from whose writings he had derived so much benefit." After an accidental delay, Gilfillan read the poems and sent Smith "so appreciative, encouraging, and eulogistic" a response that "Smith was filled with unwonted joy, incited to increase hopefulness, and stirred to greater activity in composition. Other poems, at Mr. Gilfillan's desire were transmitted for his inspection, and a friendly correspondence commenced between the poet and the critic." [4]

At the same time, Gilfillan introduced Smith to the public in a magazine article.[5] He lavishes the highest praise upon him, comparing him to the author of *The Roman*. To illustrate Smith's

1. Gilfillan, *A Gallery of Portraits*, p. 61.
2. Ibid., p. xii.
3. Rev. T. Brisbane, *The Early Years of Alexander Smith* (London, Hodder and Stoughton, 1869), pp. 111–14.
4. Ibid.
5. *The Eclectic Review*, N.S. 2 (1851), 458–62.

"exquisite thoughts and imagery," he includes a selection of beauties from the major poem of the manuscript volume, a "Life Fragment." Additional encomiums were soon sent forth by Gilfillan,[6] and the reading public grew eager to see the poems themselves. The author too became restive and overly hasty:

> Smith, knowing that the public—now prepared by the extracts which had been laid before them—awaited the appearance of his poems in their full form, devoted every available moment to preparation for publication. Mr. Gilfillan had suggested to him, however, that the select literary world would be best satisfied with some longer poem than any he had yet written, in which the sustained concentration of his powers might be shown; and at once he perceived the justness of the suggestion. But as no subject for such an effort had yet occurred to his mind, he began to entertain the thought of attempting to fuse the detached pieces he had already composed into one extensive mould, formed after the plan of one of them, entitled "A Life Fragment." . . . This was to become, when thus expanded, "A Life Drama."[7]

A Life-Drama was thus the result of much "detaching, transposing, piecing, uniting, and supplementing."[8]

Another ominous portent for the coming *Life-Drama*, also traceable to Gilfillan,[9] was Smith's sudden admiration for *Festus*. Brisbane, his close friend during this period, remarks:

> Keats was no longer now the chief controlling spirit of his genius. The spell of Bailey's "Festus," rather, was now upon him. And too much under his influence, it is to be feared, the composition of the work was commenced and carried out. Evidence of this is very apparent when one compares "A Life Drama," with the previously written "Life Fragment," of which it was to some extent an expansion. The latter is throughout in conception, spirit, and treatment, far more Keatsean,—quiet, hazy, dreamy. It is a very different spirit

6. *The Critic* (Dec. 1, 1851), p. 567; *Hogg's Instructor*, N.S. *10* (1853), 649.
7. Brisbane, *Alexander Smith*, pp. 130–31.
8. Ibid., p. 132.
9. *The Eclectic Review*, N.S. 2 (1851), 459.

which animates "A Life Drama." The mind of Smith, in fact, was never in such an abnormal state as when he wrote that work.[1]

Nevertheless, *A Life-Drama* attained a remarkable, initial success;[2] now it was Smith's turn to wake to find himself famous.[3] Meredith wrote him a sonnet, hailing "The mighty warning of a poet's birth," and Herbert Spencer was "strongly inclined to rank him as the greatest poet since Shakespeare."[4] After *Firmilian,* however, people recognized Smith's poetic faults, and his reputation dropped rapidly. Gilfillan had done much to ensure Smith's immediate success, but he must share the blame for the ultimate failure of Smith's major attempt for permanent poetic standing.

Once the public had been prepared for the work of Smith, Gilfillan subjected *A Life-Drama* to a more judicial examination.[5] His evaluation remained favorable: he had special praise for the young poet's heart, music, and "unexcelled" imagery. But now he found fault with Smith's "vague and unformed" intellectual views; the minister expressed concern that no deep vein of reflection ran into religion. Smith's creed seemed to stop at "Beauty is truth—truth beauty." He was not, as yet, the looked-for poet to express "the spirit of the age" or to reconcile religion and art. When Smith, as a result of the Spasmodic controversy, turned to a more objective and restrained style of poetry and later to prose, Gilfillan repudiated him, regretting his failure to fulfill his youthful promise.[6]

A LIFE-DRAMA

The Spasmodic hero dominates *A Life-Drama.*[1] Walter is a poet: "For Poesy my heart and pulses beat,/For Poesy my blood runs red and fleet" (p. 1). One might question the pertinence of "red"

1. Brisbane, *Alexander Smith,* pp. 145–46.
2. See *Putnam's Monthly Magazine,* 2 (1853), 94–100, for a summary of the enthusiastic reception of the volume.
3. Watson, *George Gilfillan,* p. 200.
4. David Duncan, *Life and Letters of Herbert Spencer* (2 vols. New York, D. Appleton and Company, 1908), *1,* 87.
5. Gilfillan, *A Third Gallery,* pp. 130–43.
6. Watson, *George Gilfillan,* pp. 292–93.
1. Alexander Smith, "A Life-Drama," *The Poetical Works of Alexander Smith,* ed. W. Sinclair (Edinburgh, W. P. Nimmo, Hay, and Mitchell, 1909).

here, but no one can doubt Walter's feverish devotion to his art. He draws the familiar analogies between the poet and the eagle and between the poet and God (pp. 26, 90, 127). In one of his striking individual lines he describes poetry as "The grandest chariot wherein king-thoughts ride" (p. 17). It is through poetry that he hopes to realize his personal ambition: "O Fame! Fame! next grandest word to God!/I seek the look of Fame!" (p. 5).

Walter's notions of the poet closely resemble those of Festus and Gilfillan. The poet is a natural. His heart alone makes him a poet (p. 90); it is his nature "to blossom into song" (p. 13); he writes books when his "soul is at spring-tide," "When it is laden like a groaning sky/Before a thunderstorm" (p. 12). The poet is the spokesman of his own age: he sets the contemporary subject to music and, somehow, by this process, he hopes "to ease the earth" (pp. 18, 71, 72). Hence arises what may be called the "Spasmodic paradox." Gilfillan urged Smith and Dobell to attain poetic greatness in order to help convert the world, and Marston, Smith, and Dobell stress the ultimately social function of their work. Yet the poetry itself stands as an example of the most subjective and isolated kind; it withdraws almost completely from the outside world in *A Life-Drama,* and completely in *Balder.*

Walter's grand work, for instance, which was to "sun-crown this age" (p. 17), turns out to be "only written for two souls"—his own and his love's (p. 134). Smith, however, occasionally expresses impatience with the limitations of his hero. As Brisbane emphasizes throughout his biography, Smith was writing away from his natural bent in *A Life-Drama;* he could accept Aytoun's criticisms generously because he himself had never completely lost the ability to view his hero objectively. In *A Life-Drama,* subsidiary characters direct telling criticisms against the protagonist. The "critic-worms" describe a dead poet who is remarkably like Walter:

> Poet he was not in the larger sense;
> He could write pearls, but he could never write
> A poem round and perfect as a star. (p. 25)

Walter's first love leaves him with this advice:

> Strive for the poet's crown, but ne'er forget
> How poor are fancy's blooms to thoughtful fruits;
> That gold and crimson mornings, though more bright
> Than soft blue days, are scarcely half their worth. (p. 56)

And Edward, the practical man of the world, has the following reaction to Walter's thinly disguised self-portrait:

> Now, what a sullen-blooded fool was this,
> At sulks with earth and Heaven! Could he not
> Outweep his passion like a blustering day,
> And be clear-skied thereafter? He, poor wretch,
> Must needs be famous! Lord how poets geck
> At Fame, their idol. (p. 94)

Indeed, the movement of the poem is away from Spasmodic individuality and toward social responsibility: Walter violates Violet, wanders alone, writes a great poem, rejoins Violet, and accepts the world. In the final two pages, he expresses his new Victorian outlook:

> My life was a long dream . . . .
>
>   .   .   .
>
> I will go forth 'mong men, not mailed in scorn,
> But in the armour of a pure intent.
> Great duties are before me and great songs,
> And whether crowned or crownless, when I fall
> It matters not, so that God's work is done.
> I've learned to prize the quiet lightning-deed,
> Not the applauding thunder at his heels
> Which men call fame.
>
>   .   .   .
>
> A star's a cold thing to a human heart,
> And love is better than its radiance. Come!
> Let us go in together. (pp. 138, 139)

"Together" is the key, final word of *A Life-Drama*, but final words, or even the final two pages, do not make a long dramatic poem. They do not supersede the first 137 pages, especially since the final conversion appears a rather arbitrary affair. The lasting impression made on the reader by Walter is overwhelmingly that of the Spasmodic individual rather than of the regenerate citizen. Just as Gilfillan was justified in believing that Smith had not gone beyond Keats to do "God's work," so Aytoun was justified in believing that *A Life-Drama* challenged established order and morality.

Walter also displays other characteristics of the Spasmodic hero. In fact, he probably comes closer to the popular conception than either Festus or Balder; as we shall see, contemporary criticism of the Spasmodics tended to concentrate on and generalize from the work of Smith. Walter is a lover of "rich soul" (p. 13) and has two burning affairs. He is the solitary, "Lonely as God" (p. 90), who turns away from the cities of men to find consolation in nature (pp. 19, 89, 91, 106, 107). Often he reveals his Byronic origins, partially derived by way of *Festus*, and even seems to single out Byron for acknowledgment as one of his models:

> Beside that well I read the mighty Bard
> Who clad himself with beauty, genius, wealth,
> Then flung himself on his own passion-pyre
> And was consumed. (p. 38)

Walter exposes to view his own weariness, restless flitting, and remembrance of dreadful sins (pp. 60–61), his "strange sorrow" to which "all his thoughts did tend" (pp. 129), his loneliness "upon his waste and dreary road" (p. 130). He is finally advised:

> If thy rich heart is like a palace shattered,
> Stand up amid the ruins of thy heart,
> And with a calm brow front the solemn stars. (p. 55)

(These lines come directly out of *Festus;*[2] indeed, Bailey accused Smith, both in conversation and print, of plagiarism.[3] Finally, Walter exhausts all human experience, except "the cold feel of Death" (p. 70), and it is precisely at this point that *Balder* begins.

A Life-Drama has the fitful structure that one would expect from its method of composition, its models, and its thin plot.

2. Bailey, *Festus,* p. 237.
3. See Gilfillan, *A Gallery of Portraits,* p. xvii.

Smith works originally separate poems into his work. In theory, such a technique seems unpromising, and, in practice, the joints show frequently, and isolated purple passages result. Especially common are Walter's long descriptions of unfortunate young poets, who always turn out to be Walter himself (pp. 14–16, 61–69, 89–94). The concept of digression reaches its reductio ad absurdum with the inclusion of long digressive poems within long digressive poems (pp. 41–43).

A Life-Drama gained its initial success because of its sensuousness and spectacular imagery; Smith seemed to be a new Keats at a time when Keats had become extremely popular. Walter describes his own practice when he reports,

> our chief joy
> Was to draw images from everything
> And images lay thick upon our talk,
> As shells on ocean sands. (p. 104)

It is undeniable that Smith had a remarkable ability for image-making, but his very felicity seems detrimental:

> The lark is singing in the blinding sky.
> Hedges are white with May. The bridegroom sea
> Is toying with the shore, his wedded bride
> And, in the fulness of his marriage joy,
> He decorates her tawny brow with shells,
> Retires a space, to see how fair she looks,
> Then proud, runs up to kiss her. All is fair—
> All glad, from grass to sun! Yet more I love
> Than this, the shrinking day, that sometimes comes
> In Winter's front, so fair 'mong its dark peers,
> It seems a straggler from the files of June,
> Which in its wanderings had lost its wits,
> And half its beauty; and when it returned,
> Finding its old companions gone away,
> It joined November's troop, then marching past;
> And so the frail thing comes, and greets the world
> With a thin crazy smile, then bursts in tears
> And all the while it holds within its hand
> A few half-withered flowers. (pp. 75–76)

Each image is rich—yet, when together, too opulent, and, in juxtaposition, somewhat incongruous. It is certainly not the sort of poetry which lends itself to dramatic movement. Sometimes, Smith's individual images are arrestingly extravagant:

> come to-morrow
> And I will pasture you upon my lips
> Until thy beard be grown. (p. 52)

The usual cliché is that he exercised little restraint.

Ruskin chose two examples of the "pathetic fallacy" from *Maud;* he could also have gone to the Spasmodics. Smith's stars, as Aytoun was to emphasize, are especially active: they are always throbbing, shuddering, or panting with passion (pp. 3, 65, 81, 87, 93). And here is discovered another difficulty: Smith always turns to the same sources for his imagery, particularly to the sky and the sea. He will make use of Antony and Cleopatra four times in the same way, but never another pair of lovers (pp. 4, 28, 49, 114).

Smith's sensuousness generally takes the form of reveling in color. Walter describes his own technique as a limning, "with words like colours," on the canvas of the sense (p. 105). Thus, we find frequent scene-painting:

> On balcony, all summer roofed with vines,
> A lady half-reclined amid the light,
> Golden and green, soft-showering through the leaves,
> Silent she sat one-half the silent noon;
> At last she sank luxurious in her couch,
> Purple and golden-fringèd, like the sun's,
> And stretched her white arm on the warmèd air. (pp. 39–40)

Walter's description of a poet as "an April tree" with "vermeil-loaded boughs" (p. 25) may have suggested to Aytoun the title *Firmilian.*[4]

Finally, Smith is the most extreme delineator of "the over-loaded heart." In *A Life-Drama,* the heart is likened to a hut and a palace full of music (pp. 101, 111); there are references to the

---

4. See *The London Quarterly Review,* 2 (1854), 587, for a cogent description of the Spasmodic poems as "colour without form."

heart's chariot, rivers, fissures, green fields, and torn red tendrils (pp. 47, 97, 112, 110, 68). Similarly, the heart has a basement and cope, an arrow, and a finger (pp. 2, 3, 100); it is like an eagle, a forest haunted with pagan shapes, and a mountain range whose sides feed sheep (111, 108, 110, 74). Here, as elsewhere in Smith, Spasmody has come a long way.

BALDER

Spasmody reaches its extreme limits in Sydney Dobell's *Balder*. The poem so shocked Victorian readers when it first appeared in the last week of 1853 that, when the second edition came out in 1854, Dobell added a preface defending himself. He explains that he intends to portray, in three parts, the Progress "of a doubtful mind to a faithful mind." The first part, now before the public, presents merely "the egoistic hero of isolation and doubt" (pp. 333–34).[1] Unfortunately, because of Aytoun's *Firmilian* and the subsequent reaction, Balder's Progress was never completed.

As Dobell's remarks testify, *Balder*, in contrast to the philosophical *Festus* and the unfocused *Life-Drama*, is a psychological study. Dobell is unwilling to remain in "this sun-light world" and dives down into "the gulphs and deeps" with his hero (pp. 460, 511). His chief concern is the exposure of Balder's mind:

> The cavernous and windy mysteries;
> Yea, all the creeping secrets of her maw,
> The busy rot within her, and the worm
> That preys upon her vitals. (p. 379)

As in all Spasmodic writings, external action remains subordinate. Balder feels that he must experience everything before he can complete his great poem. Since death, the ultimate experience, has always eluded him, he seeks it by killing his own daughter. This act unnerves both him and his wife Amy. He slowly recovers, but she grows insane, and as the first part ends, Balder is about to kill her also. This bare plot may sound absurd, but its function is to allow for the examination of abnormal states of mind; and,

---

1. Sydney Dobell, *Poems* (Boston, Ticknor and Fields, 1860).

as Dobell dissects Balder's mind through a series of reveries, the
whole situation becomes fearfully believable.

Balder contains all of the familiar Spasmodic elements, but
Dobell pushes them to the breaking point—and sometimes beyond. Balder himself tends to make the other protagonists appear
rather pale. Like Gerald, the omens of his greatness have always
been clear; he put his "question to the universe,/And overhead
the beech-trees murmured 'Yes' " (p. 341). He has enjoyed all
of the experiences of Festus, without need of supernatural aid:

> Bound helpless on the fury of the winds,
> To scour the plains I seek not, scale the height
> Where my brain swims, and leap, as in a dream,
> Down into the unfathomable void. (p. 375)

Like Faust, he has tried all philosophies in vain: his pride has
climbed above earth, yet Heaven is no nearer (p. 499). Still, his
insatiability surpasses that of all his predecessors; only he could
speak of

> mine hunger, unappeased
> That sucks Creation down, and o'er the void
> Still gapes for more. (p. 366)

Balder is also a Poet-God (p. 348). He has been chosen by
Nature, "the one Teacher whom the Poet needs" (pp. 433, 506),
and he "attains in solitude" (p. 345). Like the others, he writes
about his own heart's woe (pp. 348, 381) but, to accomplish his
work, Balder goes far beyond them:

> Who is to die? It is not credible
> That this I have begun should come to end
> For lack of human lives, or that a pang
> Not mortal should fly wide of me; of me
> Who had I the round earth within my hand
> O'er populous as a green water-drop,
> Would swallow it to taste a novel savour. (pp. 382–83)

He frequently displays egotism and destructiveness unprecedented
in the Spasmodic tradition and, I believe, in English poetry.

Whereas Walter would have been satisfied with fame, Balder

wants "The seat of templed Power. Not Fame but Power./Or Fame but as the noise of Power" (p. 345). But he too falls into the "Spasmodic paradox." This most egotistic, isolated, and destructive of all individuals seeks power for the public good. He wants to be "the King of men" in order to "beget a better world" (p. 341). He is a god, but "In the form/Of manhood I will get me down to man" (p. 441)! He understands the deadness of "Society consorted to no end" and is the "One Infallible" to "make these dry bones live" (p. 496).

Dobell, in his preface of 1854, explains his seeming paradox. He had a moral purpose in the creation of such an amoral character—the exposure of the Romantic-Spasmodic hero.

> I understand that the public press have described my hero to be egoistic, self-contained, and sophistical, imperfect in morality, and destitute of recognized religion, mistaken in his estimate of his own powers and productions, and sacrificing to visionary hopes and dreamy distant philanthropies the blessing that lay in his embrace, and "the duty that was nearest."
>
> This is precisely the impression which I wished the readers of this volume to receive, and I owe some acknowledgement for such loud and emphatic testimony that exactly what I desired to attain has been attained. I have reason, however, to blame some of these powerful witnesses for the indecorous haste and uncharitable dogmatism with which, as I have seen, and am informed, they have taken for granted that I must personally admire the character I think fit to delineate, and that I present as a model what, in truth, I expose as a warning. (p. 334)

As to the propriety of the creation of such a character, Dobell replies that all the "elements of my hero" are already well known and refers to such popular writings as the autobiography of Haydon, the letters of Keats, the life of David Scott, and sundry incidents in the history of Goethe (p. 335).

The rub comes with the realization that *Balder* was never completed. Only the model appeared, not the exposure. Thus, although Dobell began on Aytoun's side with the moralist's intention of ridiculing the Romantic-Spasmodic hero in the interests of established order, his own hero justifiably became the chief butt of Aytoun's ridicule.

Dobell also differs from the other Spasmodics in his poetic manner. Although he cannot build a long dramatic poem, he can write excellent poetry.[2] By following Bailey's advice to work all things into his poem,[3] he spoiled the artistic unity of *Balder;* almost half the poem is composed of extraneous passages. These isolated passages, however, are often of fine quality and run the gamut from Wordsworthian quiet in the song for Amy (pp. 528–29) to Miltonic violence in the description of Tyranny (pp. 368–69). Dobell also excels in the undramatic device of working variations upon a theme. He selects a subject such as the supreme excess of Nature (pp. 433–34), or relief from pain (pp. 501–02), or the honoring of a favorite (p. 342) and then reels off one felicitous simile after another as illustration. Unlike the other Spasmodics, he exhibits a mastery of blank verse; he can sustain his power over the length of a paragraph. Like the others, however, he was often content to aim for the striking line. Swinburne believed "he never wrote a bad verse,"[4] but this is debatable, for in a line of iambic pentameter even more daring than Lear's use of "never" five times, Balder exclaims, "Ah! ah! ah!/Ah! ah! ah! ah! ah! ah! ah! ah! ah!" (p. 520). The Spasmodic cannot go further than this.

Dobell introduces one important element of psychological realism into the Spasmodic tradition. At crucial moments in the story, he has his hero examine minutely some extrinsic object (pp. 490, 533, 534). A student of psychology, Dobell believed that in moments of extreme tension the mind seeks an outlet by fastening its attention upon some unessential aspect of the immediate environment. This technique is burlesqued in *Firmilian,* used and speculated upon in the celebrated shell passage of *Maud,* and employed in much pre-Raphaelite poetry.

2. "Keith of Ravelston" is probably his most admired work. D. G. Rossetti thought it "one of the finest, of its length, in any modern poet—ranking with Keats's La Belle Dame sans Merci" (see W. M. Rossetti, ed., *Dante Gabriel Rossetti; His Family Letters* (2 vols. London, Ellis and Elvey, 1895), *1,* 420.

3. Jolly, *Sydney Dobell, 1,* 389.

4. Gosse, *Works of Algernon Charles Swinburne, 19,* 268.

Unlike Smith, Dobell does not try to load every rift with ore, but his imagery is more daring and more varied. Balder says,

> the bare hill-top
> Shines near above us; I feel like a child
> Nursed on his grandsire's knee that longs to stroke
> The bald bright forehead; shall we climb? (p. 438)

Later, he describes

> the man-fruit on the gallows-tree;
> It hung up like a fruit and like a fruit
> Shook in the wind, like a fruit was plucked down
> And the dark wintry branch stood bare. (p. 493)

The miserable Amy asks her husband to "ope the lattice of my soul," and finally Balder agrees to "let her forth/As a poor bird out of a burning cage" (p. 370). The only sure thing in *Balder* is the unusual. Even the individual words are uncommon. What are the meanings of "lunation" (p. 488), "susurrent" (p. 504), "snood" (p. 527), and "parhelion" (p. 538). With the publication of *Balder,* poetry seemed to Aytoun like "Pegasus run wild," and he determined to do something about it.

THE SPASMODIC CONTROVERSY

Numerous articles of the period dealt with Spasmodic poetry, and the most famous critical document of the decade, Arnold's 1853 Preface, developed out of the immediate controversy. From the mass of available material, it is possible to illustrate the positions taken by the pro- and anti-Spasmodics by examining the writings of five prominent men of letters: Herbert Spencer, J. M. Ludlow, Arthur Hugh Clough, Matthew Arnold, and Charles Kingsley. It is to be noted that whereas the pro-Spasmodics begin their arguments with the poet and his style, the anti-Spasmodics start with the poem and its structure.

Herbert Spencer asserts his viewpoint so dogmatically that the issues of the difficult problem are clearly outlined. His "Philosophy of Style" [1] establishes, incidentally, a rationale for Spasmodic poetry. With regard to style, his general principle is "that the force of all verbal forms and arrangements is great in proportion as the time and mental effort they demand from the recipient is small" (p. 450). Such forcible expression is the result of an excited state of mind: "mental excitement spontaneously prompts the use of those forms of speech which have been pointed out as the most effective" (p. 452). Spencer advocates a highly emotional, spontaneous mode of expression for that "peculiarly impressive species of composition which we call poetry." He is concerned that the poet develop "from the typical expressions in which men utter passion and sentiment, those choice forms of verbal combination in which concentrated passion and sentiment may be fitly presented" (p. 453). He champions the purple passage and

---

1. *The Westminster Review*, N.S. 2 (1852), 435–59.

quotes Shakespeare, Milton, Scott, Coleridge, Shelley, Keats, Tennyson, and Alexander Smith as established masters. It is not surprising to learn that, with such a philosophy of style, Spencer was "strongly inclined to rank him [Smith] as the greatest poet since Shakespeare." [2]

J. M. Ludlow offers a more challenging rationale for the practice of the Spasmodics, challenging enough to evoke a reply from Matthew Arnold. In an article of August 1853, "Theories of Poetry and a New Poet," [3] ostensibly devoted to the *Poetics* of E. S. Dallas and the *Poems* of Alexander Smith, Ludlow develops his own theory of poetry and then judges Smith's performance on the basis of that theory. He divides poetic theory into classical and Romantic camps: Aristotelian theory stresses the mimetic nature of poetry, while Baconian theory emphasizes the imaginative passion of the poet. He aligns himself with the latter, beginning his discussion with the mind of the poet: "The poetical tendency, then, is the tendency to that kind of mental activity which consists in the production, we might almost say secretion, by the mind of an artificial concrete; and the poetic genius is that kind of condition of mind to which this kind of activity is constitutionally most delightful and easy" (p. 311). He points out that Romantic theory favors an allegory of the poet's own mind:

> Indeed, Goethe's theory of poetical or creative literature was, that it is nothing else than the moods of its practitioners objectivized as they rise. A man feels himself oppressed and agitated by feelings and longings, now of one kind, now of another, that have gathered upon him till they have assumed the form of a definite moral uneasiness . . . if he is a literary man, then the uneasiness is but the motive to creation, and the result is—a song, a drama, an epic, or a novel. (p. 318)

Or, as Ludlow sums it up, "The subject chosen by a poetical writer, we have already said, is a kind of allegory of the whole state of his mental being at the moment" (p. 321).

2. Duncan, *Life and Letters of Herbert Spencer, 1*, 87.
3. *The North British Review, 19* (1853), 297-344.

When Ludlow examines the "artificial concrete" itself, he disregards the classical criteria of unity and structure and concentrates on imagery and verse. Imagery, the most prominent of Spasmodic elements, becomes the touchstone by which to judge an author's ability: "Now, as the very essence of the poet consists in the incessant imagination of concrete circumstance, a language rich in imagery is in itself a proof of the possession of poetical faculty in a high degree" (p. 326) . Verse comes with passion: "We incline to the belief that, though poetry and passion, like two inseparable friends that have taken up house together, have metre for their common servant, it is on passion, and not on poetry, that metre holds by legal tenure" (p. 328) .

Finally, Ludlow evaluates Smith's *Poems*. Although he censures some aspects of the achievement, he likes Smith's approach and rates him highly as a poet. This is understandable, for Smith satisfies Ludlow's requirements for poetic success: he writes an allegory of the poet's mind, his language is opulent with imagery, and he is passionate. Ludlow's method of evaluating the poems is characteristic of the pro-Spasmodic critics: the poet himself is dragged in, and emphasis is laid upon individual passages and images, in other words, upon "beauties."

> This is daring, almost to the limit of the lawful; but the words are not more solemn than the mood in which the author has written them. And, in any case, such a passage is decisive at least of the fact, that the author is a poet, and a poet of no common order . . . . If we take, for example, the theory of poetical genius which we have been expounding, and which, we believe, is identical, in the main, with all that is vaguely felt on the subject by some, and more explicitly stated by others, there is scarcely a volume from which a greater number of passages could be selected, illustrative of that theory. The poet, we have said, is "of imagination all compact;" his peculiarity is that he cogitates in a language of concrete circumstances—that, whatever meaning lies in his mind, that meaning takes the form not of abstract proposition, but some imagined scene, object, or incident, or some imagined tissue of scenes, objects, and in-

cidents. Apply this to Mr. Smith, and every page will furnish
an example in point. (p. 335)

Matthew Arnold must have shuddered when he read this article.

Arnold disliked the kind of poetry that Smith was writing [4]
and therefore showed considerable interest when he learned his
own poetry was to be compared with Smith's by Arthur Hugh
Clough. He wrote to his friend:

> I should like to read an article of your's on me—I should
> read it with a curious feeling . . . .
>
> As to Alexander Smith I have not read him—I shrink from
> what is so intensely immature—but I think the extracts I
> have seen most remarkable—and I think at the same time
> that he will not go far. I have not room or time for my
> reasons—but I think so. This kind does not go far: it dies
> like Keats or loses itself like Browning.[5]

Several years earlier in a letter to Clough (1848–49), Arnold
had stated his objections to Keats and Browning more explicitly:

> What a brute you were to tell me to read Keats' Letters.
> However it is over now: and reflection resumes her power
> over agitation.
>
> What harm he has done in English Poetry. As Browning
> is a man with a moderate gift passionately desiring move-
> ment and fulness, and obtaining but a confused multitudi-
> nousness, so Keats with a very high gift, is yet also consumed
> by this desire: & cannot produce the truly living and moving,
> as his conscience keeps telling him. They will not be patient
> neither understand that they must begin with an Idea of the
> world in order not to be prevailed over by the world's multi-
> tudinousness . . . .
>
> But what perplexity Keats Tennyson et id genus omne
> must occasion to young writers of the ὁπλίτης sort: yes and
> those d----d Elizabethan poets generally. Those who cannot

4. For an excellent discussion of this subject, see H. W. Garrod, "Matthew
Arnold's 1853 Preface," *Review of English Studies, 17* (1941), 310–21.

5. Letter of May 1, 1853. All quotations from Arnold's letters are from Arnold,
Matthew, *Letters to Arthur Hugh Clough,* ed. H. F. Lowry (London, Oxford University Press, 1932).

read Greek should read nothing but Milton and parts of Wordsworth: the state should see to it.

On October 28, 1852, he had again written to Clough:

Keats and Shelley were on a false track when they set themselves to reproduce the exuberance of expression, the charm, the richness of images, and the felicity of the Elizabethan poets. Yet critics cannot get to learn this, because the Elizabethan poets are our greatest, and our canons of poetry are founded on their works. They still think that the object of poetry is to produce exquisite bits and images . . . it must not lose itself in parts and episodes and ornamental work, but must press forwards to the whole.

Thus, the ideas of Arnold's 1853 Preface had long been developing in his mind, and Clough was well aware of them when he compared the classicist with the Spasmodist.

"Citizen Clough" has a thesis to push in his article [6] and does not scruple to distort the works under review in order to make his point. He wants modern poetry to deal with "the actual, palpable things with which our every-day life is concerned" (p. 357). Thus, he contrasts Smith, the "Glasgow mechanic," writing about "something substantive and lifelike, immediate and firsthand," favorably with Arnold, the "scholar and gentleman," "reflecting, pondering, hesitating, musing, complaining" (pp. 358, 370). *A Life-Drama,* however, does not deal with "every-day life"; its resolution is Walter's realization that his isolated existence was a "long dream" and his determination to "go forth 'mong men." Lionel Trilling offers a generous explanation of Clough's misunderstanding of Smith: "He [Smith] had been a mechanic and this seems to have induced Citizen Clough to read into his pretentious work a democratic significance which was simply not there." [7] Whether an accidental or a willful error, Clough, like Dipsychus, contrasts "the extremes of ascetic and timid self-culture, and of unquestioning unhesitating confidence" and resolves the *"antinomy"* to his own satisfaction.

6. "Review of Some Poems by Alexander Smith and Matthew Arnold," *Prose Remains* (London, MacMillan and Co., 1888), pp. 355–78. Originally in *The North American Review,* 77 (1853), 1–30.

7. Lionel Trilling, *Matthew Arnold* (New York, Meridian Books, 1955), p. 134.

Clough manifests more critical acumen in his remarks on style; in fact, he criticizes Smith for the same faults that Arnold would have emphasized:

> He writes, it would almost seem, under the impression that the one business of the poet is to coin metaphors and similes. . . . But simile within simile, after the manner of Chinese boxes, are more curious than beautiful; nor is it the true aim of the poet, as of the Italian boy in the street, to poise upon his head, for public exhibition, a board crowded as thick as they can stand with images, big and little, black and white, of anybody and everybody, in any possible order of disorder, as they happen to pack. (pp. 374–75)

Although he finished second in the two-man competition, Arnold probably understood that Clough had made the comparison for his own purposes and undoubtedly appreciated his remarks on style: "They think here that your article on me is obscure and peu favorable—but I do not myself think either of these things" (letter of August 25, 1853). Trilling believes that Arnold's Preface is an answer to Clough's July review.[8] This may seem exaggerated in view of Arnold's long preoccupation with the subject, but it must be granted that the essay is, in effect, an answer because it makes quite clear Arnold's opinion of the contemporary subject and "every-day life" in poetry. It is also, of course, much more than an answer. Arnold's 1853 Preface formulates anew a classical principle of poetry and is, for this reason, still famous today. But while admiring this quality of timelessness, it is also wise to remember that the essay had a particular relevance for the period in which it was written.

Arnold introduces his discussion of the proper subject for poetry with an explanation of the omission of his own most ambitious poem, "Empedocles on Etna," from the present volume. He emphasizes that "Empedocles" reveals much that is considered "exclusively modern": "the dialogue of the mind with itself has commenced; modern problems have presented themselves; we hear already the doubts, we witness the discouragement, of Ham-

8. Ibid., p. 135.

let and of Faust." [9] Arnold's particular reasons for the omission of such a subject apply exactly to Balder's problem, a problem which Maud's lover solves by going to war:

> What then are the situations, from the representation of which, though accurate, no poetical enjoyment can be derived? They are those in which the suffering finds no vent in action; in which a continuous state of mental distress is prolonged, unrelieved by incident, hope or resistance; in which there is everything to be endured, nothing to be done. In such situations there is inevitably something morbid, in the description of them something monotonous. (p. 284)

Arnold stresses that he did not exclude "Empedocles on Etna" because the subject came from a distant time and country; he does not want to be confused with those critics who believe that only modern subjects should be chosen. He even quotes "an intelligent critic" who promulgates the doctrine of "matters of present import"; the critic is Rintoul but could have been Clough or Gilfillan. To the refutation of this contemporary view he now devotes himself.

The classicist begins not with the mind of the poet, but with the poem itself. Excellent actions, "those which most powerfully appeal to the great primary human affections," are the eternal objects of poetry. "The modernness or antiquity of an action, therefore, has nothing to do with its fitness for poetical representation; this depends upon its inherent qualities" (p. 286). The great action itself, that which is to produce "the one moral impression," must be the primary concern of the poet:

> A modern critic would have assured him that the merit of his piece depended on the brilliant things which arose under his pen as he went along. We have poems which seem to exist merely for the sake of single lines and passages; not for the sake of producing any total impression. We have critics who seem to direct their attention merely to detached expressions, to the language about the action, not to the

9. Matthew Arnold, "Preface to First Edition of Poems," *Irish Essays and Others* (London, Smith, Elder, and Co., 1882), pp. 281–305.

action itself. I verily think that the majority of them do not in their hearts believe that there is such a thing as a total impression to be derived from a poem at all, or to be demanded from a poet; they think the term a commonplace of metaphysical criticism. They will permit the poet to select any action he pleases, and to suffer that action to go as it will, provided he gratifies them with occasional bursts of fine writing, and with a shower of isolated thoughts and images. That is, they permit him to leave their poetical sense ungratified, provided that he gratifies their rhetorical sense and their curiosity. (p. 292)

From this general attack on contemporary criticism, Arnold narrows his focus to deny the prescription of a particular critic, Ludlow:

But the modern critic not only permits a false practice; he absolutely prescribes false aims.—"A true allegory of the state of one's own mind in a representative history," the poet is told, "is perhaps the highest thing that one can attempt in the way of poetry." [1] And accordingly he attempts it. An allegory of the state of one's own mind, the highest problem of an art which imitates actions! No assuredly, it is not, it never can be so: no great poetical work has ever been produced with such an aim. (p. 293)

Just as Aytoun was to tell Mrs. Browning that plot and arrangement must precede expression,[2] so Arnold advises "the individual writer" to avoid critics like Ludlow and learn of the classics "the all-importance of the choice of a subject; the necessity of accurate construction; and the subordinate character of expression" (p. 300).

Aytoun and Arnold took the same position toward the popular poetry of that day, and, because of the opposite reactions to their works, it is tempting to contrast the effects of parody and argument. *Firmilian* was popular in its own time and laughed the Spasmodics out of court; the Preface of 1853 was little known

1. Arnold quotes inexactly. See his letter of October 10, 1853, to Clough for his inability to relocate Ludlow's article and hence his need to rely upon his memory.
2. *Blackwood's, 81* (1857), 40.

and had little practical effect. Today, few people know *Firmilian,* while the Preface stands secure as a classic. It is often true that, where a reasonable statement of general principles will have no effect on reigning taste, a burst of laughter startles the public into an awareness of its error. Once the objects of laughter have been forgotten, however, the parody loses its point, while the statement of principles retains its somewhat independent character. Thus, a successful parody of vicious models seems to carry within itself the germ of its own destruction.

Charles Kingsley completes the critical trio aligned against the poetic practice of the time. He probably deserves credit for suggesting to Aytoun the deadly name with which he characterized the school. "Spasmodic," of course, is not unusual and had been used by Carlyle, Horne, and *Tait's* to characterize, respectively, Byron, Browning, and Smith.[3] Never before, however, had it described a school of poetry, and precisely that school which Aytoun was to satirize. In "Thoughts on Shelley and Byron,"[4] Kingsley argues against the conception of Byron as the chief influence upon the young poets and tries to foist the parentage upon Shelley. He uses "spasmodic" early in the article, but the key sentence comes later: "And thus arose a spasmodic, vague, extravagant, effeminate, school of poetry, which has been too often hastily and unfairly fathered upon Byron" (p. 318). If Aytoun borrowed the term anywhere, it was here. "Spasmodic" stuck like a burr, being more accurately suggestive than other famous names for schools of poetry.

The preceding month, Kingsley had written another pertinent article, "Alexander Smith and Alexander Pope."[5] He reproaches Smith less than "Smith's models and flatterers," especially Bailey. Whereas Arnold advised a study of the Greeks and Milton, and Aytoun favored ballad models and Homer, Kingsley pleads with the young poet to emulate the common sense and control of the great neoclassicist. Again unlike Arnold and Aytoun, he does not

3. Alexander Smith, *Last Leaves,* ed. Patrick Proctor Alexander (Edinburgh, William P. Nimmo, 1869), p. lxv; Horne, *A New Spirit of the Age,* p. 278; *Tait's,* 20 (1853), 303.

4. Charles Kingsley, *Miscellanies* (London, John W. Parker and Son, 1859), pp 304–24. Originally in *Fraser's* (Nov. 1853,) pp. 568–76.

5. Ibid., pp. 269–303. In *Fraser's* (Oct. 1853), pp. 452–66.

argue from the classical position of form and unity but attacks Smith at his strongest defense, his "beauties." The passage should rank as an important one in Victorian criticism, for it is a striking anticipation of Ruskin's remarks on the pathetic fallacy:

> And hundreds, nay, thousands more in this book, whereof it must be said that beautiful or not, in the eyes of the present generation—and many of them are put into very beautiful language, and refer to very beautiful natural objects— they are not beautiful really and in themselves: because they are mere conceits; the analogies in them are fortuitous, depending not on the nature of the things themselves, but on the private fancy of the writer, having no more real and logical coherence than a conundrum or a pun; in plain English, untrue: only allowable to Juliets or Othellos, while their self-possession, almost their reason, is in temporary abeyance under the influence of joy or sorrow. Every one must feel the exquisite fitness of Juliet's "Gallop apace, ye fiery-footed steeds," etc., for one of her character in her circumstances: every one, we trust, and Mr. Smith among the number, will some day feel the exquisite unfitness of using such conceits as we have just quoted, or any other, page after page, for all characters and chances. For the West is not wretched; the rains never were brutal yet, and do not insult the sun's corpse, being some millions of miles nearer us than the sun, but only have happened once to seem to do so in the poet's eyes. (pp. 293–94)

Gilfillan, however, defended Smith and the other Spasmodics against such attacks.[6] Thus, throughout the critical writings of the early fifties, the charges and countercharges fly back and forth, pro and con, each side reassuring itself but unable to make an impression upon the other.

AYTOUN'S CRITICAL POSITION

In his early literary works, Aytoun indicated the position he was to take in the Spasmodic controversy. In *The Book of Ballads,* he

6. See *Eclectic Review, 98* (1953) , 541–53, and *A Third Gallery of Portraits,* esp. pp. 131–35.

appeared as the conservative critic: he upheld established standards by ridiculing antisocial declamation, obscurity, and impiety. In *Lays of the Scottish Cavaliers,* he cast his lot with the balladists and, in prose, contrasted such objective poetry favorably with poetry of "rhetorical artifice" and allegory. His later critical writings elucidate his position.

Aytoun never promulgated a philosophy of criticism or proclaimed a series of literary principles. But after the defeat of the Conservative party in December 1852, which officially marked the death of the Protection policy in Britain, he turned away from politics and devoted himself to practical literary criticism. It is from these articles on the state of literature and these reviews of contemporary works that we can induce Aytoun's "philosophy." He makes the job easy, for, just as in political and social questions, he maintains a remarkably consistent and confined attitude.

Aytoun believed that literary criticism was of great importance. He frequently speaks of the "grave duty" of the critic,[1] and he defends his own assault against Tennyson's *Maud* as a performance of duty with regard to the poetic literature of the country (*78* [1855],321). Aytoun considered the function of the critic so important because literature itself was bound up intimately with life, ultimately with moral questions. Therefore, he warns the poets, "the dispensers of glory," "to whom a mighty trust is committed, and who have a high function to discharge," that they "ought most assuredly, for the common interest of mankind, to be rigidly impartial in their judgments, to abstain from giving even a modified approval to actions which cannot be traced either to a regard for the ordinances of God, or a sincere desire for the welfare of the human race" (*85*[1859],770). From here, it is a short step to poetic justice:

> It is, we think, a most desirable thing, that in all works of fiction, whether high or low, there should be a distinct development of the Nemesis, or retributive power—that vice or fraud, however exhibited, should not be portrayed as finally triumphant—but that each action, according to its

---

1. *Blackwood's 66* (1849), 341; *81* (1857), 358–59. All subsequent references to *Blackwood's* in this section are found in parentheses in the text.

merit or demerit, should have its proper moral consequence, and produce its legitimate effect. (77[1855],187)

Aytoun understandably expressed his highest praise for Arnold's Preface of 1853 (75[1854],305–07). With regard to the art of poetry, he maintained the same principles and had anticipated many of Arnold's remarks on structure. Aytoun always emphasized unity of tone and effect (71[1852],216). The art of poetry is "no other than the art of giving adequate expression to an idea"; [2] the sine qua non is the idea, never the expression for its own sake. Thus, the poet first selects a major theme; then he arranges the various parts of his subject; finally, he concentrates on adequate expression (81[1857],40).[3] If the basic theme is incomprehensible, or the arrangement "vicious," then no brilliance of execution can redeem the work (71[1852],224). Episodes especially mar the unity of contemporary poetry (73[1853],245); wanted are purity and simplicity of form (71[1852],217).

Like Arnold, Aytoun believes that the major theme of non-lyric poetry should be a great action (76[1854],698; 81[1857],362). The poet "must deal with such passions as lie near the surface. Love, hatred, revenge, ambition, remorse, heroism—these are his materials" (76[1854],706). "Works of fiction are, or ought to be, representations of the general feeling of mankind" (77[1855],629). Literature of the opposite nature—individualistic, subjective, reflective—should be avoided: "The reader may well be excused for experiencing an occasional qualm, when he finds the author recounting, with unnecessary minuteness, the sensations which beset his inner man when suffering under extreme tribulation, his manifold perspirations and toils, and a great deal more which had better have been left untold (72[1852],745). Arnold had used his doctrine of the great action to show that the modernity of a subject was unimportant. Aytoun goes one step further and argues that a contemporary subject is detrimental to a poet:

It is not the province of the poet to depict things as they are, but so to refine and purify as to purge out the grosser matter; and this he cannot do if he attempts to give a faithful pic-

2. *The Times* (May 21, 1853), p. 7.
3. Ibid.

ture of his own times. For in order to be faithful, he must necessarily include much which is abhorrent to art, and revolting to the taste, for which no exactness of delineation will be accepted as a proper excuse. All poetical characters, all poetical situations, must be idealised. . . . Whilst dealing with a remote subject the poet can easily effect this, but not so when he brings forward characters of his own age. (*81*[1857],34–35)

Elsewhere, Aytoun discards theory and points out that, in fact, the giants of poetry—Homer, Shakespeare, Milton, Scott—all went back to the past for their subject matter (*75*[1854],754–55).

Style, like structure, should be pure and simple. Indeed, simplicity of expression is called "the criterion of a genuine poet" (*71*[1852],215) and, elsewhere, "the highest excellence in poetry" (*78*[1855],319). Aytoun explains that "By simplicity we do not mean bald diction, or baby utterance;—we use the term in its high sense, as expressive of the utmost degree of lucidity combined with energy, when all false images, far-fetched metaphors and comparisons, and mystical forms of speech, are discarded" (*78*[1855], 319–20). Thus, he complains of Mrs. Browning's "The Dance": "Criticism, as well as sense, is utterly baffled by such images as the overskying blue swooning with passion, and mountains, heaving mighty hearts, sighing a rapture in a shadow" (*87*[1860],494). Similarly, he attacks George Borrow for his strange "jargon" (*69*[1851],328); using his favorite epithets, he calls for "pure and simple diction" (*71*[1852],217) or "pure and masculine diction" (*97*[1865],331). Naturally, the author must show propriety in his selection of words. He must overcome the "tendency to clothe trivialities in lofty language, quite unsuited to the nature of the theme—a common but a great fault in composition" (*72*[1852],749). Aytoun criticizes the "grandiose style and pomposity of language" in Macaulay's speeches on precisely these grounds (*75*[1854],200). Finally, even in metrics "poetic licence may sometimes be carried too far"; Aytoun would like to limit the poet "to the safe, familiar, and yet ample range of recognized Saxon metres" (*71*[1852],216,217).

This last sentence almost epitomizes Aytoun's attitude not only

toward literature, but also toward politics, religion, and society:
trust to the safe, familiar, ample guides of the past. Elsewhere,
he summed up:

> Artists, like architects, must work by rule—not slavishly in-
> deed, but ever keeping in mind that there are certain prin-
> ciples which experience has tested and approved, and that
> to deviate from these is literally to court defeat. Not that we
> should implicitly receive the doctrines laid down by critics,
> scholiasts, or commentators, or pin our faith to the formula
> of Longinus; but we should regard the works of the great
> masters, both ancient and modern, as profitable for instruc-
> tion as well as for delight, and be cautious how we innovate.
> We may consider it almost as a certainty that every leading
> principle of art has been weighed and sifted by our prede-
> cessors; and that most of the theories, which are paraded as
> discoveries, were deliberately examined by them, and were
> rejected because they were false or impracticable. (*81*[1857],34)

Experimentation is dangerous; Aytoun refers to it as the "besetting sin" (*71*[1852],217) of the age, "simply a token of a morbid craving for originality," and "the bane of many poets" (*81*
[1857],39). He grudgingly admits that "in art, novelty is much"
but insists that "that does not last long; and the enterprising in-
novator must either fall back upon the principles of common
sense, or submit to become a laughingstock" (*74*[1853],535).
When Aytoun realized that the new poets were not going to fall
back upon the principles of common sense, he personally made
sure that they became laughingstocks.

AYTOUN'S EARLY ATTACKS ON
THE SPASMODICS

Aytoun launched his first extended attack on modern poetry in
February 1852 in a review of "Longfellow's Golden Legend." [1]
As the title indicates, Longfellow bears the brunt of the assault:
The Golden Legend is "an ill-constructed drama, almost aimless
in purpose, and without even an intelligible moral" (p. 224).

---

1. *Blackwood's, 71* (1852), 212–25.

But Aytoun is after bigger game; he is criticizing the whole tendency of modern literature:

> In the acted drama we know very well that a bad or uninteresting plot can never be redeemed, even by the most brilliant speeches. To the epos, or narrative tale, the same rule applies; for episodes, however spirited or pathetic, never can make up for the want of interest in the leading story. The fault is not peculiar to Mr. Longfellow—it is discernible in most of the compositions, both in prose and poetry, of the present age. Aptitude of handling is considered a greater accomplishment than unity or strength of design; and the consequence is that we lay down works, written by many of our best authors, with a vague feeling of disappointment, which can be attributed only to their total disregard of that preliminary consideration of story and plan which occupied the attention, as it constituted the triumph, of our older literary masters. (p. 225)

In the article, he traces much of this deplorable tendency back to Goethe's *Faust,* for reasons already noted.

The harshest words, however, are directed against Philip James Bailey. Even the maligned Longfellow "is infinitely his superior in poetical accomplishment, in genius, in learning, and in delicacy of sentiment" (p. 213). Aytoun attacks *Festus* on literary and especially on moral-religious grounds:

> From Byron to Festus Bailey—a sad declension, we admit— poets and poetasters have thought it their privilege to make free with the Satanic character, and to introduce the author of evil, or at least one of his subordinate imps, in the capacity of a tempter. . . . Mr. Bailey knows all about him— nay, has no doubt whatever as to his ultimate felicitous destination. He is several universes beyond Milton. He foresees restoration to the whole powers of evil; and having thus, in his philosophy, kindly reinstated the fallen angels, of course those who have fallen by their agency become at once immaculate. . . . Great allowance is always to be made for poetic licence; but there is a bound to everything; and we

are compelled to record our deliberate opinion, that nowhere, in literature, can we find passages more hideously
and revoltingly presumptuous than occur in the concluding
pages of the *Festus* of Mr. Bailey. (pp. 212–13)

This attack ignited the smoldering feud between Aytoun and
Bailey's standard-bearer, George Gilfillan.

It seems inevitable that Aytoun and Gilfillan would come into
violent opposition: Aytoun, the Jacobite, author of *Lays of the
Scottish Cavaliers,* and Gilfillan, the Covenanter, author of
Martyrs, Heroes, and Bards of the Scottish Covenant; Aytoun,
the Conservative, writing for *Blackwood's Edinburgh Magazine,*
and Gilfillan, the Liberal, writing for *Tait's Edinburgh Magazine;* Aytoun, the attacker and destroyer of the Spasmodics, and
Gilfillan, their inspirer and defender. If ever two contemporaries
have had entirely opposed views of their common world, they
were Aytoun and Gilfillan. Originally, they opposed each other
over a political-historical question. In his introduction to "The
Execution of Montrose," Aytoun described the Covenanters as
"a party venal in principle, pusillanimous in action, and more
than dastardly in their revenge." [2] Gilfillan retaliated in *Martyrs,
Heroes, and Bards of the Scottish Covenant.* He attacked the
historical views offered in the prose introductions to Aytoun's
ballads, presented the Covenanters' interpretation of the facts,
and ended by calling his antagonist "a vulgar volunteer in the
bad cause." [3]

The literary opposition smoldered dangerously. In 1850, Gilfillan classified Aytoun with Robert Montgomery, saying that he
believed in the poetic ability of neither.[4] Two years later, he
criticized Aytoun's *Lays* and concluded with a personal assault
upon the author: "Aytoun's [insulting tone] is the small spite of
a school-boy who confounds impudence with cleverness, and
thinks that, because connected with Christopher North, he may
indulge in similar freaks of fancy, and present the distaff without
the Hercules—the contortions without the inspiration—the buf-

2. Ibid., *56* (1844), 289.
3. George Gilfillan, *Martyrs, Heroes and Bards of the Scottish Covenant* (Edinburgh, Gall and Inglis, 1864), pp. 256–64.
4. *The Eclectic Review, 91* (1850), 270.

fooneries or profanities of Falstaff without his wit, his bon-
hommie, or his rich originality." [5] Then Aytoun attacked Bailey,
and Gilfillan rushed to the defense of his favorite. Writing in
April 1852,[6] he begins his own review of Longfellow's *Golden
Legend* with a reference to Aytoun's article: "We have been led
into these remarks by a glance we accidentally took at the last
February number of 'Blackwood,' containing a review of the
'Golden Legend,' and a comparison, most uncalled-for and unjust,
between Longfellow and Bailey, of 'Festus'" (p. 455). Gilfillan
goes on to make the same comparison but reaches quite a different
conclusion: "Why, this 'Golden Legend'—fine as it is—might
have been a slip, fallen and never missed out of one corner of
'Festus' . . . in quantity and grandeur of thought, variety of
image, and power of language, there seems no comparison, any
more than between the elegant little jets of gas in a sea-coal fire
and the red rivers of lightning which run down a stormy midnight heaven" (p. 456). He ends the review in his familiar stance
of expectation, expressed in his typically excited, highly figurative
prose:

> Surely some great poetic orb must be nearing the verge of
> the horizon! What a flush of fine poetry, both at home and
> from abroad, we have had lately in the rich and eloquent
> writings of a Longfellow, an Emerson, a Lowell, a Poe, a
> Croly, an Aird, a Yendys,[7] (who, we are glad to hear, has a
> new poem on the anvil,) a Tennyson, a Marston, a Brown,
> the Brownings, an Alexander Smith, (who is collecting his
> beautiful verses into a separate form,) a Scott, a Bailey, a
> Jameson, (the author of "Nimrod,") and some more genu-
> ine bards of greater or less promise! We have a strong sus-
> picion, that somewhere or other, from among this number,
> is to arise the poet of our period; and we would advise star-
> gazing critics to watch *this cluster* well, to mark attentively
> all its movements and mutations, to report their observa-
> tions candidly, lest in it there should appear, before their
> telescopes are in order, some star brighter than his fellows,

5. Gilfillan, *Martyrs*, p. 263.
6. *The Eclectic Review*, N.S. 3 (1852), 455–67.
7. The pen name of Dobell.

forming the central sun to a great system, and a star of hope, promise, and prophecy to the coming age. (p. 467)

Besides stargazing, Gilfillan delighted in the "negative comparison." He described what a poet was by describing what he was not: "Gerald Massey has not the voluptuous tone, the felicitous and highly wrought imagery, or the sustained music of Smith; nor the diffusive splendour and rich general spirit of poetry in which all Bigg's verses are steeped; nor the amazing subtlety, depth, and pervasive purpose of Yendys's song." [8] Aytoun was noting these eccentricities of the Dundee critic and preparing to burlesque them.

He began his major offensive against the Spasmodics in March 1854. In "The Two Arnolds," [9] devoted ostensibly to the work of Matthew and Edwin Arnold, he refers slightingly to Bailey and Dobell and exposes Gilfillan to censure and laughter. He begins:

> We have not for a considerable time held much communing with the rising race of poets, and we shall at once proceed to state the reason why. Even as thousands of astronomers are nightly sweeping the heavens with their telescopes, in the hope of discovering some new star or wandering comet, so of late years have shoals of small critics been watching for the advent of some grand poetical genius. These gentlemen, who could not, if their lives depended on it, elaborate a single stanza, have a kind of insane idea that they may win immortal fame by being the first to perceive and hail the appearance of the coming bard. Accordingly, scarce a week elapses without a shout being raised at the birth of a thin octavo.

Then, anticipating the bogus review of *Firmilian* which was to appear in two months, Aytoun turns to burlesque:

> "Apollodorus,[1] or the Seraph of Gehenna, a Dramatic Mystery, by John Tunks," appears; and we are straightway told, on the authority of Mr. Guffaw,[2] the celebrated critic, that:

8. Gilfillan, *A Third Gallery*, p. 163.
9. *Blackwood's*, 75 (1854), 303–14.
1. The pen name of Gilfillan.
2. Gilfillan.

—"it is a work more colossal in its mould than the unde-
fined structures of the now mouldering Persepolis. Tunks
may not, like Byron, possess the hypochondriacal brilliancy
of a blasted firework, or pour forth his floods of radiant
spume with the intensity of an artificial volcano. He does
not pretend to the spontaneous combustion of our young
friend Gander Rednag [3] (who, by the way, has omitted to
send us his last volume), though we almost think he possesses
a diviner share of the poet's ennobling lunacy. He does not
dive so sheer as the author of *Festus* into the bosom of far
unintelligibility, plummet-deep beyond the range of compre-
hension, or the shuddering gaze of the immortals. . . . He
may not, like Shakespeare, etc., etc." And then, having occupied many columns in telling us whom Mr. Tunks does
not resemble, the gifted Guffaw concludes by an assurance
that Tunks is Tunks, and that his genius is at this moment
flaring over the universe, like the meteor-standard of the
Andes! (pp. 303–04)

Aytoun concentrated his attack upon Gilfillan because he considered him fundamentally responsible for the vicious practices
of the Spasmodic school. Gilfillan's ecstatic, undiscriminating
praise prevented young poets from attaining the "proper culture"
necessary for the slow maturation of their abilities. Long after the
publication of *Firmilian*, Aytoun admitted that Bailey and Dobell
had "intellect and power; but they do not know how to apply it." [4]
He was especially impressed by Smith, believing he exhibited
"unmistakable marks of genius": "Alexander Smith possesses
abilities which, if rightly directed, cannot fail to make him eminent as a poet. The real danger to which he is exposed arises
from the superlative commendation lavished upon him by men
who, in the present deluge of cheap literature, have been let
loose upon the public as critics. Worse supporters for a young
author could not be found." [5] Gilfillan had failed in the "grave
duty" of critic and was, in the final analysis, morally reprehensible.

3. Gander Rednag, a squib on "Sydney Yendys," is Dobell. See Gilfillan's last
paragraph in his review of *The Golden Legend* (*The Eclectic Review*, N.S. *3*
[1852], 455–67), and Jolly, *Sydney Dobell*, *1*, 342.
4. *Blackwood's 81* (1857), 41.
5. Ibid., *76* (1854), 712.

"Little, indeed, do the tribe of the Guffaws care for the mischief they are doing." [6]

In March 1854, Aytoun was beginning to perceive his own duty as a critic; the idea of *Firmilian* was taking shape:

> It is really very difficult to know what to do in such cases. On the one hand, it is a pity, without an effort, to allow a likely lad to be fly-blown and spoiled by the buzzing blue-bottles of literature; on the other, it is impossible to avoid seeing that the mischief has been so far done, that any remedy likely to be effectual must cause serious pain. To tie up a Guffaw to the stake, and to inflict upon him condign punish-ment—a resolution which we intend to carry into effect some fine morning—would be far less painful to us than the task or duty of wounding the sensitiveness of a youth who may possibly be destined to be a poet. (pp. 304–05)

His discussion of the faults of the Guffaws leads easily into praise of Arnold's Preface of 1853, and this is followed by an examination of the poetry of Matthew and Edwin Arnold. At the end of the article, however, Aytoun returns to the Spasmodics. He praises Edwin Arnold for

> not treading in the footsteps of the "intense" school, and that he always writes intelligibly—a virtue which we observe a good many modern poets hold utterly in derision. Let him go on in his vocation, cultivating his taste, improving his judgment, observing nature, and eschewing gaudy ornament —and he may hope to win a name which shall be reverenced, when those of the utterers of fustian and balderdash, dear to the heart of Guffaw, are either wholly forgotten, or re-membered only with ridicule. (p. 314)

Thus we see that Aytoun had not yet selected the name "Spas-modic" for the school but had already designated its chief mem-bers. Gilfillan and Smith had been referred to in the first part of the article, and now came the turn of Bailey and Dobell, for "fustian" was Aytoun's favorite word for *Festus* and "balderdash" for *Balder*. *Firmilian* was about to appear, and we must turn to it now.

6. Ibid., 75 (1854), 304.

FIRMILIAN

THE BURLESQUE REVIEW

In May 1854, *Blackwood's* published a review, with copious extracts, of *Firmilian; or, The Student of Badajoz: a Tragedy* by T. Percy Jones.[1] The burlesque review had appeared in English literature at least as early as *The Rolliad*. *Blackwood's* itself had scored a hit in 1820 with Maginn's "Horae Scandicae No. II," a review of an imaginary play by Oehlenschlaeger.[2] But if Aytoun drew his inspiration from any single source, it was from his old collaborator, Theodore Martin. Martin had published in 1841 a burlesque review of a thieves' anthology, "Flowers of Hemp; or, The Newgate Garland. By One of the Family."[3] Aytoun liked the strategy so much that he sought the acquaintance of the author and formed the Bon Gaultier partnership. As Kitchin points out, however, although there were earlier models, "the idea comes to full fruitage" in *Firmilian*.[4]

The review opens in an apparently innocent manner:

We have great pleasure in announcing to our readers the fact, that we have at last discovered that long-expected phenomenon, the coming Poet, and we trust that his light will very soon become visible in the literary horizon. We cannot, however, arrogate to ourselves any large share of merit in this discovery—indeed, we must confess, with a feeling akin

1. *Blackwood's* 75 (1854), 533–51.
2. Ibid., 7 (1820), 674–79.
3. See *The Book of Ballads* (16th ed.), pp. vii–xvi.
4. Kitchin, *A Survey of Burlesque and Parody in English*, p. 293.

to shame, that we ought to have made it at a much earlier
date. *Firmilian* is not altogether new to us. We have an in-
distinct recollection of having seen the tragedy in manuscript well-nigh two years ago; and, if we remember aright,
a rather animated correspondence took place on the subject
of the return of the papers. We had, by some untoward ac-
cident, allowed them to find their way into the Balaam-box,
which girnel of genius was at that particular time full up to
the very hinges. We felt confident that *Firmilian* lay under
the weight of some twenty solid layers of miscellaneous literature . . . we now remark a degree of vivacity and force of
expression, however extravagant many of the ideas may be,
which had escaped our previous notice. We hope that, by a
tardy act of justice, we shall offer no violence to that amiable
modesty which has, in the mean time, restrained him from
asking the verdict of the general public. (p. 533)

Even in the most innocent-looking passages of *Firmilian*, however, Aytoun is "taking off" from some specific model or models.
Gilfillan had introduced Smith to the public over two years before in a similar manner:

Some four months ago we received a packet of poetry from
Glasgow, accompanied with a very modest note, signed "Alex.
Smith." Encumbered with many duties, and with an immense
mass of MS., good, bad, and indifferent, we allowed the
volume to lie by us for a long time, till at last, lifting it up
carelessly, we lighted upon some lines that pleased us, were
tempted to read on—did so—and ere the end, were all but
certain we had found a Poet—a new and real star in those barren Northern skies.[5]

Aytoun did not necessarily remember Gilfillan's introduction of
Smith; more probably, he worked with the text before him. Again
and again in his political articles for *Blackwood's,* he quotes
periodicals from various times and places. As chief writer for that
huge periodical organization, he had command of all of its facili-
ties for fingering topical literature.

5. *The Critic, 10* (1851) , 567.

Aytoun soon begins his literary criticism. His strategy is to attack vigorously the "Spasmodic" school, including T. Percy Jones, but to contrast him favorably with the other members:

> Those who admire spasmodic throes and writings may possibly be inclined to exalt him to a very high pinnacle of fame; for certainly, in no modern work of poetry—and there have been several recently published which might have borne the *imprimateur* of Bedlam—have we found so many symptoms of unmistakable lunacy. Still there is a method in his madness—a rapidity of perception and originality of thought, which contrasts very favourably with the tedious drivellings of some other writers of the same school. His taste is not one whit better than theirs, but he brings a finer fancy and a more vivid imagination to the task; nor is he deficient in a certain rude exaggerated dramatic power, which has more than once reminded us of the early style of Marlowe and the other predecessors of Shakespeare. (p. 533)

He turns to an examination of the doctrine of the school and complains, "It is not very easy to comprehend the exact creed and method of the new school of poets, who have set themselves to work upon a principle hitherto unknown." However, their basic notion seems to be to "regard poetry not only as a sacred calling, but as the most sacred of any—that, in their opinion, every social relation, every mundane tie, which can interfere with the bard's development, must be either disregarded or snapped asunder—and that they are, to the fainting race of Adam, the sole accredited bearers of the Amreeta cup of immortality." The reviewer retaliates with the practical, the societal attitude: "Poets are, like all other authors or artisans, valuable according to the quality of the article which they produce. If their handiwork be good, genuine, and true, it will pass at once into circulation and be prized—if the reverse, what title can they prefer to the name which they so proudly arrogate to themselves." He does not, however, quarrel with the poet so much "for having an exalted idea of his art"—such a belief may be necessary—as for his inability "to acquire its rudiments": "When one of our young poetical aspirants, on the strength of a trashy duodecimo filled with unintelligible ravings, asserts his claim to be considered as a prophet and a teacher, it is beyond the power of humanity to check the intolerable tickling of the midriff" (p. 534). Aytoun then examines the "practice of the poets of the Spasmodic School" and enumerates four particular vices:

> In the first place, they rarely, if ever, attempt anything like a plot. After you have finished the perusal of their verses, you find yourself just as wise as when you began. You cannot tell what they would be at. You have a confused recollection of stars, and sunbeams, and moonbeams, as if you had been staring at an orrery; but sun, moon, and stars, were intended to give light to something—and what that something is, in the poet's page, you cannot, for the life of you, discover. In the second place, we regret to say that they are often exceedingly profane, not, we suppose, intentionally, but because they have not sense enough to see the limits which decency, as well as duty, prescribes. In the third place, they are occasionally very prurient. And, in the fourth place, they are almost always unintelligible. (p. 534)

Now the reviewer is ready to narrow his focus to T. Percy Jones. Jones is "a decidedly favourable specimen of his tribe" because his work has "if not a plot, at least some kind of comprehensible action." Still, *Firmilian* serves as an excellent example of Spasmodic practice, for "in it he has portrayed the leading features of the poetical school to which he belongs with so much fidelity and effect." Lengthy extracts from the latest Spasmodic tragedy follow, interspersed with the reviewer's criticisms, which are both humorous and serious and mix praise with censure.

Aytoun ends the article by widening his view again to include the entire school and launching his most determined attack against it:

> It is rather difficult to give a serious opinion upon the merits of such a production as this. It is, of course, utterly extravagant; but so are the whole of the writings of the poets of the Spasmodic school; and, in the eyes of a considerable body of modern critics, extravagance is regarded as a proof of extraor-

dinary genius. It is, here and there, highly coloured; but
that also is looked upon as a symptom of the divine afflatus,
and rather prized than otherwise. In one point of proclaimed
spasmodic excellence, perhaps it fails. You can always tell
what Percy Jones is after, even when he is dealing with
"shuddering stars," "gibbous moons," "imposthumes of hell,"
and the like; whereas you may read through twenty pages of
the more ordinary stuff without being able to discern what
the writers mean—and no wonder, for they really mean
nothing. They are simply writing nonsense-verses; but they
contrive, by blazing away whole rounds of metaphor, to
mask their absolute poverty of thought, and to convey the
impression that there must be something stupendous under
so heavy a canopy of smoke. If, therefore, intelligibility,[6]
which is the highest degree of obscurity, is to be considered
a poetic excellence, we are afraid that Jones must yield the
palm to several of his contemporaries; if, on the contrary,
perspicuity is to be regarded as a virtue, we do not hesitate
in assigning the spasmodic prize to the author of *Firmilian*.
(p. 551)

With those words, Aytoun thought he had heard the last of
Firmilian, but he had done the job too well. He had tempered
his critical attack with enough praise to give the whole an appearance of sincerity. To the lovers of Spasmody, the poetic extracts seemed no more suspicious than the serious productions of
their favorites. Aytoun, the most surprised man of all, wrote to
Martin in late May:

> Did you see the sham notice of "Firmilian" in Blackwood
> for May? Strange to say, the newspapers (with but four or five
> exceptions) have treated it as an actual production, and some
> of them declare that the review is grossly unfair, and entreat
> Percy Jones to give his volume to the public! Between you
> and me, I intend, for the sake of mystification, to gratify
> them, and have already done a good bit, so that you may
> expect one of these days to see a real roaring tragedy. I in-
> tend to introduce a good many hits by way of spice. It is very

6. A serious misprint. The word should be "unintelligibility."

curious, when you sit down to write this sort of thing, to find how very closely some of the passages approximate to good poetry; and I am really of opinion that the best things in Marlowe were owing mainly to a fine rhythmical ear and a reckless energy. I wish I could show you some of my lines, written *currente calamo,* for this sort of crambo comes out as fluently as prose. Here is a short sample—

> I clove my way
> Right eastward, till I lighted at the foot
> of holy Helicon, and drank my fill
> At the clear spout of Aganippe's stream.
> I've rolled my limbs in ecstasy along
> The self-same turf on which old Homer lay
> That night he dreamed of Helen and of Troy;
> And I have heard at midnight the sweet strains
> Come quiring from the hill-top, where, enshrined
> In the rich foldings of a silver cloud,
> The Muses sang Apollo into sleep.

Damme, sir, if crambo isn't the thing after all! And the advantage is, that you can go on slapdash, without thinking!

Don't say anything about this at present. I want to mystify the London humorists.[7]

Aytoun incorporated the published extracts, introduced "a good many hits," provided the necessary connections, and, by July 16, mailed off the last proofs to *Blackwood's.*[8] In late July of that same year, William Blackwood and Sons published, in London and Edinburgh, the complete 153-page "Spasmodic Tragedy," *Firmilian.*[9]

THE POEM

Firmilian is more than an attack upon local eccentricity; it is a classical protest against extravagance. In literature it goes beyond

7. Martin, *Memoir,* pp. 146–47.
8. Letter of July 16, 1854.
9. T. Percy Jones, *Firmilian: or The Student of Badajoz. A Spasmodic Tragedy* (Edinburgh and London, William Blackwood and Sons, 1854). The complete edition of 1,048 copies was sold immediately, at five shillings a copy.

the Spasmodic school to expose exorbitant prose, the *Faust* tradition, and all ultra-romantic drama; it extends beyond the realm
of literature to expose excess in religion, social criticism, science,
and popular belief. *Firmilian* is a plea for sanity.

The burlesque begins immediately. In a preface, T. Percy Jones
defends himself against critics like the *Blackwood's* reviewer. It
is a takeoff on the combination of mock modesty and boastfulness
to be found in many a young poet's disclaimer. He concludes:

> I am not arrogant enough to assert that this is the finest
> poem which the age has produced; but I shall feel very much
> obliged to any gentleman who can make me acquainted with
> a better. (p. xi)

The supporters of the Spasmodics were arrogant enough to make
such assertions for their favorites. One Festonian, for example,
gathered the "beauties" of Bailey's work together and introduced
them as follows:

> To pronounce his work, as a whole, faultless would be to
> ascribe to him a success which mortal, as yet, has not at-
> tained in any effort. But to declare it less abounding in
> merit, in the manifold and distinctive parts of which it is
> composed, than the production of any other author of mod-
> ern times, would be equally distant from impartial truth.[1]

The bulk of Jones' preface seems to be a parody of Dobell's
preface to the second edition of *Balder*. Jones defends himself
against the "accusation of extravagance" leveled at "the moral
obliquity of the character of Firmilian." "To that I reply, that
the moral of a play does not depend upon the morals of any one
character depicted in it; and that many of the characters drawn
by the magic pencil of Shakespeare are shaded as deep, or even
deeper, than Firmilian" (pp. viii–ix). Similarly, Dobell defends
himself against the charge that Balder is "egoistic, self-contained,
and sophistical, imperfect in morality, and destitute of recognized
religion." He points out that it is wrong to think "that I must
personally admire the character I think fit to delineate, and that

---

1. *The Beauties of Festus:* Compiled, with a Copious Index, By a Festonian
(Boston, B.B. Mussey and Co., 1851), p. 6.

I present as a model what, in truth, I expose as a warning"
(p. 334). Jones suggests Mesdames de Brinvilles and Laffarge
and the Borgias as parallels in nature to Firmilian; Dobell points
to the autobiography of Haydon, the letters of Keats, the life of
David Scott, and incidents in the history of Goethe. The most
interesting aspect of this parallelism is that *Firmilian* was published in late July, while the second edition of *Balder* did not
appear until after November 17.[2] Aytoun understood his opponents well enough to parody them in anticipation.

The career of the hero, Firmilian, serves as the vehicle for the
parody of the *Faust*-Byronic-Spasmodic tradition. "Firmilian" implies both the literary and moral bases of Aytoun's attack. On the
one hand, it suggests "vermilion," a bright red pigment. Vivid
coloring had always been one of the distinguishing traits of the
Spasmodics: one contemporary magazine characterized their writings as "colour without form." [3] Aytoun distrusted the artist who
"carries his colour-box with him, and never hesitates, for effect,
to dash in the carmine" [4] and, in the burlesque review of *Firmilian*, had complained that the school's high coloring was mis-
takenly regarded as a symptom of the divine afflatus.[5] On the
other hand, "Firmilian" suggests a "Familiar," a spirit of supernatural origin who has traffic with men. Aytoun never did con-
done this notion (see p. 113), and, in one of his last articles, in
which he discussed the use of the Familiar in Marlowe's *Faustus*
and Goethe's *Faust*, the moralist pointed out that "Indeed,
throughout the whole Bible, no sin is more severely and em-
phatically denounced than that of holding traffic or communion
with familiar spirits." [6]

Firmilian is a unique creation, incorporating the major characteristics, occasionally inverted, of previous Spasmodic heroes.
His "life-drama" parodies at times a specific predecessor but more
frequently suggests the constituents and atmosphere of the entire
tradition. Aytoun evokes reminiscence; he points a direction
more often than he pinpoints.

2. Jolly, *Sydney Dobell*, *1*, 380.
3. *The London Quarterly Review*, 2 (1854), 587.
4. *Blackwood's*, 72 (1852), 683.
5. Ibid., 75 (1854), 534.
6. Ibid., 97 (1865), 207.

Scene One opens, true to the Spasmodic tradition, with the hero musing in his study. The general atmosphere is reminiscent of *Faust* and helps to establish it as the source of Spasmodic drama. Firmilian, like Faust, begins abruptly by expressing his disgust with study:

> Three hours of study—and what gain thereby?
> My brain is reeling to attach the sense
> Of what I read, as a drunk mariner
> Who, stumbling o'er the bulwark, makes a clutch
> At the wild incongruity of ropes,
> And topples into mud. (i.1–6)

These lines do not parody any particular poet but suggest the attempted ingenuity, often undignified, of all of the Spasmodics.

Aytoun indicates the values of his hero right at the start by having him attack a great representative of the classical world. Firmilian has been studying Aristotle and now turns against that "especial fool." The "vile imposter" having been disposed of, he wonders, in another unhappy figure of general Spasmodic relevance,

> Who shall take his place?
> What hoary dotard of antiquity
> Shall I invite to dip his clumsy foot
> Within the limpid fountain of my mind,
> And stamp it into foulness? (i.26–30)

He rejects law, theology, and medicine as mercenary; his social criticism here is alien to the contemporary Spasmodic school and comes closest to *Faust*. But even if the public professions were honorable, Firmilian would not work at them: he is the antisocial genius. Here Aytoun's parody of Spasmodic theory begins. In the sham review, he had singled out for exposure the notion of the sacred, all-licensed poet; now Firmilian recalls his personal vision:

> Then came the voice of universal Pan,
> The dread earth-whisper, booming in mine ear—
> "Rise up, Firmilian—rise in might!" it said;

"Great youth, baptised to song! Be it thy task,
Out of the jarring discords of the world,
To recreate stupendous harmonies
More grand in diapason than the roll
Among the mountains of the thunder-psalm!
Be thou no slave of passion. Let not love,
Pity, remorse, nor any other thrill
That sways the actions of ungifted men,
Affect thy course. Live for thyself alone.
Let appetite thy ready handmaid be,
And pluck all fruitage from the tree of life,
Be it forbidden or no. If any comes
Between thee and the purpose of thy bent,
Launch thou the arrow from the string of might
Right to the bosom of the impious wretch,
And let it quiver there! Be great in guilt!
If, like Busiris, thou canst rack the heart,
Spare it no pang. So shalt thou be prepared
To make thy song a tempest, and to shake
The earth to its foundation—Go thy way!" (i.69–91)

Having had this vision, Firmilian has tried "To paint the mental
spasms that tortured Cain" (i.96). This is unusual: the other
Spasmodic heroes write poetry about themselves, but Aytoun
gives Firmilian a specific theme. I believe he wants to indicate
that his hero is in the Byronic tradition, just as throughout the
scene he reveals his relation to *Faust*.

   At this point, the story takes its permanent direction. Aytoun
has chosen to follow the plot of *Balder,* and consequently most
of the specific parody will be directed against that extreme
example of Spasmody. Firmilian, attempting "to paint the mental
spasms that tortured Cain," complains:

How have I done it? Feebly. What we write
Must be the reflex of the thing we know;
For who can limn the morning, if his eyes
Have never looked upon Aurora's face?
Or who describe the cadence of the sea,

Whose ears were never open to the waves
Or the shrill winding of the Triton's horn? (i.97–103)

These lines illustrate that Aytoun occasionally introduces serious passages in order to prevent the continual play of wit and sarcasm from becoming tedious. Firmilian will have to kill in order to experience Cain's remorse. The suffering Amy had begged Balder to "ope the lattice of my soul" (p. 370), and he finally decided to "let her forth/As a poor bird out of a burning cage" (p. 524). Firmilian determines: "I'll ope the lattice of some mortal cage,/And let the soul go free!" (i.112–13).

After a lengthy digression in the Spasmodic manner, Firmilian "requires a pause of thought" to choose an appropriate victim. It must be someone dear to him, "or else the deed/Would lose its flavour and its poignancy" (i.135–36). He coolly considers his three loves and his "especial friend" Haverillo but finally fixes on three of his drinking companions. The entire passage is a burlesque of Balder's search, beginning "Who is to die?" and ending with the murder of his own daughter (pp. 382–83). The scene concludes with an address to the moon, reminiscent of that in the first scene of *Faust* but closer still to that which closes the first scene of *A Life-Drama*. Here, as so often in *Firmilian*, Aytoun can caricature more than one work at the same time because the themes and techniques of the Spasmodic tradition are so consistent.

A friend had written to Dobell about the preface to *Balder:* "You have explained on the ground where your reader might fairly own himself perplexed—Your philosophical intention; the cause of the difficulty being, in my mind, the absence of any character in the work to show the *author's* moral status, and so to contrast it with the aberrations of the hero." [7] The same difficulty applies to *A Life-Drama* in which Smith reveals his "moral status" in the abrupt conclusion. Although their purpose was ultimately moral, the Spasmodic poets had offered only the negative model and had failed to establish their own convictions. Aytoun does not make the same mistake. In Scene Two, he introduces his mouthpiece, Firmilian's "especial friend" Haverillo. The "Hav-

7. Jolly, *Sydney Dobell, 1*, 327–28.

erel" appeared recurrently in the writings of Aytoun; he is "an ancient and garrulous gentleman, who persisted in telling us everything that we knew before, with a prolixity which nothing could check, and a monotony that sounded like the eternal ticking of a clock." [8] So must Haverillo have seemed to Firmilian, for he represents the man of common sense and moderation.

When Haverillo describes to Mariana the activities of her betrothed, Firmilian, Aytoun is able to offer his own literary criticism of the Spasmodic school:

> He's wayward, doubtless,
> And very often unintelligible,
> But that is held to be a virtue now.
> Critics and poets both (save I, who cling
> To older canons) have discarded sense,
> And meaning's at a discount. Our young spirits,
> Who call themselves the masters of the age,
> Are either robed in philosophic mist,
> And with an air of grand profundity,
> Talk metaphysics—which, sweet cousin, means
> Nothing but aimless jargon—or they come
> Before us in the broad bombastic vein,
> With spasms, and throes, and transcendental flights,
> And heap hyperbole on metaphor. (ii.2–15)

When Mariana asks Haverillo whether Firmilian can be honorable in love, Aytoun presents his own moral criticism of the Spasmodic hero:

> You must remember what Firmilian is—
> A Poet. He is privileged to sing
> A thousand ditties to a thousand maids.
> Nine Muses waited at Apollo's beck—
> Our modern poets are more amorous,
> And far exceed the stint of Solomon:
> But 'tis mere fancy, inspiration all;
> Pure worthless rhyming.   (ii.47–53)

8. *Blackwood's,* 77 (1855), 631.

Unlike the Spasmodic poets, Aytoun leaves no doubt about his moral status.

In Scene Three, Firmilian becomes a murderer like Balder, but the parody is of *Festus* and *A Life-Drama*. He meets his three victims at a tavern, and the discussion turns on the relative merits of national beauties. Aytoun is parodying the same discussion in the Party and Entertainment Scene in *Festus*.[9] But when Firmilian offers his opinion, Aytoun caricatures Smith. The passage begins as a parody of Walter's poetry about himself and soon includes Smith's sensuality and style, even down to his references to Mark Antony:

> I knew a poet once; and he was young,
> And intermingled with such fierce desires
> As made pale Eros veil his face with grief,
> And caused his lustier brother to rejoice.
> He was as amorous as a crocodile
> In the spring season, when the Memphian bank
> Receiving substance from the glaring sun,
> Resolves itself from mud into a shore.
> And—as the scaly creature wallowing there,
> In its hot fits of passion, belches forth
> The steam from out its nostrils, half in love,
> And half in grim defiance of its kind;
> Trusting that either, from the reedy fen,
> Some reptile-virgin coyly may appear,
> Or that the hoary Sultan of the Nile
> May make tremendous challenge with his jaws,
> And, like Mark Anthony, assert his right
> To all the Cleopatras of the ooze—
> So fared it with the poet that I knew.
>
> He had a soul beyond the vulgar reach,
> Sun-ripened, swarthy. He was not the fool
> To pluck the feeble lily from its shade
> When the black hyacinth stood in fragrance by.
> The lady of his love was dusk as Ind,

9. Bailey, *Festus,* p. 195.

Her lips as plenteous as the Sphinx's are,
And her short hair crisp with Numidian curl.
She was a negress. You have heard the strains
That Dante, Petrarch, and such puling fools
As loved the daughters of cold Japhet's race,
Have lavished idly on their icicles:
As snow meets snow, so their unhasty fall
Fell chill and barren on a pulseless heart.
But, would you know what noontide ardour is,
Or in what mood, the lion, in the waste,
All fever-maddened, and intent on cubs,
At the oasis waits the lioness—
That shall you gather from the fiery song
Which that young poet framed, before he dared
Invade the vastness of his lady's lips. (iii.67–105)

Broad as the parody is, it is still difficult to go back to Smith and read *A Life-Drama* without an intolerable tickling of the midriff.

D'Aguilar, one of the auditors, prevents a recitation of "the fiery song" by striking Firmilian and challenging him to a duel. The cowardly Firmilian surprises his companions with his valor:

O, you have much mista'en me, if you think
That some slight spurting of Castilian blood,
Or poet's ichor, can suffice to lay
The memory of tonight's affront asleep. (iii.193–96)

Again Aytoun has descended to minute details. "Ichor" appears in *Balder* (p. 369) and is used here in mimicry of Dobell's affected diction. Firmilian accepts the challenge, defies his companions to appear, and then poisons them.

Firmilian succeeds in the murder but fails in his purpose. In Scene Four, he complains that "Keen-beaked Remorse" has not settled on his soul, but, after all, no harm done:

If I have gained no knowledge by this deed,
I have lost none.

·   ·   ·

> I have but shot an idle bolt away,
> And need not seek it further. (iv.41–42, 47–48)

Fate soon offers another chance. Firmilian overhears a Graduate
raving to a Priest and threatening to blow up the accursed
churches. Here is the perfect scapegoat for Firmilian's next
crime:

> As he spoke,
> Methought I saw the solid vaults give way,
> And the entire cathedral rise in air,
> As if it leaped from Pandemonium's jaws. (iv.120–23)

As for the raving Graduate, we shall return to him later, for he
is none other than John Ruskin.

When Firmilian next appears, in Scene Six, he is all ready to
blow up the Cathedral of St. Nicholas. His "terrestrial thunder
lies prepared" in the vault and "only waits a spark to be dis-
solved." His only fear is that the lightning of the storm outside
may fire the "flagrant stuff" before he can. In destructive, cosmic
imagery, reminiscent of the final scenes in *Festus* and various outbursts by Balder, Firmilian exclaims:

> Let the hoarse thunder rend the vault of heaven,
> Yea, shake the stars by myriads from their boughs,
> As Autumn tempests shake their fruitage down;—
> Let the red lightning shoot athwart the sky,
> Entangling comets by their spooming hair,
> Piercing the zodiac belt, and carrying dread
> To old Orion, and his whimpering hound;—
> But let the glory of this deed be mine! (vi.11–18)

Suddenly, the cathedral chorus breaks in with a Latin chant.
This is a parody of the cathedral scene in *Faust* in which Latin
choruses punctuate the speeches of Gretchen and the Evil Spirit.[1]
Firmilian feels a momentary pity as he imagines the thousand
"wretches" inside:

> Censers steam
> With their Arabian charge of frankincense,

1. Goethe, *Faust*, pp. 143–45.

> And every heart, with inward fingers, counts
> A blissful rosary of prayer.   (vi.30–33)

Aytoun scores a palpable hit at the "overloaded heart" common to
all Spasmodic poems, and especially heavy in *A Life-Drama;*
indeed, Walter had spoken of "the finger of my soul" (p. 100).
When the organ and choir break in again, Firmilian is so
affected that he must remind himself of his noble purpose:

> Lose this one chance,
>   Which bears me to th' Acropolis of guilt,
> And this, our age, foregoes its noblest song. (vi.76–78)

Fortunately for the age, the next chorus deals with the baptizing
of Jews; the religious Firmilian is outraged:

> What! would they venture to baptize the Jew?
> The cause assumes a holier aspect, then;
> And, as a faithful son of Rome, I dare
> To merge my darling passion in the wrong
> That is projected against Christendom! (vi.96–100)

He hesitates no longer; as a faithful Catholic, he blows up the
cathedral.

   The multiple murder is a glorious success. In Scene Nine,
Aytoun gives Firmilian a speech of triumph aimed at the entire
Spasmodic school:

> 'Twas a grand spectacle! The solid earth
> Seemed from its quaking entrails to eruct
> The gathered lava of a thousand years,
> Like an imposthume bursting up from hell!
> In a red robe of flame, the riven towers,
> Pillars and altar, organ-loft and screen,
> With a singed swarm of mortals intermixed,
> Were whirled in anguish to the shuddering stars,
> And all creation trembled at the din.
> It was my doing—mine alone! (ix.1–10)

But, alas, Firmilian still cannot feel remorse. Having killed a
thousand random people, he admits he has "been too coarse and

general in this business." After all, "what were the victims unto
me?" he asks, and answers in the manner of Balder:

> Nothing! Mere human atoms, breathing clods,
> Uninspired dullards, unpoetic slaves,
> The rag, and tag, and bobtail of mankind;
> Whom, having scorched to cinders, I no more
> Feel ruth for what I did, than if my hand
> Had thrust a stick of sulphur in the nest
> Of some poor hive of droning humble-bees,
> And smoked them into silence. (ix.36–43)

He must murder a dearer victim and has already selected
Haverillo,

> Who was my friend and brother. We have gazed
> Together on the midnight map of heaven,
> And marked the gems in Cassiopeia's hair—
> Together have we heard the nightingale
> Waste the exuberant music of her throat,
> And lull the flustering breezes into calm—
> Together have we emulously sung
> Of Hyacinthus, Daphne, and the rest
> Whose mortal weeds Apollo changed to flowers. (ix.49–57)

This parody of Smith's common use of "friendship" poetry,[2]
astronomical allusions, classical mythology, and the pathetic fallacy is done in a manner remarkably similar to Smith's own.

The end of this scene is a direct parody of the end of Scene
XXVIII in *Balder*. Just as Balder lures Doctor Paul to the ramparts
to kill him, so Firmilian invites Haverillo to the Pillar of St.
Simeon Stylites. After the difficult ascent, Doctor Paul complains
"That winding stair—two hundred steps and more—/My head
swims" (p. 490); Haverillo gasps, "These steps have pumped the
ether from my lungs,/And made the bead-drops cluster on my
brow" (ix.77–78). Neither hero shows much interest in his
guest's discomfort, however. In a psychological shift typical of
Dobell, Balder relieves his mind at this critical moment by fixing
on something irrelevant:

2. See Smith, *The Poetical-Works*, pp. 103–04, 17–19.

> 'Tis a fearful height. My Dog
> Whose stature thou didst praise seen hence appears
> Notably less. His kennel which thou knowest
> Befits a mastiff of the English breed,
> Might house a cur.   (p. 490)

Firmilian observes:

> A moment.—Do you see
> Yon melon-vender's stall down i' the square?
> Methinks the fruit that, close beside the eye,
> Would show as largely as a giant's head,
> Is dwindled to a heap of gooseberries!
> If Justice held no bigger scale than those
> Yon pigmy seems to balance in his hands,
> Her utmost fiat scarce would weigh a drachm! (ix.104–11)

Aytoun adds just that little touch to push the realism of Dobell into the realm of the ridiculous. Both murderers disbelieve the promises of their victims to do their bidding, but whereas Balder contemptuously sends Paul away, Firmilian hurls Haverillo to his death below.

Firmilian does not reappear until Scene Thirteen. He has decided to relinquish Cain as his subject, though without regretting his manifold murders:

> Could I undo, even by a single word,
> All my past actings, and recall to life
> The three companions of my earlier years—
> The nameless crowd that perished in the church—
> The guileless poetaster—and the rest
> Who indirectly owe their deaths to me—
> Would I exert the power? Most surely not.
> Above the pool that lies before my foot
> A thousand gnats are hovering—an hour hence
> They'll drop into the mud! Should I lament
> That things so sportive, and so full of glee
> So soon must pass away? In faith, not I!
> They all will perish ere the sun goes down,
> And yet tomorrow night that self-same pool

Will swarm with thousands more. What's done, is done;
I'll look on it no further.   (xiii.51–66)

Aytoun is hitting hard at the casual morality of the Spasmodic
poets. Festus destroys the world and is rewarded in Heaven;
Walter rapes Violet and gains her love; Balder kills his daughter,
recovers from transient remorse, and prepares to kill his wife—
not exactly what Aytoun considered poetic justice.

Firmilian abandons Cain as his subject because he is too
strong to feel remorse:

> Some other bard
> With weaker nerves and fainter heart than mine
> Must gird him to the task.

He continues with what the bogus review called the Spasmodic
"view of the powers of poets and poetry":

> 'Tis not for me
> To shrine that page of history in song,
> And utter such tremendous cadences,
> That the mere babe who hears them at the breast
> *Sans* comprehension, or the power of thought,
> Shall be an idiot to its dying hour!
> I deemed my verse would make pale Hecate's orb
> Grow wan and dark; and into ashes change
> The radiant star-dust of the milky way.
> I deemed that pestilence, disease, and death,
> Would follow every strophe—for the power
> Of a true poet, prophet as he is,
> Should rack creation!   (xiii.76–88)

Instead, Firmilian decides on "love, love, love!—the master of
the world" for his subject, feeling that he is "a graduate . . . in
Cupid's lore." In order to make his song perfect, however, he
must attain a "frank communion," which means that he must
enjoy his three women simultaneously.

Firmilian gathers all three together in Scene Fourteen, and
Aytoun launches his major attack against the lasciviousness and
promiscuity of the Spasmodics. Mariana's opening extravaganza

is less a parody than a condensed reproduction of Smith's episode
of the Indian Page: [3]

> O my beautiful!
> My seraph love—my panther of the wild—
> My moon-eyed leopard—my voluptuous lord!
> O, I am sunk within a sea of bliss,
> And find no soundings!　　　　　(xiv.1–5)

Even the symbolic presentation of the three women as rose, lily,
and night-stock is reminiscent of Walter's two loves, the daisy
and the violet.[4] The basic situation, however, is a parody of
Festus' professions of fidelity to Angela, and Clara, and Marian,
and Helen, and Elissa. But whereas Festus was allowed to enjoy
his women, Firmilian loses them all when he broaches his com-
munal plan. Aytoun the parodist, having completed his work,
fades into the background, while Aytoun the serious moralist
comes to the fore.

In the next and final scene, Firmilian becomes unique among
Spasmodic heroes: he suffers retribution. Aytoun believed it
desirable that "in all works of fiction, whether high or low, there
should be a distinct development of the Nemesis, or retributive
power—that vice or fraud, however exhibited, should not be
portrayed as finally triumphant—but that each action, according
to its merit or demerit, should have its proper moral consequence.[5] Parody must retreat before higher claims. The agent
of nemesis in this case is conscience, which Aytoun believed "in-
destructible, and certain to return at last with an aspect of tenfold
terror." [6] Chased by members of the Inquisition onto a barren
moor, Firmilian recalls that this is the same place where, two
years before,

> An old blind beggar came and craved an alms,
> Thereby destroying a stupendous thought
> Just burning in my mind—a glorious bud
> Of poesy, but blasted ere its bloom!

3. Ibid., pp. 45–52.
4. Ibid., pp. 56, 97.
5. *Blackwood's*, 77 (1855), 187.
6. Ibid., *90* (1861), 310.

I bade the old fool take the leftward path,
Which leads to the deep quarry, where he fell. (xv.12–17)

Now he himself falls victim to a chorus of ignes fatui, "the echo
of an inward voice, or spirit words," which plagues him with a
summary of his crimes and lures him to the same deep quarry
where he plunges to his death. Ironically, he finds remorse at
last. So ends the career of Firmilian and, with it, Aytoun's
criticism of the Spasmodic poets.

The career of the hero occupies only one-half of *Firmilian,*
and Aytoun attacks much more than the Spasmodic poets. His
most vicious assault is against their advocate, George Gilfillan.
Aytoun usually had trouble controlling his criticism of this
archenemy, and here he breaks into vituperation. Apollodorus,
the critic, soliloquizes:

> Why do men call me a presumptuous cur,
> A vapourizing blockhead, and a turgid fool,
> A common nuisance, and a charlatan?
> I've dashed into the sea of metaphor
> With as strong paddles as the sturdiest ship
> That churns Medusae into liquid light,
> And hashed at every object in my way.
> My ends are public. I have talked of men
> As my familiars, whom I never saw.
> Nay—more to raise my credit—I have penned
> Epistles to the great ones of the land,
> When some attack might make them slightly sore,
> Assuring them in faith, it was not I.
> What was their answer? Marry, shortly this:
> "Who in the name of Zernebock, are you?" (x.1–15)

Bentley's Miscellany explains the import of the last lines:

> Mr. Gilfillan has, in some one of his sketches, made a com-
> plaint against Mr. Macaulay, on the score of contemptuous
> rudeness—the ground of offence being, that when the histo-
> rian's *magnum opus* was mauled by a personal adversary in
> the *Quarterly,* a friend of Mr. Gilfillan's was kind enough to

write a letter of condolence to him, Thomas Babington Macaulay—and that the only response elicited was a haughty expression of indifference on the historian's part, as to what Mr. Gilfillan's "friend" might think or feel, one way or the other. If Mr. Gilfillan's friend was not Mr. Gilfillan himself, he managed his report of the snubbing affair maladroitly, and rumour maliciously wrongs him.[7]

Apollodorus hears a costermonger singing in the street and rhapsodizes over this "genuine bard," "a creature of high impulse," unsoiled "By coarse conventionalities of rule." He advises his most recent discovery:

> thine ass should be a Pegasus,
> A sun-reared charger snorting at the stars,
> And scattering all the Pleiads at his heels—
> Thy cart should be an orient-tinted car,
> Such as Aurora drives into the day,
> What time the rosy-fingered Hours awake. (x.61–66)

Only threats of violence from the costermonger prove sufficient to disenchant this searcher after genius. Apollodorus ends in his usual posture of expectation:

> Towards the firmament
> I gaze with longing eyes; and, in the name
> Of millions thirsting for poetic draughts,
> I do beseech thee, send a poet down!
> Let him descend, e'en as a meteor falls,
> Rushing at noonday—   (x.76–81)

Ironically obtaining his wish, he is crushed to death by the falling body of Haverillo.

The Spasmodics are not the only poets who attract the attention of Aytoun. The reference to the Pillar of St. Simeon Stylites is a glance at the poet laureate, although of no burlesque value. More significance attaches to the relationship of Firmilian's three loves: Mariana, "the blooming mistress of the moated grange," "the tender, blushing, yielding Lilian," and Indiana, "that full blown beauty of Abassin blood." The first two are early Tenny-

---

7. *Bentley's Miscellany, 38* (1855) , 138.

sonian maids, while the third is the Creole heroine of George Sand's first independent novel, *Indiana*.[8] Firmilian asks the rose and the lily to share their claims on him with the night-stock: Mariana is outraged, "A filthy negress! Abominable!" and Lilian is amazed, "Mercy on me! what blubber lips she has!" The withered Mariana and "airy, fairy" Lilian pale before a full-blooded woman. Aytoun is criticizing the album pictures of the young Tennyson, but only lightly; he usually expressed warm admiration for "Prince Alfred" [9]—at least until the appearance of *Maud*.

Aytoun deals more intently with another subject of greater dimensions. Kitchin points out that *Firmilian* "has a larger application to all ultra-romantic drama from the Elizabethans down." [1] This would seem to be a difficult assertion to make convincing. Certainly the particular in literature is subject to generalization; certainly the extreme romanticism of the Spasmodics often recalls that of their predecessors; but is there any specific evidence to prove that Aytoun aimed beyond the contemporary school and at "all ultra-romantic drama"?

In the burlesque review of May, the *Blackwood's* reviewer points out that T. Percy Jones has "a certain rude exaggerated dramatic power, which has more than once reminded us of the early style of Marlowe and the other predecessors of Shakespeare." [2] He praises Jones for not carrying "his imitative admiration of Goethe's *Faust* so far, as personally to evoke Lucifer or Mephistopheles" (p. 534). As we have seen, Goethe's drama is a principal object of the parody. The *Blackwood's* reviewer informs his readers that Jones has borrowed an idea from Victor Hugo's tragedy of *Lucrèce Borgia* (p. 536). He compliments the author for managing the first part of Scene Fourteen "with a dexterity which old Dekker might have applauded" (p. 548). And his final words on Jones are:

8. The novel was well known in Victorian England. Matthew Arnold compares its *"heaven born character"* with "the undeniably powerful but most un-heaven-born productions" of Thackeray and Mrs. Stowe (*Letters to Arthur Hugh Clough*, p. 133; see Clough's opinion on p. 58).

9. See *Blackwood's*, 66 (1849), 343–44, and 75 (1854), 303.

1. Kitchin, *A Survey of Burlesque and Parody in English*, p. 293.

2. *Blackwood's*, 75 (1854), 533.

To him the old lines on Marlowe, with the alteration of the
name, might be applied—
  "Next Percy Jones, bathed in the Thespian Springs,
  Had in him those brave sublunary Things
  That your first Poets had; his Raptures were
  All Air and Fire, which made his Verses clear;
  For that fierce Madness still he did retain,
  Which rightly should possess a Poet's Brain." (p. 511) .

Aytoun is not merely making the incidental comparisons common to the critique of a new play; he is deliberately associating
Firmilian with a whole class of dramatic writings. This evidence
of a relationship gains corroboration from his letter to Martin:
"It is very curious, when you sit down to write this kind of
thing, to find how very closely some of the passages approximate
to good poetry; and I am really of opinion that the best things
in Marlowe were owing mainly to a fine rhythmical ear and a
reckless energy." [3] Aytoun was cognizant that the difference between good Romantic drama and bad Spasmodic drama depended
largely on the sensibility of the artist, that that sensibility was
subject to error, that Spasmody was not limited to the Spasmodics.

T. Percy Jones has the romantic tendencies of a Marlowe,
without the sensibility. Thus, in his preface to *Firmilian,* he
compares his work to the dark tragedies of Shakespeare, Goethe's
Faust, and "any of the great works which refer to the conflict of
the passions" (p. vii) . In a sense he is right, just as he is correct
in designating Addison's *Cato* as the absolute antithesis of *Firmilian.* The difficulty in accepting his comparisons arises from
his inability to distinguish any difference more subtle than that
between black and white.

Within *Firmilian* itself, Aytoun keeps the reader aware of the
extensive relevance of his parody. Besides the passages which
caricature the extravagant quality of Romantic verse in general,
particular echoes of Elizabethan drama can be distinguished. In
the letter to Martin, for instance, immediately after Aytoun
likens "this sort of crambo" to the poetry of Marlowe, he offers
the following sample from *Firmilian:*

3. Martin, *Memoir,* p. 146.

> I clove my way
> Right eastward, till I lighted at the foot
> Of holy Helicon, and drank my fill
> At the clear spout of Aganippe's stream.
> I've rolled my limbs in ecstasy along
> The self-same turf on which old Homer lay
> That night he dreamed of Helen and of Troy. (i.59–64)

This sounds more like Marlowe than any of the Spasmodics, and the two lines immediately following reinforce the Elizabethan impression. They seem intended to recall Falstaff's "We have heard the chimes at midnight": "And I have heard at midnight the sweet strains/Come quiring from the hill-top" (i.65–66). Marlowe handled the exotic East with fervor and wielded proper names with Miltonic strength; the following passage from *Firmilian* is alien to the Spasmodic school:

> The caliph of Baldracca crossed their path,
> Him they took captive, with three princes more,
> And made them stand to ransom. All the East,
> As I have heard—Chaldea, Araby,
> Fez, Tunis, India, and the far Cathay—
> Was racked for tribute. From the Persian Gulf
> There came huge bags of large and lustrous pearl,
> Which in the miry bottom of the sea
> The breathless diver found.   (vii.19–27)

In addition, Elizabethan conventions, foreign to the Spasmodics, subserve a humorous purpose. The final couplet, for instance, was used in a continuous Elizabethan drama in order to indicate to actor and audience the end of a scene. Such a contrivance was understandably absent from the closet dramas of the Spasmodics, yet Aytoun mimics it four times.[4] The archaic "soft you now!"[5] seems to serve no purpose other than to point to an earlier era. Two references to Faustus[6] and frequent echoes of Shakespeare keep reminding the reader of the relevance of *Firmilian* to Elizabethan writings. It may be impossible for a British dramatist

4. The end of scenes i, viii, xiii, and xiv.
5. ii.53 and iii.65.
6. xii.12–14, 18.

to avoid Shakespearean echoes, but they occur so often in Jones' work that they seem purposeful.[7]

Finally, Jones deviates from Spasmodic practice and follows the Elizabethans in the matter of artistic propriety. In a review of Mrs. Browning's *Aurora Leigh,* Aytoun complained that, unlike Shakespeare, modern dramatists put all of their material into verse.[8] He allows Jones, on the other hand, to use prose for transitions and low comedy. All of his prose passages, however, are so coarse that they caricature the vulgarity which Aytoun found so offensive in the Elizabethans, especially Beaumont and Fletcher.[9]

Coventry Patmore was aware of Aytoun's purpose in *Firmilian* and, in a discussion of the influence of Fletcher and his contemporaries upon Bailey and Smith, referred to the Elizabethans as "the early 'spasmodic school' of English dramatists." [1] Other readers of *Firmilian* may tend to overlook the larger relevance of the parody to all ultra-romantic drama—not because of its unobtrusiveness, but because the parody of the Spasmodics is the immediate object and is accomplished so effectively.

Aytoun designated a prose counterpart to the Spasmodic school of poetry, and the select membership was composed of John Ruskin and Thomas Carlyle. Martin believed that the Graduate in *Firmilian* "typified" the "Oxford undergraduate" speaking "with Ruskin-like vehemence." [2] This misses the point, however, for the Graduate is Ruskin himself. In June 1854, the month between the appearance of the burlesque review and the completion of *Firmilian* itself, Aytoun published a review of Ruskin's *Lectures on Architecture and Painting.*[3] Ruskin had

7. There are at least four echoes of lines from *Hamlet* (vii.86–88, ix.82, x.43, xiii.71–72) and one each from *Henry IV,* Pt. 2 (i.65–66), *Othello* (i.139), and *Richard III* (xii.95). The words of Firmilian to Haverillo on the Pillar of St. Simeon Stylites (ix.104–11) parody those of Edgar to Gloucester "on the cliffs" at Dover (IV, vi.11–24).

8. *Blackwood's, 81* (1857), 37.

9. *The Times* (May 21, 1853), p. 7.

1. *The Edinburgh Review, 104* (1856), 341.

2. Martin, *Memoir,* p. 158.

3. *Blackwood's, 75* (1854), 740–56.

delivered these lectures at Edinburgh in November 1853 and had roused the ill will of his auditors by decrying the architecture of their city. Like many of his fellow citizens, Aytoun was angered, and he soon made his answer.

The review establishes that Aytoun considered Ruskin a prose Spasmodic: "We have perused a good deal of undaunted nonsense in our day, but never aught like this. It is a first-rate specimen of what our French neighbours term *galimatias*—in the vernacular, balderdash" (p. 745). Ruskin may even be more blameworthy than the poets, for he advises and decries without attempting to create anything himself: "If the weakest poet of the new Spasmodic school had, in the preface to his own effusions, declared his conviction that Homer was an ass, and Shakespeare an impostor, this much might be said for him, that he at least challenged comparison. Mr. Ruskin takes a safer, but, we must be allowed to say, a much more pusillanimous line. He has nothing whatever of his own to show" (pp. 744–75).

Aytoun attacks Ruskin at all points. Personally this "Prophet" displays "excessive puppyism and calm pretension" (p. 744). A "contradictory and arraigning spirit characterizes the whole of his writings" (p. 740). Stylistically "he confounds eloquence with bombast; and when he means to be particularly sublime, becomes absolutely unintelligible" (p. 756). Ultimately he is a danger to the established order: "He affects the utmost reverence for Scripture, and yet quotes it in a way which cannot be designated by a milder term than irreverent . . . indeed it is woeful, when shallow impertinence attempts to obscure the lights of other ages, and when the great men of antiquity who have been honoured for centuries, and still are honoured, are assailed, not by candid criticism, but by downright dogmatic abuse" (p. 756). Aytoun consequently "introduces a hit" at the Graduate [4] in *Firmilian*. It is interesting to view his unusual method in this particular case: he combines three passages from Ruskin's *Lectures* and writes them out in blank verse, adding nothing. In other words, he thought Ruskin's writing so ridiculous as to parody itself. The first words of the Graduate are:

4. Ruskin had used that sobriquet on the title page of *Modern Painters*.

Believe me, father, they are all accurs'd!
These marble garments of the ancient Gods,
Which the blaspheming hand of Babylon
Hath gathered out of ruins, and hath raised
In this her dark extremity of sin;
Not in the hour when she was sending forth
Her champions to the highway and the field,
To pine in deserts and to writhe in flame—
But in the scarlet frontage of her guilt,
When, not with purple only, but with blood,
Were the priests vested, and their festive cups
Foamed with the hemlock rather than the wine. (iv.49–60)

The original passage, quoted and underlined by Aytoun in his review of Ruskin's *Lectures,* reads as follows:

Accursed, I call it, with deliberate purpose. It needed but the gathering up of a Babylonish garment to trouble Israel; —these marble garments of the ancient idols of the Gentiles, how many have *they* troubled! Gathered out of their ruins by the second Babylon—gathered by the Papal Church in the extremity of her sin—raised up by her, not when she was sending forth her champions to preach in the highway, and pine in the desert, and perish in the fire, but in the very scarlet frontage and fulness of her guilt, when her priests *vested themselves not with purple only, but with blood, and bade the cups of their feasting foam not with wine only, but with hemlock.* (p. 745)

The self-parody continues throughout the Graduate's lengthy speech.

Because of his threats against the churches, the Graduate is brought to the stake after Firmilian blows up the Cathedral of Saint Nicholas. In a summary of the last words of the Graduate, Aytoun makes clear that his principal objection to Ruskin is his spirit of contradiction, holding nothing sacred and challenging the established social and religious orders:

His speech was worse than any commination.
He curs'd the city, and he curs'd the church;

He curs'd the houses, and he curs'd their stones.
He cursed, in short, in such miraculous wise,
That nothing was exempted from his ban. (xi.36–40)

Immediately after the death of the Graduate, another victim is led forth, a fellow "rejoicing in the name of Teufelsdröckh."

Aytoun criticized Carlyle for the same faults he parodied in Ruskin. As early as 1846, he called him "very deep sounding and unintelligible," [5] and in the publication of *Latter-Day Pamphlets*, he saw another challenge to established institutions. In his review of the pamphlets in 1850,[6] he characterizes them as "the silliest productions of the day" (p. 657). He points out that, like Ruskin, Carlyle "is anything but a man of practical ability"; he "can never stir one inch beyond the merest vague generality" (p. 642). Yet this sluggard has the excessive puppyism and calm pretension to abuse everyone else:

> It must be admitted that our author is perfectly impartial in the distribution of his strokes . . . . Clenching both his fists, he delivers a facer to the Trojan on the right, and to the Tyrian on the left. Big with the conviction that all Governments are wrong, as presently or lately constituted, he can see no merit, but the reverse, in any of the schemes of progress, or reform, or financial change, which have yet been devised. (p. 644)

Carlyle's unique prose also comes under assault: "As to his style, it can be defended on no principle whatever . . . in Mr. Carlyle's sentences, there is no touch or sound of harmony. They are harsh, cramped, and often ungrammatical; totally devoid of all pretension to ease, delicacy, or grace" (p. 658). Consequently, the description of Teufelsdröckh in *Firmilian* emphasizes Aytoun's two objections to Carlyle—his universal abuse and his unique style.

> Six times the Inquisition held debate
> Upon his tenets, and vouchsafed him speech,
> Whereof he largely did avail himself.

5. *Blackwood's, 60* (1846), 229.
6. Ibid., *67* (1850), 641–58.

But they could coin no meaning from his words,
Further than this, that he most earnestly
Denounced all systems, human and divine.
And so, because the weaker sort of men
Are oft misled by babbling, as the bees
Hive at the clash of cymbals, it was deemed
A duty to remove him. He, too, spoke.
But never in your life, sir, did you hear
Such hideous jargon! The distracting screech
Of waggon-wheels ungreased was music to it;
And as for meaning—wiser heads than mine
Could find no trace of it. 'Twas a tirade
About fire-horses, jötuns, windbags, owls,
Choctaws and horse-hair, shams and flunkeyism,
Unwisdoms, Tithes, and Unveracities.
Faith, when I heard him railing in crank terms,
And dislocating language in his howl
At Phantasm Captains, Hair-and-leather Popes,
Terrestrial Law-words, Lords, and Law-bringers—
I almost wished the Graduate back again:
His style of cursing had some flavour in't;
The other's was most tedious. By and by,
The crowd grew restive; and no wonder, sir;
For the effect of his discourse was such,
That one poor wench miscarried in affright.   (xi.56–83)

So ends Aytoun's attack on Spasmodic prose—a brief skirmish,
but closely related to the major assault against Spasmodic poetry.

Firmilian includes a significant amount of nonliterary satire.
Aytoun was a fierce adversary of Roman Catholicism, writing
against Peel's attempts to relax restrictions and denouncing the
movement of his own Conservative party toward an endowment
of the priesthood.[7] In *Firmilian*, however, he concentrates on
aspects of Catholicism which have constantly provided material
for the satirist. He presents the members of the Inquisition as
hypocritical, sensual, and ignorant; the Chief Inquisitor closes

7. Ibid., *69* (1851), 491–512; *71* (1852), 132.

the judgment scene with the expressive "Put out the lights!" The confessor of the Countess D'Aguilar, the mother of one of Firmilian's victims, proves to be a grasping knave. When he is warned that the D'Aguilars' treasure room is guarded by a magic effigy, he scornfully replies:

> Reserve thy tales
> For gaping crones, and idle serving-men!
> Can I not make an image stare and wink,
> Exhibit gesture with its painted hands,
> Yea, counterfeit the action of a saint—
> And dost thou hope to scare me with a lie. (viii.80–85)

Even in his prose articles, Aytoun identified the sacred relics of Catholicism with the magic exhibitions so popular at the time:

> John Bull laughs with scorn at the mention of Popish relics, and professes himself unable to comprehend the imbecility of those who make pilgrimages to visit them; yet within half an hour afterwards, the excellent man takes Mrs. Bull and the junior members of his family to see the wonderful exhibition of two infant priests, brought from a mysterious city in Central America, as detailed in a newspaper account which he read that morning with infinite gratification and amazement! [8]

Aytoun wrote frequent articles in the early fifties, such as "Spiritual Manifestations," "Rapping the Question," and "Revelations of a Showman," [9] attacking the gullibility of John Bull for magic shows. When Firmilian gives up his original theme of Cain, he thinks:

> What if I chose
> A theme of magic? That might take the ear;
> For men who scarce have eyesight to discern
> What daily passes underneath their nose,
> Still peer about for the invisible. (xiii.97–101)

In 1854, magic was the particular channel along which ran the continual search for a panacea; if *Firmilian* had been written a

8. Ibid., 77 (1855), 200.
9. Ibid., 73 (1853), 629–46; 74 (1853), 711–25; 77 (1855), 187–201.

decade earlier, Aytoun would have satirized the railway mania. It was his countrymen's resilient faith in happy miracles that Aytoun always attacked.

If faith in magic is an improper attitude, however, so is un-imaginative belief in science. Speaking of the charms of nature, Firmilian observes:

> Why, none but fools affect to seek them now
> For the mere sense of grandeur. To a painter,
> Yon crag might seem magnificent indeed,
> With its bold outline. A geologist
> Would but regard it as a pillar left
> To mark some age that was pre-Adamite,
> And, with his hammer, excavate the bones
> Of brutes that revelled in the oozy slime,
> Ere yet a bud had burst in Eden's bower.
>
> .   .   .
>
> Such men are wise.
> They overlook the outward face of things;
> Seek no sensation from the rude design
> Of outward beauty; but fulfill their task
> Like moles, who loathe the gust of upper air,
> And burrow underneath. (xiii.5–13, 27–32)

Aytoun also ridiculed scientists, especially geologists, in several prose articles.[1] Like many religious men at mid-century, he feared that the new discoveries would jeopardize established truths.

The nonliterary, as well as the literary, criticism in *Firmilian* is the expression of a distrust and fear of the new, the extreme, the unusual; Aytoun is pleading for an adherence to established forms in poetry, prose, and social organization. *Firmilian* is a great burlesque of the Spasmodic poets, but it is also the em-bodiment of its author's philosophy.

Firmilian gained great critical acclamation.[2] Two obtuse re-viewers mistook the parody for a genuine Spasmodic production:

1. Ibid., *67* (1850), 95; *68* (1850), 231; *71* (1852), 748.
2. *Graham's Magazine, 45* (1854), 491; *The Literary Gazette* (1854), pp. 747–49; *The New Monthly Magazine, 102* (1854), 140–47; *The Westminster Review*, N.S. *6*

John Bull attacked "the enormity of Firmilian's character" and took "exception to the entire ἦθος" of the poem;³ the *Press* ended its attack with the well-meaning statement that "in the race of absurdity Mr. Percy Jones has fairly distanced all competitors, and set a brand of ridicule upon the 'spasmodic' school which we sincerely trust may soon have the effect of banishing it from print, though it may still drivel in manuscript."⁴ *Tait's,* which had formerly opposed Aytoun in politics and literature, carried a favorable review of the poem.⁵ The *Times* simply called *Firmilian* "the most perfect, as it is the most elaborate and the most legitimate, parody that has ever been written."⁶ Of the two captious reviews, one was merely part of a general argument against humor as a fit subject for literature.⁷ Twenty years later, *St. James's Magazine* summed up the early Victorian reaction when it said, "his 'Firmilian' places him apart from, and in some respects above, all other recent writers of humorous verse."⁸

The early reaction has been corroborated by later critics. Millar, a historian of Scottish literature, calls *Firmilian* "a masterpiece," Walker, a historian of Victorian literature, "one of the keenest parodies ever written," and Kitchin, the historian of burlesque and parody in English, "a great dramatic burlesque."⁹ Saintsbury sums up: "Firmilian and the pilot-article on it in *Blackwood* at once attracted the popularity they deserved, and have received honourable mention from almost all critics and literary historians of competence who have mentioned them since."¹

Indirect praise was accorded Aytoun by two of the great Eng-

(1854), 614–15; *The Dublin University Magazine, 44* (1854), 488–92; *The Press, 2* (1854), 761; *The National Magazine, 5* (1854), 476–77; *Norton's Literary Gazette* (1854–55), p. 461; *Bentley's Miscellany, 38* (1855), 137–39; *The New Quarterly Review, 4* (1855), 82–85.

3. *John Bull* (1854), p. 602.
4. *The Press, 2* (1854), 761.
5. *Tait's* (1854), pp. 557–61.
6. *The Times* (Dec. 27, 1856), p. 4.
7. *The Eclectic Review,* N.S. *9* (1855), 39–49; *The Athenaeum* (1854), p. 1165.
8. *St. James's Magazine, 2* (1876), 270.
9. Millar, "William Edmondstoune Aytoun," p. 110; Walker, *The Literature of the Victorian Era,* p. 513; Kitchin, *A Survey of Burlesque and Parody in English,* p. 293.
1. Saintsbury, *The Cambridge History of English Literature, 13,* 179.

lish parodists, Swinburne and Beerbohm: they followed with works in the manner of *Firmilian*. Swinburne had been "violently attracted" to *Balder* in his boyhood but later was repelled by its incoherence. Gosse reveals that the carefully balanced form of *Atalanta* "was a protest against the shapelessness of the 'spasmodical' types of lyrical but essentially untheatrical drama, such as were much admired at that time . . . some of us still recall Swinburne's attitude towards Alexander Smith's *Life Drama*, Sydney Dobell's *Balder*, and the whole set of rhapsodical works of which they were the type. We know how resolutely and designedly he set his face against their excesses." [2] Swinburne desired no less than "to reform the idea of poetical drama, based on the Elizabethans, which had been illustrated by Beddoes, P. J. Bailey, and particularly by Dobell in his *Balder* (1853) . . . . He saw that these so-called dramas were really incoherent masses of dexterous or impressive verse in its essence lyrical." [3] As an initial volley in this crusade, he published "The Monomaniac's Tragedy. By Ernest Wheldrake" in *Undergraduate Papers* for 1858.[4] It is a burlesque review, with extracts, of the work of a Spasmodist and is in obvious imitation of *Firmilian*.[5]

The relationship between *Firmilian* and Beerbohm's "Savonarola" [6] is more difficult to determine. At first glance, both dramas form part of an English tradition which parodies the high-flown Romantic manner.[7] On closer examination, however, these two seem to have especially "interesting similarities," [8] from minute details to the bogus prose introduction and the blank-verse parody of Elizabethan tragedy. Nothing in the literature on Beerbohm, however, indicates that he was acquainted with *Firmilian;* he seems to have achieved his method independently.

2. Gosse, *Works of Algernon Charles Swinburne, 19,* 104.

3. Ibid., p. 73.

4. *Undergraduate Papers,* No. 2, Pt. 3 (1858) , pp. 97–102.

5. "The Monomaniac's Tragedy" has recently been republished for the first time, in *New Writings by Swinburne or Miscellanea Nova et Curiosa,* ed. Cecil Y. Lang (Syracuse, Syracuse University Press, 1964) , pp. 81–87.

6. Max Beerbohm, "Savonarola," *Seven Men and Two Others* (London, W. Heinemann Ltd., 1950) .

7. *Tom Thumb* and *The Critic* are early successful members of the tradition.

8. MacDonald, ed., *Parodies: An Anthology from Chaucer to Beerbohm—and After,* p. 562.

THE NEW CRITICAL CLIMATE

The finest tribute paid to Aytoun was the critical revolution that *Firmilian* helped to effect. The Spasmodics had been unusually popular poets; after *Firmilian,* they were widely condemned. The *London Times* said of Aytoun, "to him alone almost belongs the merit of actively opposing and protesting against the system. . . . Firmilian has proved to be a most salutary discipline." [1] Proof of this salutary discipline can be found in an examination of the general criticism of the post-*Firmilian* period, the future careers of the Spasmodics themselves, and the critical reception of the three most famous poetical works of 1855–56, *Maud, Men and Women,* and *Aurora Leigh.*

Tait's Edinburgh Magazine epitomized the general shift in critical opinion. In "The Last Spasm," this former organ of Gilfillan burlesqued the Spasmodic school; [2] even Aytoun expressed surprise at such apostasy. [3] *Blackwood's,* on the other hand, intensified its earlier campaign. Remarking "the entire family aspect and resemblance" of *A Life-Drama, Balder, Maud, Men and Women,* and the work of Mrs. Browning, it belittled this "secondary age" of poetry and called for "manfuller voices." [4] Now it had considerable support.

The *North British Review,* in "Poetry—The Spasmodists," [5] decried the subject matter of the Spasmodics. They deal with the

---

1. *The Times* (Dec. 27, 1856) , p. 4.
2. *Tait's* (1854) , pp. 557–61.
3. Undated letter to John Blackwood.
4. *Blackwood's, 79* (1856) , 125–38.
5. *The North British Review, 28* (1858) , 231–50.

"rare and peculiar" rather than the universal; "they refine upon reality till it becomes the faintest shadow, and only attempt to grasp it at the stage in which it cannot be laid hold of" (p. 238) ; they concentrate too much upon the "perplexed thought and uncertain feeling" of Doubt (p. 237) ; they are not men speaking to men:

> We urge a return to the lasting and true subject-matter of poetry, and a firmer reliance on primal truths; for it is this which has so often given fresh life to both poetry and painting in the past. . . . Anything that has in it a genuine human interest is sure to win its way to the heart, so irresistible is the touch of real truth . . . we must have poetry for men who work, and think, and suffer, and whose hearts would feel faint and their souls grow lean, if they fed on such fleeting deliciousness and confectionery trifle as the spasmodists too frequently offer them—we must have poetry in which natural emotions flow, real passions move, in clash and conflict—in which our higher aims and aspirations are represented, with all that reality of daily life which goes on around us. (pp. 249–50)

The *New Quarterly Review,* in "The Anti-Spasmodic School of Poetry," [6] condemned the Spasmodics' poetic method. Every work of art

> may be analyzed into three separate elements, regarded under three different points of view—the Idea, the Plan, and the Execution. To the "Idea" belongs the "moral" or "purpose" intended to be conveyed; the "Plan" includes the choice of a story, and the machinery of narrative, drama, etc., by which it is to be worked out; the "Execution," of course, comprises the language, style, and every other matter of detail, by which the Idea is ultimately brought before the reader. (p. 123)

Like Aytoun and Arnold, this writer emphasizes the primacy of the "Idea": "As the test of a work of art is the impression it produces on the mind; and as, if the idea be absent there is nothing to be impressed, we shall hardly be wrong in concluding that, of

6. *The New Quarterly Review,* 7 (1858) , 123–35.

the three possible defects we have implied, the want of a leading purpose is the most fatal" (p. 124). Since the Spasmodics lack such purpose and perversely expend their talents on execution, their poetry is ultimately worthless: "Mannerism is the result to which the practice of the spasmodic school is inevitably tending. There is a want of serious purpose about them—a disposition to be satisfied with any kind of canvas, provided it will bear gorgeous embroidery, which augurs ill for the stability of their work, or its adaptation to any thing but the uses of transient enjoyment" (p. 125).

The *Edinburgh Review* also criticized various Spasmodic practices.[7] "We find literally nothing but an aimless and incoherent succession of 'striking things,'" and thus "to a reader of old-fashioned mental habits, one who has been accustomed to expect and require purpose, unity, and vital sequence in all kinds of intellectual products, and, in return, to give habitually that attention which such qualities demand for their appreciation, the writings in question are absolutely unreadable" (p. 341). These writers parade "an eager and feverish craving for poetic reputation, far different from the calm confidence, often boldly expressed by great poets, in ultimate fame." "The most remarkable quality common to these writers is their surprising lack of acquaintance with all that is the true poet's chief material, namely, the ordinary realities of human nature" (p. 343). On the other hand, "Mr. Matthew Arnold's poems are very refreshing and instructive contrasts to the works of the writers who engaged our attention in the first part of this article. Mr. Arnold seems to have been driven, by the consideration of the faults of those writers, into almost an affectation of indifference to minute verbal beauties" (pp. 358–59).

This contrasting of Arnold with the Spasmodics was employed by other Victorian critics. Aytoun used the contrast, as we have seen, in his important article of March 1854. Similarly, the *London Quarterly* said:

Not more highly gifted as a poet than many of his young contemporaries, with whom so much fault has recently been

7. *The Edinburgh Review, 104* (1856), 337–62.

found, he writes much better poems. The sentiment diffused throughout their formless rhapsodies, with him acknowledges the subtle laws of taste,—finds order and coherence. . . . Mr. Arnold's style is simple, almost to baldness, and contrasts strongly with the profuse ornaments of the school of "Balder." Yet this is the triumph of genuine poetry, when its suggestions of beauty, novelty, and grace, arise from the use of language apparently not one degree removed from artless prose.[8]

On the other hand, the *Eclectic Review*, that nonconformist organ of Gilfillan in which *A Life-Drama* was brought to light, remained loyal to the Spasmodics and attacked Arnold's Preface of 1853. It depreciated his objectivity: "The sweetest songs ever sung do not necessarily relate an action, they chronicle a thought, or a sentiment . . . we believe there is a world of unuttered thought yet to be uttered subjectively, and that it affords as great and glorious a field for the poet as all the great actions of the past." It objected that Arnold's turning to the past was more suitable to the historian than to the poet: "how shall we deal with this wondrous living age of ours, so transitionary, so full of hopes and fears; its fettered energies, its phases of faith, its mental revolutions." [9] Finally, with regard to style, "we would not have poetical expression become bald and meagre. We would not have paltriness and triviality mistaken for simplicity. After Shakespeare, we can never return to the severity of the Greek tragedians. We are more pictorial, and have a stronger sense of colour than they had" (p. 280). But the *Eclectic* was fighting a lonely battle.

Eight years after its criticism of the Spasmodics, the *North British Review* announced the death of the school. James Hannay wrote as though his readers had forgotten that the Spasmodic school ever existed:

About a dozen years ago, there existed a bad school of poetry, encouraged by an absurd school of criticism, and owing its origin ultimately to the *Festus* of Mr. Bailey. No doubt

8. *The London Quarterly Review, 4* (1855), 274.
9. *The Eclectic Review, N.S. 9* (1855), 279.

there were men among them whose natural poetic power was greater than Aytoun's own. But the power was absurdly used; was employed on extravagant conceptions clothed in extravagant expression; and the result was something offensive to all who had formed their taste on the great models whether of antiquity or of England. Aytoun's sympathies in these matters were sound; indeed, if they erred at all, they erred from a certain narrowness on the sound side. So he did what his talents exactly suited him for. . . . The "spasmodic school" no longer exists as a school.[1]

THE REACTION AGAINST THE SPASMODICS

The criticism of the post-*Firmilian* period shows that the designation "Spasmodic" was gaining currency and that more classical standards were being applied in considerations of poetry. The careers of the Spasmodics themselves reveal even more dramatically the change that *Firmilian* helped to effect. Gilfillan, the spokesman for the school and the butt of Aytoun's vituperation, reacted the most violently to the parody. Before the publication of the poem, he had written in an essay on "Hazlitt and Hallam":

The first twenty-five volumes of "Blackwood's Magazine" are disgraced by incessant, furious, and scurrilous attacks upon the person, private character, motives, talents, and moral and religious principles of Hazlitt, which future ages shall regard with wonder, indignation, and disgust. . . . "Old Maga" has greatly improved in this respect since; but there is at least one of its present contributors who would perpetuate, if he durst, similar enormities of injustice, and whose maximum of will to injure and abuse all minds superior to his own, is only restrained by his minimum of power.

1. *The North British Review*, 45 (1866), 83–88. See also *The Saturday Review*, *1* (1855), 34; *Hogg's Instructor*, *3* (1854), 187; and W. H. Mallock, *Every Man His Own Poet; or The Inspired Singer's Recipe Book* (London, Whittaker and Co., 1873), pp. 24–27. Mallock wrote in answer to Robert Buchanan, *The Fleshly School of Poetry* (London, Strahan and Co., 1872), p. 15, and *A Look Round Literature*, pp. 185–203.

After the publication of *Firmilian,* Gilfillan added this footnote: "He has since dared! Vide that tissue of filthy nonsense, which none but an ape of the first magnitude could have vomited, yclept 'Firmilian.' " [1]

Putnam's Monthly referred to "his funny rage at Firmilian," [2] and *Bentley's Miscellany* wrote:

"Firmilian's" *quid* for Mr. Gilfillan's *quo,* was at least its equipollent and equivalent in smartness and severity. The Spasmodic tragedian gave quite as good as he took, and rather better. The Rowland was more than a match for the Oliver. That Apollodorus winced under the infliction is only too evident. . . .

Supposing it delightful to a satirist to see the absolute writhing of his victim, the author of "Firmilian" has unmistakable reason for exultation. [3]

The *London Quarterly Review* launched a long attack, emphasizing that Gilfillan "is a corrupter and misleader of youth . . . not free from faults of language which would disgrace the themes of a third-class boy. . . . His rashness hurries him into assertions of the wildest nature, and his freedom borders closely upon profanity." [4] *Tait's* commended the attack in the *London Quarterly* and added its own strictures. [5] The *North British Review* also emphasized Aytoun's major complaint against Gilfillan: "One critic like Mr. George Gilfillan can do infinitely more harm to literature than any number of spasmodic poets. For he is the prime source of mischief: he it is who calls these poets into their brief but harmful existence." [6] As *Harper's* summed up the situation, "George is now on the fair way to a reputation, for he is being abused by everybody." [7]

Gilfillan himself summarized the year 1854: "It was a disastrous year to me on the whole. My good old mother died on the 8th

1. Gilfillan, *A Third Gallery*, p. 177.
2. *Putnam's Monthly, 5* (1855), 332.
3. *Bentley's Miscellany, 38* (1855), 138.
4. *The London Quarterly Review, 4* (1855), 185.
5. *Tait's*, N.S. 22 (1855), 314–15.
6. *The North British Review, 42* (1865), 163.
7. *Harper's New Monthly Magazine, 9* (1854), 572.

of May; my congregation was disturbed; and Aytoun and his allies commenced a furious battery of abuse and detraction." [8] Two and a half years later, he wrote to John Stanyan Bigg:

> I have, you may be sure, something to cheer me under that systematic abuse and slander from which no one, since Hazlitt and Shelley, has suffered more. I have a good congregation, the ear of the town, an admirable wife, a decent, though not a rich, competence, a determined spirit, a firm belief in Christ as the "Coming One," and a most thorough and growing disgust at a world which I do not scruple to call "the Devil's." [9]

After Aytoun's parody, Gilfillan was no longer an influence in literature.[1]

Bailey was always known as the father of the Spasmodic poets after *Firmilian*. His new work, *The Mystic* (1855), was condemned as a Spasmodic poem, and *Festus* was reexamined more critically.[2] Whereas Ebenezer Elliott had claimed that *Festus* contained enough poetry to set up fifty poets, Coventry Patmore now said, "It contains enough poetry to have set-up a dozen minor poets, yet is Mr. Bailey no more than such a poet himself, and his work is just such a production as might have been looked for from a minor poet attempting to write the greatest poem of the world." [3] Instead of individual "beauties," critics were beginning to look for overall unity and coherence. Because of its poverty of thought "gilded with a lavish wealth of imagery," its egotistical hero, and its dissociation from "the world of reality," *Festus* was now characterized as "the poem which has been most harmful, and has wrought most evil to the young poetic mind of our time." [4] Although *Festus* retained its popularity among religionists, it never regained the esteem of the literati.[5] The egotistical

---

8. Watson, *George Gilfillan*, p. 389.

9. Ibid., pp. 414–15.

1. See Gilfillan, *A Gallery of Portraits*, p. vii.

2. See *The Saturday Review, 1* (1855), 34; *Bentley's Miscellany, 38* (1855), 609; *The North British Review, 38* (1858), 242–45, and *45* (1866), 83; *The Edinburgh Review, 104* (1856), 354–55; *Blackwood's, 79* (1856), 128–35.

3. *The Edinburgh Review, 104* (1856), 354.

4. *The North British Review, 38* (1858), 243.

5. Gosse, "Philip James Bailey," pp. 92–93.

Bailey refused to comment on the linking of his name with those of the younger Spasmodics, but, in 1893, he was finally "induced" to set forth his views:

> As regards the especial school of poetry to which you refer, I am only so far interested or concerned with the members of it as to acknowledge, along with both public and publicist, the generally bright colouring, pure morality, happy imagery, and exquisite similitudes manifest in one or two of their poems; but I have no sympathy with their works specially, nor with their ways.[6]

This jars a little with Bailey's charges of plagiarism against Smith.[7] After comparing *Festus* favorably with the works of Milton, Byron, and Shelley, and explaining what a magnificent poem it really is, he finally allows his resentment against Aytoun to seep out:

> In this light, and as completive of what may be called a synoptic view of the moral evangels of various poetical messengers, the work may now be regarded, and will repay the study of any reader interested in serious and elevated thought. It is not criticism of it that is wanted. There are volumes of it, several of the writers of which, from the cheery and voluminous balladist of his day to the literary Caliban of the current hour, have endeavoured to perpetuate, with an eye to their own renown, their self-inflicted stigmata of ignorance and incompetence.[8]

Through the silent years, Bailey was well aware of the source of his literary decline.[9]

Smith and Dobell, though they were the chief butts, appreciated Aytoun's parody. Dobell wrote to his parents about the burlesque review:

6. "The Author of 'Festus' and the Spasmodic School," *Literary Anecdotes of the Nineteenth Century*, eds. W. R. Nicoll and Thomas J. Wise (2 vols. London, Hodder and Stoughton, 1896), 2, 413.

7. Gilfillan, *A Gallery of Portraits*, p. xvi.

8. "The Author of 'Festus,'" 2, 417–18.

9. John Westland Marston, Bailey's friend, refused to include *Gerald*, one of his most ambitious efforts, in his complete works. See J. Westland Marston, *The Dramatic and Poetical Works* (2 vols. London, Chatto and Windus, 1876), 1, xi.

I laughed more, on first reading it, than at anything I have read lately. It is wonderfully well done (by Aytoun), and professes to be a critique on a new tragedy, of which specimens are given: said tragedy being a happy burlesque on me and Alexander; the incidents of "Balder" being travestied in a style intended for his and mine. The thing is so finely done that hardly anyone but those in the secret will know what it means. Poor _____ entering as Apollodorus is slain by the friends whom Balder throws from the Tower. But you must read it.[1]

He also met Aytoun on amicable terms.[2]

Smith became even more friendly with Aytoun. He had put together *A Life-Drama* hurriedly, under public pressure, and not entirely true to his natural bent. He had even undercut his protagonist, though insufficiently. Smith was therefore quite capable of valuing an exposure of his major defects:

Smith was wont to laugh heartily over several passages of this book which most directly referred to himself; always spoke of it as a production of true genius, and never bore any malicious grudge against its author. But, at the same time, he did not altogether enjoy its allusions to himself: indeed, no man in his circumstances could do so. Nothing so prejudices the mass of men against a public man or author as, though excessive, deserved, and so successful, ridicule. And as this was achieved in "Firmilian" with superlative cleverness, public sentiment which had, perhaps, become already sated with its own over-rapturous applause at "A Life Drama," began to look shy at its author . . . .

Commercially, it marred the sale of his books, and so pecuniarily he suffered by it; while, at the same time, it sobered his poetic genius, and purged it of the sins of his youth. His own spirit had, indeed, of itself begun to recoil against the spasmodic character of his first book, but the chastising hand of Aytoun confirmed his repentance.[3]

1. Jolly, *Sydney Dobell*, *1*, 353–54.
2. Ibid., *1*, 342, and 2, 50.
3. Brisbane, *Alexander Smith*, pp. 189–91.

Firmilian did not merely mar the sale of *A Life-Drama:* once the epithet "Spasmodic" had been pinned on Smith, his future poetic career was doomed to failure. Aytoun regretted this; he thought Smith exhibited "marks of genius" and, under proper discipline, could create something valuable.[4] But the damage had been done: Smith's poetry went nowhere, and he had to support a growing family out of the small income of a secretary to Edinburgh University. His colleague Aytoun came to him one morning and said:

> "You're now married, Smith, and have got a household and family to care for. What we give you here is, sooth to say, no very fat provision. Poetry is well; but it don't *pay* for the most part. Why not try a little prose? Suppose you write something for *Blackwood; try;* write the stuff, and let me know when you send it in. I'll do what I can for you in that quarter, and I don't much doubt I'll be able to get it admitted. Thereafter as may be. An occasional cheque coming in, of fifteen or twenty guineas, under these new conditions, might not perhaps inconvenience you." [5]

Smith wrote "the stuff," and it was, of course, admitted; he was off again, this time to a quieter but more abiding fame. Thus, if English literature lost a promising poet because of the author of *Firmilian,* it also gained a pleasing prose stylist, the author of *Dreamthorp.*

Smith appreciated and returned Aytoun's kindness. In a late poem, "Wardie—Springtime," he enumerates the literati of Edinburgh—Scott, Jeffrey, Lockhart, Wilson—and concludes:

> Of all that noble race but one remains,
> Aytoun, with silver bugle at his side
> That rang through all the gorges of romance—
> Alas, that 'tis so seldom at his lip! [6]

In addition, he begins his essay on "Sydney Dobell" with the following personal remarks:

4. See *Blackwood's, 76* (1854), 712.
5. Smith, *Last Leaves,* pp. cxvii–cxviii.
6. *Good Words, 3* (1862), 272–73.

Ten years ago the readers of the magazines and critical reviews could hardly fail to encounter unfavourable strictures on what was called the "Spasmodic School of Poetry." The three or four writers supposed to constitute that "school" were, at the period referred to, passing through the fires of exhortation, reproof, and parody. The nickname was the invention of a brilliant poet and wit, recently gone to his rest; and it had a nickname's best prosperity—it stuck. . . . The nickname "Spasmodic School" grew popular, and in a short time it became the critical stock-in-trade of provincial newspapers, just as if they had been its sole inventors, and had taken out a patent for its exclusive use. For a while, no one of the writers could air himself in public in a volume of verse, however staid and hum-drum, without the cry of "spasmodist" being raised, here, there, and everywhere, so loudly that he was glad to retreat again into his shell. All this is a matter of ten years ago. For seven years past the magazine reader has heard nothing of the "Spasmodic School,"— it is the lost pleiad of the critical firmament.[7]

In the essay, he also pays tribute to Dobell, "by far the most important member of the school." One grows to admire Alexander Smith.

As Smith's testimony reveals, *Firmilian* ruined his poetic career and that of Dobell. "Spasmodic" stuck like a burr and predisposed critics against them. They were ambitious youths who had attempted to storm the citadel of literary fame and had succeeded only in becoming laughingstocks; they could produce "beauties" but had no conception of a unified whole; their dramas contained interminable reflections but had lost the name of action. New critical criteria seemed to justify the epithet "Spasmodic." Smith and Dobell could not escape the designation, no matter how hard they tried; their later poetry is, in fact, a search for matter and manner opposite to those of the Spasmodic school.

They collaborated on a small volume, *Sonnets on the War*, published in 1855. The thirty-nine sonnets treat conventional war themes in an undistinguished manner. It is evident that "the

7. Smith, *Last Leaves*, pp. 171–72.

Sonnet's scanty plot of ground" constrained their spraw ling talents —Smith's ability to elaborate images and Dobell's command of sustained blank verse. The little book was generally ignored by the reviewers, although *Blackwood's* kept kicking its fallen opponents.[8]

Dobell published a companion volume, *England in Time of War*, the following year. It concentrates on the home front, presenting representative people in recognizable situations: a mother dreaming of her boy's heroics, a Christian lamenting the bloodshed, a widow crying over her husband. Such characters contrast remarkably with Balder, the isolated genius brooding over his forbidden desires. Likewise, the author of the long blank-verse dramas, *The Roman* and *Balder*, has now told his story in forty-four condensed lyrics.

The critics, however, stressed that this was another publication of that Spasmodic Dobell. The *Literary Gazette* ended its article, "Alter his dress how he will, the author of 'Balder' and 'The Roman' is always apparent." [9] Gilfillan argued against this guilt by association:

> We have been thoughtfully interested by the reception of Sydney Dobell's "England in Time of War," on which the critics have so lavishly poured out the vials of their wrath. One after the other have they come on into the battlefield, like that Russian major at Inkermann, stabbing the already wounded. The chief reason for this kind of treatment, on the part of the critics, seems to lie in the fact that Mr. Dobell has written "Balder." [1]

Gilfillan's complaint was futile. The critical strategy was not to judge Dobell's individual works on their own merits but to summarize his Spasmodic reputation and use his poems as illustrations. The characteristics selected for censure reveal just how much critical standards had changed. Dobell is criticized for an inability to criticize himself, a lack of order and proportion, an

8. *Blackwood's*, 77 (1855), 533–35. See also *The Saturday Review*, 2 (1856), 304; *The Scottish Review*, 3 (1855), 355.

9. *The Literary Gazette* (1856), p. 536.

1. *The Titan*, 23 (1856), 272.

inability to make his "fine thoughts and fine images . . . living portions of a work of art," his predilection for the striking, rather than the simple, phrase, and his concentration on unique and unusual situations.[2]

Naturally, reviews which lumped all of Dobell's poetry together had a generally unfavorable opinion of *England in Time of War*. What could be expected from a Spasmodic poet? The *Saturday Review*, for example, ended its severe article with the following summation:

> In a writer of the spasmodic school one has no right to be surprised at meeting with such things; it infects the whole brotherhood. The experience of years and observation of the public taste, might, one would have thought, have warned Mr. Dobell to keep off this dangerous ground. The taint, however, appears to be too deep. All his worst faults seem only to strengthen with time. In each successive publication he shows himself more unnatural, more affected, more deficient in good taste . . . his lyrics are no more pleasing than his epics; and what these are, the prompt oblivion of the public has already proved.[3]

Even the favorable reviews must have been as wormwood to Dobell, for they praised him only insofar as he had moved away from *Balder*.[4] But *Balder*, Dobell always maintained, was his best work; these lyrics were a "mere filler" before the completion of his major epic.[5] Now these minor poems were either condemned because they seemed to resemble his best work or were praised because they differed from it, and Dobell became discouraged. Despite many plans, he never took up *Balder* again and wrote only occasional poems during the last eighteen years of his life. Most touching is his refusal to allow a friend's book to be dedi-

2. *The National Review*, *3* (1856), 442–44. See also *The Saturday Review*, *2* (1856), 304–05; *Fraser's*, *54* (1856), 269; *The Literary Gazette* (1856), pp. 535–36; *The Edinburgh Review*, *104* (1856), 349.

3. *The Saturday Review*, *2* (1856), 305.

4. See *The Oxford and Cambridge Magazine* (1856), pp. 717–24; *The North British Review*, *28* (1858), 247–48; *The Spectator*, *29* (1856), 775.

5. Jolly, *Sydney Dobell*, 2, 3.

cated to him, for fear that his name on the dedication page would ensure the failure of the volume.[6]

In his attempt to rid himself of the epithet "Spasmodic," Smith divested himself of all poetic individuality. *City Poems* (1857), a volume equal in size to *A Life-Drama*, contains six poems about relatively ordinary people. Smith selects simple themes, chastens his diction, and varies his sources of imagery more frequently; in three poems, he adds an unnecessary narrator to strengthen the impression of objectivity. The first poem, *Horton*, illustrates his change in emphasis. The hero is another gifted poet heading "for the coast of Fame"; he too experiences a crucial love for a "lily-woman." But this time the career of the poet is presented through the eyes of realistic men of the world. When one of them begins to glorify poetry, another shouts:

> Stop, for Heaven's sake,—
> All that has been said a hundred thousand times,
> And will be said as often when you're dead.[7]

Throughout the volume, Smith is struggling to keep his romantic bias under control. Because he partially succeeded, *City Poems* met with a mixed critical reception. Those who saw the volume as a movement away from *A Life-Drama* praised it, while those whose glance fixed on the lingering elements of the earlier work censured it. All concurred that another *Life-Drama* had to be avoided.

The *Dublin University Magazine* complained that *City Poems* repeated the faults of *A Life-Drama*.[8] The reviewer emphasizes the need for "Action and the Unity of Action" and quotes from Voltaire and Arnold. "Tested by these rules, 'Horton' and 'Squire Maurice,' at least, are lamentably defective. They are psychological sketches—morbid, monotonous, painful—in which there is nothing to be *done*." The want of a definite impression cannot be redeemed by "affluent imagination, and limitless wealth of language" (p. 530). In addition, "There is the want of delicate

6. Ibid., pp. 64–65.
7. Smith, *The Poetical Works*, pp. 312–13.
8. *The Dublin University Magazine*, 50 (1857), 525–39.

morality in the very choice of such a character as Horton. To
choose it, indeed, is in some sense to become not simply its apol-
ogist, but its admirer; at least without a mode of handling very
different from that which Mr. Smith exhibits" (p. 531). All of
these remarks are meant to apply not only to *City Poems* but also
to *A Life-Drama*. They illustrate once again the new critical criteria: a unified action as subject, the subordination of "poetical"
language, and the avoidance of a dubious morality.

The reviewer continues with an acute observation about the
questionable morality of the Spasmodic hero:

> It is one of the most dangerous features of the moral psychol-
> ogy of the spasmodic school that it is always splitting the
> moral character, one and indivisible, into two selves. There
> is the outward "I," given to folly and "flip," to reeking
> punch and indifferent company, possibly to borrowing money
> never to be repaid, and other questionable practices. But
> there is the inward "I," delighting in virtue, and able to
> draw fine pictures of it, which cost very little, as they were
> never intended to be more than pictures. (p. 532)

Thus, Festus had claimed "There is divorce between my heart
and me," [9] and Balder could say of his violent passions, "I see
them,—mine / Not me" (p. 512). It is this recurrent dichotomy
between "high soul-scheming" and low conduct that Aytoun
satirized so tellingly in the fourteenth scene of *Firmilian,* but all
of his criticisms are common currency now. The *Dublin* reviewer
even ends his attack on *City Poems* with Aytoun's favorite doctrine of poetry as the expression of general truths; thus, it is improper of Smith to reproduce minutely the psychology of an individual. This new volume is too similar to *A Life-Drama* and is
accordingly censured.

Apparently to bolster his own verdict against Smith, the reviewer claims "his present volume is pooh-poohed. Like the used-
up man in the farce, criticism votes that his volcanoes are bores,
and his eclipses 'shady' affairs" (p. 525). This is inaccurate. *City
Poems* evoked applause, not for its own merits, but because it

9. This particular quote is from the following edition: Bailey, *Festus: A Poem*
(New York, Worthington Co., 1889), p. 582.

indicated a movement away from *A Life-Drama*. The *North British Review* wrote, "We see many signs that the author is trying to do his best; and if there is not much new growth, he has been shedding the old, so that the new may come in season." [1] *Fraser's* praised Aytoun for his success in "putting down *spasm* summarily" and noted that "Mr. Smith's poetry is in all respects improved. It is toned down and modulated. He speaks well,— without exaggeration or bombast; like a highly cultivated Englishman." [2] Poetry as the speech of a highly cultivated Englishman! Critical standards have indeed changed since the romantic agonies of Spasmodic heroes first excited the literary world. The *Westminster Review* approved the "advance" of public taste:

> Public taste has much advanced since we had the "Life Drama," thanks to the intolerable outrages on English common sense and language of which the spasmodic poets became latterly guilty. That it does not condemn and reject the "City Poems," but accepts them, however disappointing, as a proof of sensible progress in Art, must satisfy Mr. Smith that he is in the right track, and be the present reward for his efforts.[3]

Obviously, by "sensible progress in Art" is meant a movement away from the Spasmodic.

Sensitive to critical opinion and dependent upon popular support, Smith determined to eliminate Spasmody from his work altogether. For his next, and final, volume of poetry, *Edwin of Deira* (1861), he went to history for his subject matter.[4] As he himself explained, he "chose the subject thoughtfully, as knowing that his besetting sin was a certain unstrictness and vagrancy —so call it—a want of severity in the outline of substantial forms —and seeking without in the defined Historic framework some supplement of the deficiency within." [5] He kept the main story, the career of Edwin, clearly before the reader and maintained a simple and direct style appropriate to the narrative. Basically, he

1. *The North British Review, 28* (1858) , 249.
2. *Fraser's, 57* (1858) , 110.
3. *The Westminster Review, 68* (1857) , 589.
4. Bede, *Ecclesiastical History of the English Nation,* Bk. II Chaps. 9–14.
5. Smith, *Last Leaves,* p. lxxxi.

was attempting to write a long narrative poem in the manner of Scott, the type of poem advocated by Aytoun.

The reviewers were pleased. They saw the volume, correctly, as an abandonment of Spasmody. The *Athenaeum,* which had always been the severest critic of Smith, now said:

> We have to chronicle an advance on Mr. Smith's previous poetry . . . a poem approaching so nearly to oneness of conception, manliness of feeling, and simplicity of speech. . . . Altogether, this is a piece of honester workmanship. He has not allowed either memory or fancy to play him perpetually false. He has not violated the facts of natural relationship, as of old. . . . Nor is there so much of that reference to the weather, which characterizes the spasmodists, and makes their pages meteorological. . . .
>
> . . . On the whole, we like the concluding book of the poem best; it is furthest removed from Mr. Smith's earlier manner.
>
> We have to credit the writer of it with a right effort in a right direction. By the aid of history, he has got out of a morbid consciousness of self, and, by looking outwardly on the realities of life, has seen more than he would have perceived by continually looking within. This sort of change has saved poetry, before now, in the individual and the nation.[6]

The *Spectator,* criticizing the book according to strict classical principles, still credits it for being an advance over Smith's earlier poetry:

> This is unquestionably his most temperate and healthy work. It contains nothing of the enervating worship of the grandeur of passion which inspired his earlier poems. . . . And it is something that he has perceived the necessity of imposing upon himself a principle of external unity, since he cannot evolve it from within. In the attempt before us he does at least confess that a poem ought to be a natural whole, and not a mere string of glittering metaphorical beads.[7]

6. *The Anthenaeum* (1861), pp. 179–80.
7. *The Spectator, 34* (1861), 867.

In an enthusiastic review, the *Dublin University Magazine* said, "His own good sense, aided perhaps by the bracing shower-bath of hostile criticism, has given a stronger rootage and a goodlier crown of branches to the tree of his early promise." [8]

These reviews disclose at least as much about contemporary criticism as they do about *Edwin of Deira*. The *North British Review* is especially valuable in this respect, for it evaluates the poem against the background of current taste.[9] Its review begins, "We are the advocates of the real in poetry . . . we are convinced that a greater amount of incomprehensible twaddle has been talked upon the 'ideal' than upon any other mundane matter" (p. 107). The reviewer claims that recently "the triumph of the realistic school has been nearly as complete in Poetry as in Art" (pp. 108–09). Naturally, this realist expresses satisfaction over the "abolishment" of the Romantic school but realizes that the present extreme will call its own antithesis into being: "That the recoil has been somewhat excessive need not be denied. Reactions always are; and Mr. Buckle will be succeeded by a fanatical Joe Smith or an ultramundane priesthood" (pp. 109–10). Finally focusing on *Edwin of Deira,* he presents a contemporary conception of poetic subject matter:

> We incline to prefer the claim of History. When a poem possesses a historical basis, the risk of caricature is diminished. The poet who spins his web out of his own brain for any long time, "gangs aft agee" [sic]; whereas the poet who relies upon the facts which the unimaginative annalists of a people have recorded, is protected against the deceitfulness of the imagination, and brought back incessantly to reality. And, moreover, an event, as a whole and in its completeness, may be viewed with better effect when removed a little way from us. The pressure of the crowd partly conceals its proportions; but, in the silence of the night-season, what is poetic in the story is disengaged from its casual environment, grows plainer and more distinctly articulate. (p. 111)

Judged by such standards, the new Smith easily passes muster:

8. *The Dublin University Magazine, 59* (1862), 67.
9. *The North British Review, 35* (1861), 107–12.

He has hitherto failed conspicuously in his choice of subjects; but his choice in this case is admirable. The story is rife with incident, and keeps the reader's interest awake from beginning to end. His plot, too, has been generally very defective: it wanted bone and muscle; but he has now got a historical framework which he is forced to respect, and which prevents him from running into unnaturalness. The morbid and diseased self-consciousness of the *Life-Drama* is got rid of: the author of *Edwin of Deira* is beyond dispute an eminently healthy and well-conditioned mortal. (p. 112)

Plato's thin line between the poet and the madman has widened to become an impassable gulf. In the reaction against the Spasmodics, the desirable poet is an eminently healthy and well-conditioned mortal, our "highly cultivated Englishman" again.

Smith had become respectable with a vengeance. He had eliminated not only all trace of Spasmody but also all evidence of poetic individuality. He had written an undistinguished narrative which could have been the product of any capable poetaster. As the *Critic* said:

It possesses the very considerable merit of chaste and tactful diction, *quasi*-Tennysonian rhythm, and occasional vigour of expression; oftener, however, quaint than happy. It may be our fault, but it has certainly been our misfortune, that while reading the poem in question we felt no Heliconian fumes which "ascend us into the brain," like Falstaff's sherris; and that such pleasure as we have felt in reading it has not led us to believe that any fresh chord in our feelings has been struck, any new emotion disclosed, or any old one rehabilitated.[1]

Its final verdict on *Edwin of Deira* is a condensed history of the Spasmodic school:

That once "wayward fowl"—to borrow the poet's own language—which in the "Life Drama" and "City Poems" was always in season and out of season, flying beyond our ken and amusing us with some ever fresh fantastical flight of

1. *The Critic, 23* (1861), 150.

imagination, has now degenerated into a prosy, draggle-tailed muse, who has attained a quantity of very unmanageable and unoriginal book-learning at the cost of nearly all her former vigour and eccentricity. (pp. 151–52)

Edwin of Deira was "acceptable," and a second edition was called for after "a reasonable time." [2] But Smith was just another poet now: "he neither gained pecuniarily, nor appeared to increase his fame by the publication of this book." Like Dobell, "He became, it is to be feared, a little disheartened." [3] It was at this time that Smith heeded Aytoun's counsel to turn to prose. His poetic career was over; the defeat of the Spasmodics was complete.

THE CRITICAL RECEPTION OF MAUD, MEN AND WOMEN, *AND* AURORA LEIGH

The careers of the Spasmodics reveal a significant change in Victorian literary taste. Their violent language, nonfunctional imagery, emotional vicissitudes, and poetic digressions were now censured. Classical conceptions of unity and coherence began to appear more frequently in critical reviews; heroes of dubious morality were examined more strictly. This extreme reaction against Spasmodic poetry also affected those works suspiciously close to it. Distinctions were not often made, and *Men and Women* and *Aurora Leigh* were caught in the backwash. But the charge of "Spasmodic" was most commonly directed against *Maud*.

The Spasmodic movement can be viewed as a reaction against Tennysonianism. Its poet-hero is a wild prophet, most unlike Arthur Arundel of *The Princess;* it deals directly with the large questions of the universe rather than with the Victorian milieu; and it prefers Byronic violence to ease and grace. In 1850, Gilfillan spoke for the movement when he criticized Tennyson because "his fancy loves, better than is manly or beseeming, the tricksy elegancies of artificial life—the 'white sofas' of his study—the trim walks of his garden—the luxuries of female dress—and all the tiny comforts and beauties which nestle round an English par-

2. Smith, *Last Leaves,* p. lxxxii.
3. Brisbane, *Alexander Smith,* p. 197.

lour." Gilfillan remained one of the few Victorian critics who considered Tennyson "among the minor poets of Britain." [1] This evoked the laureate's famous remark to George Meredith, "But Apollodorus says that I am not a great poet." [2] Tennyson later referred to him as "that mighty man, that pompholygous, broad-blown Apollodorus, the gifted X." [3]

Nevertheless, Tennyson always expressed admiration for the Spasmodic poets. He became especially enthusiastic about *Festus* and is quoted in the publisher's notices as saying, "I can scarcely trust myself to say how much I admire it, for fear of falling into extravagance." [4] Charles Tennyson writes that, in the last months of 1846, Alfred expressed "great admiration" for "Bailey's *Festus*, which he declared contained many grand things—grander than anything he himself had written." [5] During that same period, Alfred wrote to Edward Fitzgerald: "Order it and read. You will most likely find it a great bore, but there are really *very grand* things in *Festus*." [6] Tennyson must have felt the opulent imagery and imaginative scope of *Festus* to be liberating influences during the dull days of poetry.

When the younger Spasmodics made their auspicious debuts, Tennyson was one of the approving audience. He had met Dobell in Cheltenham sometime between 1846 and 1850, when Mrs. Tennyson was living in that city.[7] Therefore, Gosse is correct in doubting the story that Dobell "approached Tennyson at Malvern with so violent an exclamation of the introduction being 'the crowning honour of his life,' that Tennyson shrank back and said, 'Don't talk such damned nonsense!' If true, this story would date from about 1852." Gosse continues more confidently, "But what is certain is that Tennyson not merely had a very genuine admiration for Dobell's poems, but was, as I shall point out, posi-

1. Gilfillan, *A Second Gallery*, p. 215; *The Critic*, *11* (1852), 70.

2. Gilfillan, *A Gallery of Portraits*, p. xviii; Oliver Elton, *A Survey of English Literature, 1830–1880* (2 vols. London, Edward Arnold and Co., 1932), *1*, 335. The two quotes differ slightly.

3. Hallam Tennyson, *Alfred Lord Tennyson, A Memoir* (2 vols. London, Macmillan and Co., Ltd., 1897), *1*, 410.

4. McKillop, "A Victorian Faust," p. 761.

5. Charles Tennyson, *Alfred Tennyson* (New York, Macmillan Co., 1949), p. 215.

6. Hallam Tennyson, *Memoir*, *1*, 234.

7. Ibid., p. 263.

tively influenced by them." [8] Dr. Ker, writing to Hallam Tennyson about Dobell's increasing unpopularity, said, "he was no
commonplace poet your father heartily allowed." [9] With regard
to Smith, Tennyson believed "He has plenty of promise, but he
must learn a different creed to that he preaches in those lines
beginning 'Fame, fame, thou art next to God.' Next to God—
next to the Devil say I." [1] Two years after Smith's death, Tennyson again said that he had shown "considerable promise" and
this time qualified the praise by charging him with the pathetic
fallacy.[2]

Is it possible to support Gosse's contention that Tennyson not
only admired the Spasmodic poems but also was influenced by
them? The immediate impulse for the writing of *Maud* may have
been Sir John Simeon's suggestion that Tennyson make "O that
'twere possible" intelligible, but what determined the particular
form of the work? Why should the laureate, at the height of his
fame after the publication of *In Memoriam* and already at work
"on a poem about the enchantment of Merlin," [3] suddenly start
off in a new and strange direction? *A Life-Drama* was published
in late 1852; *Balder,* in the last week of 1853; Tennyson dropped
Merlin and began *Maud* in the summer of 1854.[4] It seems reasonable to conclude that, on the one hand, Tennyson determined
to surpass these anti-Tennysonians on their own terms, and, on
the other, he hoped to take advantage of the contemporary popularity of their writings. Finally, and perhaps most importantly,
he saw in their lyrical monodramas the form which would enable
him to blend most perfectly his dramatic and lyrical gifts.

Resemblances between *Maud* and Spasmodic poems also tempt
one to see the Spasmodists as an influence upon Tennyson. *Maud*
is a monodrama: " 'a little Hamlet,' the history of a morbid
poetic soul, under the blighting influence of a recklessly speculative age. . . . 'The peculiarity of this poem,' my father added,
'is that different phases of passion take the place of different char-

8. Edmund Gosse, *Silhouettes* (London, William Heinemann, Ltd., 1925) , p. 331.
9. Hallam Tennyson, *Memoir, 1,* 264.
1. Ibid., p. 468.
2. Ibid., 2, 73.
3. Charles Tennyson, *Alfred Tennyson,* p. 282.
4. Hallam Tennyson, *Memoir, 1,* 377.

acters.' " [5] *Balder,* to use its author's characterization, is also the "progress" of "the poetic type" under "the conditions of modern civilization"; [6] in it, the changing passions of the hero take the place of different characters. Tennyson's little Hamlet is akin to Balder, "the heir of madness, an egotist with the makings of a cynic," and evolves exactly like Walter:

> raised to sanity by a pure and holy love which elevates his whole nature, passing from the height of triumph to the lowest depth of misery, driven into madness by the loss of her whom he has loved, and, when he has at length passed through the fiery furnace, and has recovered his reason, giving himself up to work for the good of mankind through the unselfishness born of his great passion.[7]

This concentration on the passions of an unstable protagonist dictates an emotional, rather than a logical, development of the drama, a violent alternation between ecstasy and despair. Extreme emotional states are often exhibited by Maud's lover and the Spasmodic heroes in analogous ways. Thus, when Balder suffers a fit of madness before the murder of his wife, he cries:

> The worm crawls o'er me; the snail harbours up
> My limbs. I am as dark and all-forgot
> As any stone that never saw the sun
> And is and was and will be in the earth.
>
> I hear the sound of life above my head,
> The toads leap with it, and the very rock
> Shakes with the overgoing; but I know
> The fallen ruins lie on heap; my cry
> Can never struggle to the day; no man
> Will ever seek me.
> > Hist! they move the stones! (p. 523)

When Maud's lover becomes temporarily insane after her death, he cries:

5. Ibid., p. 396.
6. Dobell, *Poems,* p. 333.
7. Hallam Tennyson, *Memoir, 1,* 396.

Dead, long dead,
Long dead!
And my heart is a handful of dust,
And the wheels go over my head,
And my bones are shaken with pain,
For into a shallow grave they are thrust,
Only a yard beneath the street,
And the hoofs of the horses beat, beat,
The hoofs of the horses beat,
Beat into my scalp and brain. (Pt. II, ll. 239–48)

It seems inevitable that, working with the same type of story, protagonist, and lyrical monodrama, Tennyson should often produce passages similar to those of the Spasmodics.

This realization helps to explain Tennyson's, or, rather, his hero's, endorsement of the Crimean War. An important determinant of the hostile reception of *Maud* was the reaction against Spasmody, but the most important cause was "what appeared to be the false logic of Tennyson's case for war." [8] "Tennyson's case" was dramatically appropriate for Maud's lover, however, just as it would have been for the other Spasmodic protagonists. Walter says:

Weariness feeds on all.
God wearies, and so makes a universe,
And gathers angels round Him.—He is weak;
I weary, and so wreak myself in verse—
Away with scrannel pipes. Oh, for mad War!
I'd give my next twelve years to head but once
Ten thousand horse in a victorious charge.
Give me someone to hate, and let me chase
Him through the zones, and finding him at last,
Make his accursèd eyes leap on his cheeks,
And his face blacken, with one choking gripe. (pp. 127–28)

Balder enters into sympathy with a group of wandering sailors who are singing about a sea fight between the Russians and the

8. Edgar F. Shannon, "The Critical Reception of Tennyson's 'Maud,'" *PMLA*, *68* (1953), 403.

English. Later he compares his grief which "speaks with voice of fiery wrath" to

> one who crossed in hapless love
> Betakes him to the wars, and tells in blows
> His bitter need of kisses. (p. 393)

Such is the Spasmodic dilemma: these isolated, frustrated, self-centered youths must find a higher cause, excitement, and violence, and one of the natural solutions is war.

The stringing together of lyrics on a narrative thread is another resemblance that deserves mention here,[9] for it illustrates Tennyson's superior handling of the common material. His lyrics express the fluctuating moods of his hero, while those of the Spasmodic protagonists are often digressive. Similarly, his descriptions of nature reflect the speaker's state of mind, while the Spasmodics seem to delight in extravagant descriptions for their own sake. Thus, Ruskin can choose two "exquisite" instances of the pathetic fallacy from *Maud,*[1] while Kingsley attacks Smith for his "mere conceits."[2] Throbbing, shuddering, panting stars frequently embellish Spasmodic poetry, but Tennyson uses them functionally:

> Beat to the noiseless music of the night!
> Has our whole earth gone nearer to the glow
> Of your soft splendours that you look so bright?
> *I* have climbed nearer out of lonely Hell.
> Beat, happy stars, timing with things below,
> Beat with my heart more blest than heart can tell.
> (Pt. I, ll. 665–70)

It has been shown elsewhere that the imagery of *Maud* is not merely spectacular, as it too often is in Spasmodic dramas, but highly functional throughout.[3] And Tennyson also reduces the

9. Other resemblances include the use of lavish and vivid color and the attempt to provide psychological realism by having the protagonist focus on the apparently irrelevant during moments of tension. Cf. the celebrated shell passage of *Maud* with the dog passage in sec. xxviii of *Balder,* satirized in sec. ix of *Firmilian.*

1. John Ruskin, "Of the Pathetic Fallacy," *Selections,* ed. Chauncey B. Tinker (Boston, Houghton Mifflin Co., 1908), pp. 75–76.

2. Kingsley, *Miscellanies,* p. 293.

3. See E. D. H. Johnson, "The Lily and the Rose: Symbolic Meaning in Tennyson's *Maud,*" *PMLA,* 64 (1949), 1222–27, and John Killham, "Tennyson's *Maud*—

sprawling Spasmodic drama to a manageable length: a patholog-
ical monologue can be effectively maintained only so long. In
brief, the poet laureate is drawing on all of his wisdom and
experience to change the drama of Spasmodic beauties into a
drama of unified incident and tone. The beauty of the lyrics is
his own.

In 1855, however, the critics made few distinctions. They
fixed on the resemblances between *Maud* and Spasmodic poems
and censured it for the same reasons. Aytoun, who had designated
the original Spasmodic school, now admitted Tennyson to full
membership.[4] Aytoun was angry: he thought he had killed the
snake but now saw his own and the nation's favorite infusing
new life into the serpent. In the brief introduction to his con-
demnatory review of *Maud,* he speaks of the present "poem so
very spasmodic that it reminds you of the writhing of a knot of
worms." After an examination of Tennyson's earlier works, he
says, "We believe that he can, whenever he pleases, delight the
world once more with such poetry as he enunciated in his youth;
but we think that he has somehow or other been led astray by
poetic theories" (p. 315). The context makes clear that Aytoun
is referring to Spasmodic theories. He later attacks the "more
ambitious and elaborate" passages, "studded all over with those
metaphors, strange epithets, and conceits which are the disfigure-
ment of modern poetry" (p. 318). Most of all, he seemed to fear
that *Maud* would foster the production of future Spasmodic
poems: "The case is bad enough when young poetasters essay
to gain a hearing by dint of maniacal howls; but it is far worse
when we find a man of undoubted genius and widespread reputation, demeaning himself by putting his name to such absolute
nonsense" (p. 319).

In his analysis of the various sections of *Maud,* Aytoun extols
the Hall Garden Scene, a "passage of such extraordinary rhythmical music, that the sense becomes subordinate to the sound" (p.
314). Otherwise, he attacks violently: for example, he asks of
the opening stanzas, "Is that poetry? Is it even respectable verse?

The Function of the Imagery," *Critical Essays on the Poetry of Tennyson,* ed.
John Killham (London, G. Routledge and K. Paul, 1960), pp. 219–35.
    4. *Blackwood's, 78* (1855), 311–21.

Is is not altogether an ill-conceived and worse-expressed screed of bombast, set to a metre which has the string-halt, without even the advantage of regularity in its hobble?" The review richly deserves its place in *Notorious Literary Attacks*.[5]

Tennyson, well aware of the devastating effect of Aytoun's campaign against the Spasmodics, apparently feared this review more than any other and had to be reassured by his friend, F. G. Tuckerman: "As for affecting your fame . . . or influencing the motions of the masses by a magazine article, a man might as well stand upon the sea-shore in a flood-tide and attempt to put the waves back with a pitch-fork." [6] Aytoun learned of Tennyson's reaction and wrote to Blackwood in 1859:

> About Tennyson. I have as yet only read the first of the series, Enid, which I sipped like cream. It is *very good* as a whole, but somehow or other, wants finish. A dash of whiskey, now, would have made it excellent *Athol brose*. I feel rather inclined to review it, the more so because I do not wish Tennyson to remain under the impression that I depreciate him, and I can conscientiously praise this so far as I have read.[7]

Five months after Aytoun's assault, *Blackwood's* relentlessly took up the cudgel again,[8] questioning the pathetic fallacies of *Maud* and *Balder:* "When we feel Nature sympathizing with us, it is well; but it is not well when we force her to echo our own mad fancies, of themselves forced and unreal enough. The 'frantic rain,' the 'shuddering dark,' the 'maddened beach'—alas, poor poets." It reckons Maud's lover as the latest example of the Byronic-Spasmodic hero:

> He has no name, this ill-fated youth; but doubtless Balder is reckoned in his roll of cousinships, and so is Mr. Alexander Smith. There are three of them, ladies and gentlemen, and they are an amiable trio. Strangely as their garb and inten-

5. Albert Mordell, ed., *Notorious Literary Attacks* (New York, Boni and Liveright, 1926) , pp 138–61.

6. Shannon, "The Critical Reception of Tennyson's 'Maud,' " p. 406.

7. Letter of July 31, 1859.

8. *Blackwood's, 79* (1856) , 132–33.

tions are altered, there is a lingering reminiscence about them of a certain *Childe Harold* who once set the world aflame. Like him they are troubled with a weight of woe and misfortune mysteriously beyond the conception of common men.

The reviewer's first impulse is to set down *Maud* "as one of the greatest impertinences ever perpetuated by a poet," but, after another look at *Balder* and *A Life-Drama,* he adds, "It is perhaps only when we compare this with other poems of the day that we see how prettily managed is the thread of the story, and how these morsels of verse carry us through every scene as clear as if every scene was a picture." Still, this is no excuse for such a Spasmodic work from England's "best singer."

Charles Kingsley, who, as we have seen, probably deserves credit for suggesting "Spasmodic school" to Aytoun, reviewed *Maud* for *Fraser's.*[9] He decries its fragmentariness, lavish and gaudy color, lack of harmony, extreme passion which degenerates into caricature, and Byronic hero. The reader expects Kingsley to cry "Spasmodic," but in a letter to a friend he reveals why he fails to employ the common catchword which indicates all of the faults he is enumerating:

> As for poor Maud. It is a sad falling off. There are some scraps in it most exquisite: but as a whole the world (and I) view it much as you do. I think there is but one opinion, even among those who admire him most . . . . I have said all that can be said for Maud in a late no. of Fraser's Mag. I love and honour the *man,* as a private friend . . . and am in no humour to hit him as I would Balders, Baileys and other presumptuous windbags.[1]

Unlike Kingsley, other critics felt no personal affection for Tennyson and did not scruple to associate him with the Spasmodics. The *Guardian,* for instance, says:

9. *Fraser's, 52* (1855) , 264–73.
1. Margaret Thorp, *Charles Kingsley, 1819–1875* (Princeton, Princeton University Press, 1937) , pp. 94–95. Arnold, the third of the pre-*Firmilian* depreciators of the Spasmodics, also disliked the manner of *Maud* (*Letters to Arthur Hugh Clough,* letter of August 2, 1855) .

We confess to an intolerance for that dim and lazy poetry which is the fashion of the day, in which words do not represent ideas, and the writers of which do not even take the pains to think out and picture distinctly to themselves the conception they desire to convey, but envelope themselves in a cloud of vague phraseology, which they imagine, or try to lead others to imagine, to be grand and profound, because it is formless and obscure.

The reviewer criticizes Tennyson's "affectation," "eccentric diction," "rough unmetrical cadences," "harsh transitions," and "extravagance of passion" and concludes, *"Maud* is a poem in the 'Spasmodic' school of poetry, hardly superior in that kind to *The Roman,* or *Balder,* or *Festus,* and very inferior in force of thought to the verses of Mr. Browning and his wife." [2] Deploring the popularity and influence of Smith and Dobell during the early 1850s, the *Times* says:

So wide had the mischief spread, so deeply had the spasmodic poison penetrated, that at a later period the Laureate himself, in all the ripeness of his great genius, produced a poem in the very same style, starting on the basis of soliloquy, treating of disease and madness, sliding into curiosities of diction, and all with a mastery of technical detail that stamps it as the work of a master, and that would have made the reputation of any lesser man, although in coming from Tennyson it can only be accepted as a proof of his poetical apostasy. [3]

Another reviewer thought Smith had done the same job better, [4] while others saw Tennyson's career following the same downward path. [5] Dante Gabriel Rossetti believed the story worthy of Smith rather than Tennyson. [6] Aytoun's fear that the laureate's example would encourage a reemergence of Spasmodic poetry was

2. *The Guardian* (Aug. 29, 1855), p. 664.
3. *The Times* (Dec. 27, 1856), p. 4.
4. *The Irish Quarterly Review, 5* (1855), 455.
5. *The National Review, 1* (1855), 404, 409; *The Scottish Review, 3* (1855), 355, 357.
6. M. L. Howe, "Dante Gabriel Rossetti's Comments on *Maud,*" *MLN, 49* (1934), 291.

reflected in other articles,[7] one of which suggested a return to the strict manner of Henry Taylor, the author of *Philip van Artevelde,* the poem against which Bailey had reacted.[8] The wheel had come full circle.

Even the defense of *Maud* in the *London Quarterly Review* testifies to the common practice of associating Tennyson with the Spasmodics:

> Our sympathies (as the reader of this journal knows) are not deeply engaged in favour of the subjective school of poetry, with which Mr. Tennyson is commonly, but not quite fairly, identified; yet it is only just that the distinction should be made, and clearly marked, between what is genuine and original in the present claimant, and what is meretricious and extravagant in his younger rivals.[9]

The reviewer argues that Tennyson's work is "too well conceived, his thoughts too harmoniously ordered, to allow anything but recklessness or incapacity so far to misjudge his real character. He has no relation to what has been designated 'the spasmodic school of poetry.' " Finally, it is interesting to note that among the posthumous papers of Dobell was discovered a long defense against the hostile reviews of *Maud*.[1]

The inimical reviewers who do not explicitly link *Maud* with Spasmodic poetry judge it, however, according to standards which gained favor during the Spasmodic controversy. All of these reviewers, for instance, recognize the great beauty of sections of *Maud* but now subordinate this consideration to questions of unity and action. What was sufficient to obtain popularity for *A Life-Drama* two years before is now unable to earn for *Maud* anything beyond an unfavorable reception.[2] Just as Smith

---

7. *The Eclectic Review,* N.S. *10* (1855), 573; *The Irish Quarterly Review, 5* (1855), 470.

8. *The Irish Quarterly Review, 5* (1855), 467–70.

9. *The London Quarterly Review, 5* (1855–56), 213–29.

1. Jolly, *Sydney Dobell,* 2, 28. When asked to describe Tennyson, Dobell said, "If he were pointed out to you as the man who had written the *Iliad,* you would answer, 'I can well believe it.' " See Hallam Tennyson, *Memoir, 1,* 355.

2. For numerous extracts and a bibliography of the reviews of *Maud,* see Shannon, "The Critical Reception of Tennyson's 'Maud,' " pp. 397–417.

turned away from Spasmody and went to history, Tennyson again began his *Idylls of the King*.

Robert Browning has persistently been associated with the Spasmodics: sometime between 1843 and 1846, Aytoun placed him in the "school" of Bailey,[3] and, a century later, Lionel Trilling, citing his "free, even slovenly, treatment, his intimate manner, his psychologizing, his realism and—above all—his multitudinousness," called him "a Spasmodic poet who managed to be good." [4] Aytoun had *Paracelsus* especially in mind, and one assumes that the designation "Spasmodic" would apply most cogently, if anywhere in Browning, to that early soul drama. Indeed, two critics tried to foist the paternity of the Spasmodic school upon that particular work. In 1863, the *Eclectic Review* called *Paracelsus* "one of the most extraordinary poems in our language" and speculated that "it is likely to have done something in the production of 'Festus,' for it preceded it by many years." [5] Similarly, in 1876, Theodore Watts claimed, "In the study of English poetry, it is always necessary to consider the influence of 'Paracelsus' upon 'Festus,' the influence of 'Festus' upon 'Balder,' and 'England in Time of War'; and the influence of these upon most subsequent poetry." [6] The idea is tempting: *Festus* was begun one year after *Paracelsus* was published, both are imaginative soul dramas, and both contain a character with the unusual name of Festus. However, Bailey

> told his niece that when he wrote "Festus" he certainly had never seen "Paracelsus." His niece wrote: "My uncle and Mr. Browning had so great admiration for each other's genius, and each was so noble in character, that I am sure that if it had been so the influence would have been as willingly admitted by one as it would have been generously accepted by the other." [7]

3. Frykman, *W. E. Aytoun, Pioneer Professor,* p. 44.
4. Trilling, *Matthew Arnold,* p. 136.
5. *The Eclectic Review,* N.S. *4* (1863) , 438.
6. *The Athenaeum* (Apr. 1, 1876) , p. 465. See also how Gilfillan compared *Paracelsus* with *Festus* in *The Titan, 23* (1856) , 273.
7. John C. Francis, *Notes and Queries,* Ninth Series, *10* (1902) , 242.

Edmund Gosse uses this same niece's testimony: "her uncle became acquainted with 'Paracelsus' soon after the publication of 'Festus,' probably in 1840, as the gift of Westland Marston. This disposes of any idea of the influence of the earlier on the later poem." [8] If the publication of *Paracelsus* in the year 1835 made possible this ascription of paternity, it also helped the critical reception of Browning's work during a period of unimaginative poetry.[9] Had *Paracelsus* appeared twenty years later, it would have been condemned.

Browning published two volumes of poetry in 1855. He had hopes of a favorable reception for *Men and Women:* "I am writing—a first step towards popularity for me—lyrics with more music and painting than before, so as to get people to hear and see." [1] But he was to be disappointed and would have to wait another decade for popularity. Many of the reviewers characterized him as a poet of great gifts who squandered them through faulty technique,[2] and he was used to point a moral and adorn a tale "of genius unfaithful to its trust." [3] It seems almost incredible to us today, who find in *Men and Women* so much of Browning's finest poetry, that it provoked such an unfavorable reaction. Several reasons have been given which contribute toward an explanation: "In his long absence in Italy Browning had not kept his name before the British public, and when *Men and Women* appeared the Crimean war was at its height. Browning felt, also, that his publishers were not sufficiently active in his interests." [4] I would like to suggest, however, that a major reason

8. Gosse, "Philip James Bailey," p. 90.

9. For the reception of *Paracelsus*, see T. R. Lounsbury, *The Early Literary Career of Robert Browning* (New York, Charles Scribner's Sons, 1911), pp. 29–44; W. C. DeVane, *A Browning Handbook* (New York, F. S. Crofts and Co., 1935) pp. 52–54; and D. C. Somervell, "The Reputation of Robert Browning," *Essays and Studies, 15* (1929), 124–25.

1. Quoted in DeVane, *A Browning Handbook*, p. 187.

2. See *The Athenaeum* (Nov. 17, 1855), pp. 1327–28; *Fraser's, 53* (1856), 105–16; *Bentley's Miscellany, 39* (1856), 64–70; *Blackwood's, 79* (1856), 137; *The Christian Remembrancer, 31* (1856), 281–94; *The Irish Quarterly Review, 6* (1856), 1–3, 21–28; *The Westminster Review, 65* (1856), 291; *The Dublin University Magazine, 47* (1856), 673; *The North British Review, 28* (1858), 239–40.

3. *Fraser's, 53* (1856), 105.

4. DeVane, *A Browning Handbook*, p. 189.

for this adverse reception was the absorption of *Men and Women* into the reaction against Spasmodic poetry.

Many of the criticisms focused on features characteristic of Spasmodic poetry: the morbid and immoral hero, the concern with mental processes, the sudden alternations of thought, the sensuality, skepticism, and fragmentariness.[5] But the major criticism, stressed in the hostile reviews and pardoned in the favorable, was Browning's obscurity.[6] "Obscurity is the evil genius that is working the ruin of this poet: Browning is, pre-eminently, the King of Darkness."[7] The *Examiner,* always a staunch defender of Browning, devoted its entire article to establishing "beyond dispute that these volumes are not exclusively 'obscure and mystical.'"[8] The contemporary critics, contrary to Browning's efforts and expectations, even saw a decided increase in obscurity over his earlier work: these poems were "more perverse, personal, and incomplete than they were formerly,"[9] "more eccentric, affected, resolutely strange, and in parts deliberately unintelligible than [their] predecessors."[1] Today, it is difficult to understand how anyone could consider *Men and Women* more unintelligible than *Sordello* or even *Paracelsus;* however, in 1855, on the heels of the controversy that had raged over *Festus, Balder,* and *The Mystic,* the critics were especially wary of any new poetry that seemed obscure.

The reviews themselves provide explicit evidence of the contemporary association of *Men and Women* with Spasmodic poetry. *Blackwood's* calls Smith, Dobell, and the authors of *Maud* and *Men and Women* "true brothers" who "have quite a family

5. See esp. *The Christian Remembrancer, 31* (1856), 281–83; *Fraser's, 53* (1856), 107–13; *The Irish Quarterly Review, 6* (1856), 3, 22.

6. See esp. *The Irish Quarterly Review, 6* (1856), 21; *Blackwood's, 79* (1856), 136–37; *The Saturday Review, XI* (1855), 69–70; *The Athenaeum* (Nov. 17, 1855), p. 1327; *The Christian Remembrancer, 31* (1856), 282; *Bentley's Miscellany, 39* (1856), 65; *The Westminster Review, 65* (1856), 291; *The Dublin University Magazine, 47* (1856), 673.

7. *The Irish Quarterly Review, 6* (1856), 21.

8. *The Examiner* (Dec. 1, 1855), p. 757.

9. *The Athenaeum* (Nov. 17, 1855), p. 1328.

1. *The Christian Remembrancer, 31* (1856), 281. See also *The Saturday Review, I* (1855), 69; *Fraser's, 53* (1856), 108; *The Irish Quarterly Review, 6* (1856), 1, 21–22.

standard of merit by which to judge themselves." Browning is particularized as "the wild boy of the household—the boisterous noisy shouting voice." Although he alone has a talent for drama, he resembles the others in the obscurity of his work: "It is very hard to make out what he would be at with those marvellous convolutions of words." [2] The *Saturday Review* believes that Browning far exceeds his brothers in obscurity:

> Can any of his devotees be found to uphold his present elaborate experiment on the patience of the public? Take any of his worshippers you please—let him be "well up" in the transcendental poets of the day—take him fresh from Alexander Smith, or Alfred Tennyson's *Maud*, or the *Mystic* of Bailey—and we will engage to find him at least ten passages in the first ten pages of *Men and Women*, some of which, even after profound study, he will not be able to construe at all, and not one of which will he be able to read off at sight.

The "main object" of this article "has been to protest against what we feel to be the false teachings of a perverted school of art; and we have used this book of Mr. Browning's chiefly as a means of showing the extravagant lengths of absurdity to which the tenets of that school can lead a man of admitted powers." [3] The *Christian Remembrancer* also complains of the tendency of modern poets "to be guided by no canons of criticism" and moves from an examination of *Maud* and *Hiawatha* "to Mr. Browning's spasmodic whirls and eddies" and "the black gulf of Mr. Bailey's 'Mystic.' " [4] This turns out to be the severest attack against *Men and Women*.

Even the more favorable reviews noted important resemblances to the Spasmodic school. *Fraser's* ranked Browning second only to Tennyson among contemporary poets but had reservations about this latest production. After some unkind remarks about the Spasmodic elements in *Men and Women*, it concluded the negative section of its review, "Better grave dulness than this spasmodic folly; better the sober plodding of the patient ass

2. *Blackwood's, 79* (1856), 136–37.
3. *The Saturday Review, 1* (1855), 69–70.
4. *The Christian Remembrancer, 31* (1856), 267–92.

along the beaten highway of prose than this insane kicking up of heels, meaningless braying, and sportive breaches of asinine manners, in the rich pasture-meadow of poetry." [5] In "Poetry— The Spasmodists," the *North British Review* anticipated Trilling by eighty years: "It appears to us that Robert Browning is, in a sense, one of the greatest spasmodists, so far as a wilful delight in remote and involved thinking, abrupt and jerking mental movements, and 'pernickitieness' of expression, working, in the higher regions of genius, can constitute a spasmodist." [6] One might argue today that the distinction between a "good" and a "bad" Spasmodist is, after all, crucial, but few of the reviewers who were embroiled in the immediate controversy took the time to make important distinctions. Like *Maud, Men and Women* was caught in the reaction against Spasmodic poetry.

Aytoun launched his final attack against the Spasmodics in a review of Mrs. Browning's *Aurora Leigh*.[7] He is severe on the poem, calling the story "fantastic, unnatural, exaggerated" and picking out flaws in the delineation of the four major characters. But he uses the poem chiefly to exemplify modern poetic practices. Thus, after presenting an extract of Lady Waldemar's "coarse and revolting" talk, Aytoun begins to generalize:

> In poetry, passages such as that which we have quoted are intolerable, because, by juxtaposition with others, exquisite in themselves, they impair our capacity for enjoyment. . . . Hence poets, even when their situations are of the most tragic nature—even when they are dealing with subjects questionable in morality—do, for the most part, sedulously avoid anything like coarseness of expression, and frame their language so as to convey the general idea without presenting special images which are calculated to disgust. (pp. 33–34)

He doubts whether "Mrs. Browning has ever thought seriously of the principles upon which art is founded" and begins to discuss some of his own cherished beliefs.

5. *Fraser's, 53* (1856), 114.

6. *The North British Review, 28* (1858), 239–40. See also *The Guardian* (Aug. 29, 1855), p. 664.

7. *Blackwood's, 81* (1857), 23–41.

Genius alone is not sufficient in art: "There are certain principles which experience has tested and approved, and . . . to deviate from these is literally to court defeat." To learn these principles,

> we should regard the works of the great masters, both ancient and modern, as profitable for instruction as well as for delight, and be cautious how we innovate. We may consider it almost as a certainty that every leading principle of art has been weighed and sifted by our predecessors; and that most of the theories which are paraded as discoveries, were deliberately examined by them, and rejected because they were false or impracticable. (p. 34)

Aytoun examines the modern "discovery" that "the chief aim of a poet should be to illustrate the age in which he lives," a view set forth in the fifth book of *Aurora Leigh* (ll. 183–222) and exemplified by the whole poem. He fears that this theory "would lead to a total sacrifice of the ideal":

> It is not the province of the poet to depict things as they are, but so to refine and purify as to purge out the grosser matter; and this he cannot do if he attempts to give a faithful picture of his own times. For in order to be faithful, he must necessarily include much which is abhorrent to art, and revolting to the taste, for which no exactness of delineation will be accepted as a proper excuse. All poetical characters, all poetical situations, must be idealised . . . . Whilst dealing with a remote subject the poet can easily effect this, but not so when he brings forward characters of his own age. (pp. 34–35)

In his conclusion, Aytoun turns to the question of construction and makes clear that he is criticizing *Aurora Leigh* as the representative of widespread poetic practices:

> the chief defect of modern British poems consists in the carelessness of their construction. Plot, arrangement, and even probability, are regarded as things of minor moment; and the whole attention of the artist is lavished upon expression

. . . sound and pretension are becoming more esteemed than sense and deliberate purpose . . . brilliant writing, or writing which seems brilliant, is esteemed as of the highest kind, without regard to congruity or design. This is a grievous error, which cannot be exposed too broadly; and to it we trace the almost total extinction, in our own day, of the British drama. (p. 40)

Aytoun's own view is that "a plot—that is, a theme—well-considered, developed, and divided, must, to make it effective, be adequately and naturally expressed. Adequate expression is no more than the proper language of emotion; and emotion must be traceable to some evident and intelligible cause." Here, finally, he defines the true objects of attack throughout the long review: "All this is disregarded by our 'new poets,' as they love to style themselves, who come upon their imaginary stage, tearing their hair, proclaiming their inward wretchedness, and spouting sorry metaphysics in still sorrier verse, for no imaginable reason whatever." After specifying Dobell, Bailey, Smith, and J. Stanyan Bigg, Aytoun continues his attack upon the "new poets" in general and reveals his own ideal:

They think that the public will be content to receive their crude thoughts as genuine notes of issue from the Bank of Genius, if so be that they are dressed up in a gaudy, glittering, and hyperbolical form; and they ransack, not only earth and sea, but heaven itself for ornaments. All this while they forget that there is no meaning in their talk; that people who are desirous to hear a story, do not call the minstrel in for the purpose of listening to his disappointed aspirations, or the bleatings of his individual woes, but because they require of him, as a professed member of the greatest craft since the prophets disappeared, a tale of energy or emotion that shall stir the heart, or open one of the many fountains of our common sympathy. (p. 41)

It seems appropriate that Aytoun presented his fundamental literary beliefs in his last attack against Spasmodic poetry.

Mrs. Browning observed that Aytoun's article came "from the

camp of the enemy (artistically and socially)," [8] but in 1856 almost all of the reviews were artistically in the camp of the enemy. Several remarked on her resemblances to the Spasmodics; [9] more important, however, was the nature of the critical attitude, which was conservative and classical. *Aurora Leigh* was criticized for its lack of dramatic appeal, profusion of glittering and discordant imagery, alternations between inflated and vulgar styles, obscurity, and especially for its chaotic structure.[1] As one magazine summed up the critical reception, "At the time of the appearance of *Aurora Leigh,* if we trust our own memory, there were no two opinions expressed by the leading organs of our periodical literature. All admitted the power and pathos, and even depth of thought, displayed in many an individual passage. All condemned the structure of the story." [2] In 1856 individual instances of power and pathos were no longer sufficient: the popular *Aurora Leigh* was a critical failure. If it had appeared three years earlier, it would have been praised for its beauties.[3] Now, the anti-Spasmodics had won.

In a recent article on parody, John Updike writes in the *New Yorker:*

8. G. B. Taplin, *The Life of Elizabeth Barrett Browning* (New Haven, Yale University Press, 1957), p. 347.

9. *The North British Review, 28* (1858), 24; *The Press* (Nov. 22, 1856), p. 1121; *The North American Review, 85* (1857), 423; *The Dublin University Magazine, 49* (1857), 470; *The Saturday Review, 2* (1856), 776; *Blackwood's, 79* (1856), 136–37.

1. For the fullest treatment of the critical reception of *Aurora Leigh,* see Taplin, *The Life of Elizabeth Barrett Browning,* pp. 337–47, esp. his bibliography of reviews on p. 449.

2. *The Eclectic Magazine* (New York), *56* (1862), 74. The article originally appeared in *The British Quarterly.*

3. For the influence of the Spasmodics upon *Aurora Leigh,* see J. H. Buckley, *The Victorian Temper* (Cambridge, Harvard University Press, 1951), pp. 61–63. For Mrs. Browning's high praise of Bailey, see *Letters of Elizabeth Barrett Browning to Richard Hengist Horne,* ed. S. R. Townshend Mayer (New York, James Miller, 1877), pp. 222–25, and *The Letters of Robert Browning and Elizabeth Barrett Browning, 1845–1846,* ed. Robert Wiedemann Barrett Browning (2 vols., New York, Harper, 1926), *1,* 384; for her praise of Smith, see *The Letters of Elizabeth Barrett Browning,* ed. F. G. Kenyon (2 vols., New York, Macmillan Co., 1897), *2,* 112, 120, 134, 138, 161; for her admiration for *Balder,* see Buckley, *The Victorian Temper,* p. 62.

Parody becomes significant in proportion to the dimensions of the thing parodied. At the bottom of the scale are those burlesques, achieved by crude verbal substitutions, of such specific works as "Excelsior," "Hiawatha," "The Raven," and "The Charge of the Light Brigade." Their humor springs from an instinctive sense of reality that rejects the jingling high-flown; they are parody's folklore. At the middle of the scale—a temperate zone most congenial—are those comprehensive and critical imitations of the manner and style of individual authors that define our modern sense of parody. At the top, reaching into the altitude of (for want of a better word) Literature, are those imaginative creations that, taking certain writings in the air as an excuse, attack the mental climate of an age.[4]

If we accept such a scale of values for parody, *Firmilian* stands at the top. It not only defined and helped to destroy the Spasmodic school but also ridiculed the Romantic attitude out of which it developed. The attitude is recurrent and ultimately invulnerable, but in its attack upon the particular form which this attitude then exhibited, *Firmilian* was grandly successful. The Spasmodics would probably have faded into oblivion eventually, but now their fall was sudden and complete. I am not arrogant enough to assert that this is the finest parody which any age has produced, but I shall feel very much obliged to any gentleman who can make me acquainted with a better.

4. *The New Yorker* (Sept. 16, 1961), p. 168.

THE POST-SPASMODIC YEARS (1856-65)

BOTHWELL

While *Firmilian* was causing a commotion in literary circles, its author continued to enjoy a quiet life in Edinburgh. He contributed monthly to *Blackwood's,* lectured at the university, and filled the office of Sheriff and Lord High Admiral of Orkney and Zetland. Then, suddenly, in October 1855, after more than ten years of continuous service, Aytoun stopped his contributions to *Blackwood's.* He had begun work on his most serious literary endeavor, the poem *Bothwell.*

Throughout his adult life, this Jacobite wished to write a work which would vindicate Mary and show Bothwell to be the unfortunate dupe of Scottish nobles and the English queen. As early as 1834, he had shown a friend a fragment of a work he had begun, "a sketch of Bothwell." [1] In 1849, he reviewed for *Blackwood's* a historical account of Kirkaldy of Grange, one of the important personages of the period and of his own future poem. [2] He praises the book for being "strictly authentic as a history, and yet as absorbing in interest as the most coloured and glowing romance"; like "the splendid romances of Scott," he later adds. In the final paragraph, he sums up the chief reasons for his admiration: "It is seldom indeed that we find history so written—in a style at once vigorous, perspicuous, and picturesque. The author's heart is thoroughly with his subject; and he exhibits ever and anon, flashes of the old Scottish spirit, which we are glad to believe has not decayed from the land." Such were Aytoun's ideals for his own book.

1. Martin, *Memoir,* p. 49.
2. *Blackwood's, 65* (1849), 112–28.

The immediate impulse to write *Bothwell* came from a visit
to Holyrood, probably in early 1854, with Sir Edward Bulwer
Lytton.[3] On April 25, 1854, Lytton wrote to Aytoun, assuring
him of his confidence that Bothwell would "revive to grander
life under your verse—I shall indeed be proud of the Dedication
you promise me." [4] Thus, the intention to write *Bothwell* had
been formed before the appearance of the burlesque review of
Firmilian. But, encouraged to write *Firmilian* itself by his gullible readers, Aytoun put aside his serious endeavor and gleefully
entered into the midst of the Spasmodic controversy. When he
returned to his original project, it was to bear important traces
of the controversy, for Aytoun deliberately made *Bothwell* into
a model of anti-Spasmodic poetry.

Bothwell, however, would have been in opposition to Spasmodic doctrine and practice anyway. It told a clearly defined
story, the material of which was drawn from history; in form it
was a "lyrical epic," [5] resembling *Marmion* in its structural pattern and its alternation of ballad meter with rhymed octosyllabics.
But, in order to challenge the Spasmodics still more directly,
Aytoun made one drastic departure from the extended lays of
Scott: *Bothwell* became a monologue. This apparently late de-
cision caused consternation among Aytoun's friends; Martin objected that such a form would prove too great a restraint. Aytoun
replied:

> I am very much obliged to you for your criticism, and it
> gives me confidence to know that you like "Bothwell" so far
> as you have seen it. I am well aware that the form of the
> poem, which I deliberately adopted, subjects me to great
> difficulties in composition; and it may be that I cannot over-
> come them; but, if successful, it will be to a certain extent
> a triumph, for I do not know of any other poem of consider-
> able length which is constructed on the same plan.[6]

Aytoun was taking the reflective monologue of the Spasmodics
and trying to show that it could be used to narrate an extensive

3. Ibid., *80* (1856) , 223–24.
4. Letter of April 25, 1854.
5. Bulwer Lytton's phrase, in a letter of August 19, 1856.
6. Martin, *Memoir,* p. 166.

action; like Tennyson, he intended to surpass the Spasmodics on their own terms. As the *London Times* expressed it:

> He has come forward to write a tale that shall be passionate, not spasmodic; and he has chosen to fetter himself by an adoption of the form which in the hands of the other poets leads directly to spasm. He has practically said, "You soliloquizing poets, what absurdities you fall into with your eternal hysterics; now I shall take your forms; I shall write a tale in soliloquy, and I shall show you that it is possible to do so, and to fill it with action, without ever degenerating into the Spasmodic." [7]

Unfortunately, this daring strategy, arising out of a critical purpose rather than a poetic necessity, militated against the success of the poem.

Aytoun had high hopes for *Bothwell*. A popular parodist and the author of *Lays of the Scottish Cavaliers,* he still wanted to write a serious major poem. In the final lines of his attack on *Maud*, he wrote: "In virtue of the laurel-wreath, he is the poetical champion of Britain, and should be prepared to maintain the lists against all comers. Is this a proper specimen of his powers? By our Lady of the Lances! we know half-a-dozen minor poets who, in his present condition could bear him from his saddle in a canter." [8] The following month, October 1855, this minor poet began to make his attempt. In February 1856, *Blackwood's* published a critique of Smith, Dobell, Mrs. Browning, *Maud*, and *Men and Women*, in which the writer complained that "the manfuller voices are all busy with serious prose or that craft of novel-writing which is more manageable for common uses than the loftier vehicle of verse. True, there are such names as Aytoun and Macaulay, and we all know the ringing martial ballad-notes which belong to these distinguished writers; but Macaulay and Aytoun have taken to other courses, and strike the harp no more." [9] *Blackwood's* knew perfectly well that Aytoun had stopped contributing because he was once again striking the

7. *The Times* (Dec. 27, 1856) , p. 4.
8. *Blackwood's, 78* (1855) , 321.
9. Ibid., *79* (1856) , 137.

harp; this notice was merely intended to whet the public appetite for his major effort. He had been working for five months and was to work for another five. Indeed, the man who had written *Firmilian* in little over a month now worked hard enough to make himself physically ill.[1] Finally, on August 2, 1856, a volume of 300 pages was published, handsomely bound in gilt cloth and selling for twelve shillings, entitled *Bothwell—A Poem*.

From the fortress of Malmoe in which he is confined, Bothwell relates the crucial events in his life and that of Mary, Queen of Scots. The theme of the poem is close to Aytoun's heart: the conflict between the old world of chivalry and principle, represented by Mary and Bothwell, and the new world of efficiency and expediency, represented by Elizabeth and the Scottish nobles. The career of Bothwell illustrates in microcosm the historical change; Mary, on the other hand, remains as spotlessly pure throughout as the most idealized heroine of romance. Because of Aytoun's method of telling his tale chronologically, it is best to follow the narrative through its six consecutive cantos.[2]

In the first canto, Aytoun establishes the chivalric code according to which Mary and Bothwell live. Upon first seeing his queen, Bothwell relates:

> I worshipped; and as pure a heart
>   To her, I swear, was mine,
> As ever breathed a truthful vow
>   Before Saint Mary's shrine:
> I thought of her, as of a star
>   Within the heavens above,
> That such as I might gaze upon,
>   But never dare to love.
> I swore to her that day my troth,
>   As belted earl and knight,
> That I would still defend her throne,
>   And aye protect her right. (i.121–32)

1. Letter of August 22, 1856, to Blackwood.
2. Unless otherwise specified, my quotations will be from the third and revised edition of *Bothwell*, appearing in Aytoun, *Poems*, ed. F. Page (London, Oxford University Press, 1921), pp. 131–226.

That such worship of an unattainable love is the remnant of a
past tradition was made more explicit in the first edition:

>   Proclaimed myself to be her knight,
>   As in the olden time,
>   When any he who wore the spurs
>   Might love without a crime;
>   When queens were queens of chivalry;
>   And deeds of bold emprise,
>   Not flattering words or fawning speech,
>   Found grace in woman's eyes.[3]

Aytoun excised this passage because it hammers home a point
made abundantly clear throughout. The chivalric ideal involves
"deeds of bold emprise" as well as worship. Thus, Bothwell does
not object to the murder of Riccio but disdains its perpetrators;
Darnley and his henchmen have violated the code:

>   Not that I cared for Riccio's life,
>   They might have worked their will;
>   Though base it was for belted knights
>   So poor a wretch to kill.   (i.641–44)

Thinking about Mary in this practical world of Scottish intrigue,
Bothwell states his own problem:

>   Set was the star of chivalry
>   That erst had gleamed so pure
>   Upon the crests of those who lay
>   On Flodden's fatal moor.   (i.277–80)

Aytoun also establishes in this first canto the opposition between
light and dark which recurs throughout the poem. Bothwell
ascribes all of the Scottish intrigues against Mary to her cousin
Elizabeth:

>   The darkness struggles with the light,
>   The gloaming with the day,
>   Ay, even in the deeps of night
>   Will shadows force their way:

3. Aytoun, *Bothwell—A Poem* (Edinburgh and London, William Blackwood
and Sons, 1856), pp. 12–13.

> For ever, when the peerless moon
>   Is riding clear in heaven,
> Some sullen cloud, by envious winds,
>   Athwart its disc is driven.
> Yet vainly does the shadow seek
>   A borrowed light to steal,
> The cloud is darker for the orb
>   It cannot quite conceal. (i.396–407)

In the second canto, the Scottish nobles play on Bothwell's love for Mary, his hatred of her husband, and his ambition for the crown in order to persuade him to enter into their pact to murder Darnley. All three motivations are bound up with Bothwell's conceptions of chivalry. His love for Mary, for example, has grown since she came to thank him personally for his derring-do:

> "True heart! strong arm! I cannot place
>   A chaplet on your brow,
> For the old rites of chivalry
>   Are lost or banished now;
> But, trust me, never was a Queen
>   More debtor to a peer,
> Than I, brave Earl, am proud to own,
>   Before the presence here!" (ii.249–56)

They alone can appreciate "the old rites" but now move in an alien world, of which Darnley, unworthy to be either Mary's husband or a king, is a representative:

> But kings—forsooth, they called him King!—
>   Are cravens now. They claim
> Exemption from the knightly rule,
>   And skulk behind their name. (ii.648–51)

Looking back on the trap into which he was being led, Bothwell now realizes that his strength could not cope with the unprincipled maneuvers of the Scottish nobles:

> O never let the man of deeds,
>   Though strong, and bold, and brave,
> Though he has shaken thrones like reeds,

> Try issue with a knave!
> Might is no match for studied craft,
>   Which makes the best its thrall:
> When earth is mined beneath his feet,
>   The champion needs must fall. (ii.541–48)

Such is the lesson of the poem.

Darkness continues to accumulate evil connotations in this canto. After agreeing to the plot against Darnley, Bothwell dreams that Lethington is leading him to the murder scene:

> The moon was down, but myriad stars
>   Were sparkling in the sky—
> "Behold!" he said, and raised his hand—
>   They seemed to wane and die.
> They passed from out the firmament,
>   Deep darkness fell around—
> Darkness, and horror as of hell,
>   And silence most profound.
> No wind, no murmur, breath, nor stir,
>   'Twas utter blankness all,
> As though the face of God were hid,
>   And heaven were wrapped in pall. (ii.725–36)

In the third canto, Darnley is murdered by the Scottish nobles. Bothwell shares in the guilt, for, having blown up Darnley's house under the impression he was within, he has killed several "poor wretches." Instead of doing "deeds of bold emprise," Bothwell has debased himself by committing the same type of murder for which he had disdained Darnley—thus, the awful significance in the final words of the canto, as Bothwell returns to Holyrood:

> Ah! but I heard a whisper pass,
>   It thrilled me as I reached the door—
> "Welcome to thee the knight that was,
>   The felon now for evermore!" (iii.422–45)

Light had filled the hall at Holyrood before Bothwell left to attempt the murder, but to him the light was "doubly hateful." More congenial were the road to Kirk-of-Field where "No light

there was in hut or bield" and the doomed house itself where
"neither moon nor stars gave light."

   The turning point of the narrative comes in the fourth canto.
Bothwell's worldly fortunes have been steadily rising, reach their
apex, and begin to decline. He is legally absolved of any com-
plicity in the murder of Darnley because the nobles wish first
to implicate Mary and then demand justice. Consequently, Lethington offers him the Band, in which the peers of Scotland agree
to support his claim for Mary's hand. The persuasions of the
subtle statesman, appealing to the desires of the simple warrior,
convince Bothwell that his sovereignty would be best for both
Mary and the nation. Bothwell reaches the pinnacle of hubris:

> "And now," thought I, "though fortune change,
>   My place is firm, my seat secure;
> Yea, let her, like a falcon, range
>   In wilful flight o'er moss and moor!
> Nothing I feel can shake me now;
>   The strength of Scotland backs my claim." (iv.437–42)

As usual in literature, the claim of superiority over fortune
signals the downfall of the speaker. Ormiston rushes in, warns
Bothwell of the nobles' strategy, and advises:

> "Be ruled by me—forestall the time!
>   Surprise is fair in love or war;
> A little urging is no crime—
>   Take Mary with you to Dunbar!" (iv.598–601)

Bothwell agrees. Now, all is fair in love as well as war; he has
moved from the world of chivalry to that of expedience. The
opening lines of the canto come back to the reader's mind:

> In the old tales of chivalry
>   There lies more truth than priests allow;
> Valour, and strength, and courtesy,
>   Have power to make the haughtiest bow.
> The knight who by his single arm
>   Could free a lady from duresse,
> And break the fell magician's charm,
>   Had claim upon her loveliness:

Although the daughter of a king,
 She might not spurn his homage fair;
And proud was she in listed ring,
 To see him with her colours there.
Rare thoughts are these for one disgraced,
 A slave in body, racked in soul!—
My blazon has been long erased,
 My name struck off the knightly roll! (iv.21–36)

In the fifth canto, Bothwell forces Mary to marry him. His remorse for this ultimate debasement fills this part:

I have shed blood, and rued it sore,
 Because it was not knightly done;
Yet were that all my guilt—no more—
 It might well brook comparison.

   . . .

It might be foul, it might be wrong
To slay the man I hated long;
But O, what mercy from above
Can he entreat who strikes at love? (v.41–4, 67–70)

Mary, always the innocent victim, rebukes him:

"And can it be," at length she said,
"That Bothwell has his Queen betrayed?
Bothwell, my first and foremost knight—
Bothwell, whose faith I deemed more bright,
More pure than any spotless gem
That glitters in my diadem?

   . . .

Are these your thanks for all my grace,
 Is this your knightly vow?
Fie, Bothwell! hide your perjured face—
 There's falsehood on your brow!" (v.387–92, 466–69)

He, upon whom the maintenance of the chivalric code in an unprincipled world depended, has destroyed that code. Reviewing this vilest deed, Bothwell now cannot bear the light of even a single star:

> I, than all others guiltier far,
> So vile, so lost, so mean!
> O fade from heaven, thou evening star,
> I cannot bear thy sheen! (v.575–78)

In the final canto, Bothwell falls. He leads his army against the rebellious nobles and hopes for an opportunity to regain a little lost glory:

> I stood upon Carberry's height,
> Eager, intent, resolved to fight,
> Ay, to the death, as seems a knight! (vi.418–20)

But, instead of entering into battle, he issues vain challenges to personal combat. His lieutenant, Ormiston, reproves him for such "idle chivalry" and departs with many soldiers. Kirkaldy reports that no noble will fight for "chivalrous display," and Bothwell, once the foremost knight of Scotland, is forced to flee amid the hoots of the rabble.

Bothwell's fall is dramatized by a series of increasingly painful "farewells." First, he is forced to leave Holyrood, symbol of kingship, in order to give battle: "Methought it said, Farewell!" Then, because of his attempt to observe "chivalrous display," he loses Ormiston, the representative of his fighting forces: "Farewell, thou poor inconstant lord—/Farewell, it is my latest word" (vi.662–63). Finally, most painfully, Mary leaves him: "Farewell!' She passed from out the tent./O God—I never saw her more!" (vi.856–57).

By the time the reader comes to this final canto, darkness has acquired considerable symbolic significance. Originally used in connection with Elizabeth and the Scottish nobles, it is now associated with Bothwell. Kirkaldy warns him, for instance, that he can escape from Carberry only if he leaves "while the night/ Can shroud you with its gloom." In the final stanza of the poem, Bothwell begins:

> Descend, black night! Blot out thy stars;
> Nor let them through those prison bars
> Behold me writhing here! (vi.906–08)

The once ambitious nobleman expresses his last desire: "Give me one night, 'tis all I crave,/To pass in darkness to the grave" (vi.921–22).

Most of the reviews of *Bothwell* spent considerable time discussing the validity of Aytoun's historical views.[4] He had invited such extraliterary criticism by writing in the preface to the first edition, "I wish it to be distinctly understood that, except in minor and immaterial matters, necessary for the construction of a Poem of this length, I have not deviated from what I consider to be the historical truth."[5] He had even added to the two hundred pages of poetry another one hundred of historical notes. The almost unanimous verdict of the reviewers was that Aytoun had grossly distorted the facts in his desire to present a spotless Mary, Queen of Scots.

Many reviewers perceived that *Bothwell* was the logical culmination of Aytoun's campaign against Spasmodic poetry. The *Times* prefaced its review with a long account of Aytoun's previous efforts against the Spasmodics and credited him with almost single-handedly causing a critical revolution. Finally, the reviewer comes to *Bothwell:*

It is necessary to enter into these explanations, partly in assertion of our own opinion with regard to Professor Aytoun, but chiefly in order to show the significance of the poem which he has now published. Any continuous poem from the author of those stirring *Lays of the Scottish Cavaliers* which are among the finest ballads in the language would deserve a hearty welcome; and, in itself, *Bothwell* is worthy of our admiration; but as a sequel to *Firmilian,*

---

4. The important reviews of *Bothwell* are, on the favorable side, *The Times* (Dec. 27, 1856), p. 4; *John Bull and Britannia* (Aug. 18, 1856), p. 523; *The Press, 4* (1856), 784–85; *The Examiner* (1856), p. 581; *Bentley's Miscellany, 40* (1856), 276–81; and *Blackwood's, 80* (1856), 222–33; and, on the unfavorable side, *The Saturday Review, 2* (1856), 482–83; *Fraser's, 54* (1856), 347–58; *The Christian Remembrancer, 33* (1857), 1–18; *The London Quarterly Review, 7* (1856), 201–08; *The Gentleman's Magazine, 201* (1856), 402–08; *The Literary Gazette* (1856), pp. 557–59; *The Christian Examiner, 61* (1856), 462; *The Westminster Review, 67* (1857), 315; and *The Titan, 23* (1856), 280.

5. Aytoun, *Poems*, p. 133.

more than ordinary interest attaches to it, since it may be regarded not simply as a poem, but as a challenge to the poets. In choosing, at the instance of Sir Bulwer Lytton, the sad story of Mary, Queen of Scots, for his theme, the poet selected a subject full of incident and full of pathos . . . . He clings to man and human action. And, although we must regret that he has too chivalrously thrown away a most important advantage—indeed, an essential condition of success—in condescending to compose the present tale in the form of soliloquy, still there are few modern poems in which the story is more clearly told and the action is more artistically developed—all in subordination to the remorse of the captive, the expression of which is necessarily the first object of the soliloquy. Under the conditions of the problem it is impossible to produce a finer poem than *Bothwell*.[6]

The review in *Bentley's* is similar, as the opening sentence indicates: "Apart from other claims to distinction, Professor Aytoun's new poem is sure of a special welcome, as a 'relief by contrast' to the mysticism, spasmodics, and nambypambyism which have lately been rife amongst us." [7] *Fraser's,* on the other hand, censures strongly, and its attitude toward the nature of the poem is especially indicative of contemporary taste: "The tone is, in the main, healthy: we have no false views of life, no deifying 'passion' as an excuse for selfish crime, no morbid feeling—in a word, no spasm. This is slight praise, but unhappily, in our day, these negative excellences acquire an undue importance from the prevalence of the opposite evils." [8] The *London Quarterly* is more wisely eclectic than its either-or contemporaries: "Though Mr. Aytoun—in his capacity of satirist or critic—may ridicule the redundant imagery and excessive word-painting of our younger minstrels, yet when he assumes the lyre himself, it would be well if he could add something of their 'ideality' or 'language' to his own 'constructiveness.' " [9] Only the *Titan* elevated Spasmodic poetry above *Bothwell:* none other than George

6. *The Times* (Dec. 27, 1856) , p. 4.
7. *Bentley's Miscellany, 40* (1856) , 276.
8. *Fraser's, 54* (1856) , 358.
9. *The London Quarterly Review, 7* (1856) , 208.

Gilfillan humiliated Aytoun in a comparison with Smith and Dobell.[1]

Ironically, the dramatic monologue, which encouraged favorable comparisons with the Spasmodics, attracted the most censure when *Bothwell* was judged on its own merits. The reviewers complained that such a form encumbered panoramic poetry of the Scott school. "It inevitably limits the scope and freedom of the treatment, and throws a certain colouring of individual feeling over the whole, which imparts more or less monotony to the expression." [2] Also commonly questioned was the moral desirability of such a monologist. *Fraser's,* for example, hoisted Aytoun with his own petard:

> The question has been of late widely discussed, whether a poet has a right to select as a hero the victim of morbid fancies, and that the keeping of the character may be preserved, to give forth sentiments corresponding to it, as if the author's own. We believe that a writer of fiction has no such right . . . . We should not have expected the correct muse of Mr. Aytoun to have countenanced a tendency so dangerous.[3]

The other major object of critical attack was the verse form. The reviewers ridiculed Aytoun's ballad measure for its "singsong" quality,[4] "tripping" effect,[5] "monotonous . . . flow," [6] and consequent incapacity for "adapting the vehicle to the sentiment." [7] All in all, *Bothwell* was judged to be a failure. Its author was advised to resume his shorter lays, for he could not sustain his characteristic fire and energy in a prolonged poem. Ironically again, Aytoun was criticized for that which he had condemned in the Spasmodics: he could compose merely isolated passages of "beauties." He had not accomplished his goal of writing a major

1. *The Titan, 23* (1856) , 270–81.
2. *The Literary Gazette* (1856) , p. 559. See also *The Times* (Dec. 27, 1856) p. 4; *The Press, 4* (1856) , 784; and *Bentley's Miscellany, 40* (1856) , 276–77.
3. *Fraser's, 54* (1856) , 351–52. See also *The Christian Remembrancer, 33* (1857) , 10–11.
4. *The Saturday Review, 2* (1856) , 483.
5. *The Christian Examiner, 61* (1856) , 462.
6. *The Christian Remembrancer, 33* (1857) , 7.
7. *The Literary Gazette* (1856) , p. 559.

poem but had written instead a poem of "subordinate accomplishments." [8]

Aytoun could not derive consolation from popular approval this time. The book sold well at first—one thousand copies in three weeks, a second edition in December 1856, a third in January 1858 [9]—but then went nowhere. The early demand was undoubtedly from the devoted readers of *Lays of the Scottish Cavaliers*. If Aytoun felt satisfaction over *Bothwell*, it must have come from having given artistic form to a very personal feeling. The theme of the book lay as close to his heart as ever did the Spasmodic heroes' wild aspirations to their author's dreams. Aytoun cherished the world of Scottish chivalry and lamented that it had been superseded by more practical ages. He recognized the inevitability of the historical change, but this did not make him regret it any less.

8. *The Gentleman's Magazine, 201* (1856) , 408.

9. Letter of August 22, 1856, to Blackwood; the first edition consisted of 1,594 copies. The second edition was 1,030 copies; and the third, 2,096 copies, of which 2,086 were sold.

LAST YEARS

Aytoun had appeared before the public as a poet, balladist, parodist, literary and social critic, and short story and political writer. In the next five years, he was to publish a two-volume edition of *The Ballads of Scotland* (June 1858), a translation of Goethe's minor poetry (December 1858), and a three-volume novel, *Norman Sinclair* (November 1861). As the *Times* had said of its political opponent, "There are few things that come amiss to the learned and accomplished Professor of Rhetoric in the University of Edinburgh. He would have made a rare walking dramatist for the actors at the Court of Denmark." [1]

Aytoun was returning to his favorite genre in *The Ballads of Scotland*. He had first thought of editing his country's ballads in 1846, when he wrote an angry letter to John Blackwood about Sheldon's recent *Minstrelsy of the English Border:*

> It is without exception the most shameful book I have ever read. He says it is a collection of old ballads. That is a lie. There is not in the whole volume *one* original line, and many of them are cool travesties of the Scottish ballads by the author himself. I am quite indignant about it, and want to show the impostor up, for if I know any subject thoroughly it is that of the British ballads. . . . In my eyes it is a worse sin than an attempt to corrupt the Iliad. Damn their egos! what right has the English border to have any Minstrelsy at all? [2]

1. *The Times* (May 31, 1849), p. 6.
2. Letter of Nov. 29, 1846.

Obviously, Aytoun's chauvinism was bound up with his love of
the genre; as the *Saturday Review* said, "The old national ballads
still constitute the most undisputed claim which Scotland can put
forward to superiority over every rival." [3] Now that Aytoun had
published his own *Lays* and had made his try for poetic fame
with *Bothwell,* he could return to this pet project. He must have
begun intensive work soon after the completion of *Bothwell,* for
he wrote to Blackwood in the middle of 1857, "I have been working at the Scottish ballads, and have already collected and prepared a good lot of them." [4] Two months later, he described his
exertions over the book and his "hope to make this the standard
and complete edition." [5]

Aytoun's purpose was to publish in their original forms all
Scottish ballads of "real intrinsic merit," which had been "composed previous to the Union of the Kingdoms." [6] He collated
extant versions, chose among variants, and excised all modern
interpolations. In a few cases, Aytoun's scholarly reconstructions
were artistically inferior to the versions popular in his own day.[7]
More frequently, however, the original ballads justified themselves. For example, Percy's version of "Gil Morice" includes the
following stanzas:

> Gil Morice sate in gude grene wode
>   He whistled and he sang':
> O what mean a' the folk coming,
>   My mother tarries lang.

> His hair was like the threeds of gold,
>   Drawne frae Minervas loome:
> His lipps like roses drapping dew,
>   His breath was a' perfume.

> His brow was like the mountain snae
>   Gilt by the morning beam:

3. *The Saturday Review, 6* (1858), 137.
4. Letter of July 7, 1857.
5. Letter of Sept. 16, 1857.
6. Aytoun, ed., *The Ballads of Scotland* (2 vols. Edinburgh and London, William
Blackwood and Sons, 1858) , *1,* lxxxix.
7. His version of "Annie Laurie," for example, is noticeably inferior.

His cheeks like living roses glow:
His een like azure stream.

The boy was clad in robes of grene,
Sweete as the infant spring:
And like the mavis on the bush,
He gart the vallies ring.

The baron came to the grene wode,
Wi' mickle dule and care,
And there he first spied Gil Morìce
Kameing his yellow hair:

That sweetly wavd around his face,
That face beyond compare:
He sang sae sweet it might dispel,
A' rage but fell despair.[8]

Aytoun excised the last twenty lines. Whereas Robert Chambers, who had anticipated Aytoun in the principle of restitution, had given sixty-eight Scottish ballads to the public, Aytoun offered one hundred and thirty-nine.[9]

The reviewers almost unanimously extolled *The Ballads of Scotland*.[1] They recognized in the editor a perfect blend of love for and knowledge of his material—what one review called a combination of "the ardour of a runaway match, with the deliberate prudence of a French *mariage de convenance*."[2] The *Times* called it "the standard" and the *London Review* "the complete" edition.[3] The *Quarterly Review* claimed that "we have

8. Thomas Percy, *Reliques of Ancient English Poetry* (3 vols. London, Swan Sonnenschein and Co. Ltd., 1910), *3*, 97–98.

9. In his revised edition of 1859, Aytoun withdrew two of these ballads and added six others.

1. See esp. *The Quarterly Review, 105* (1859), 305–41, for an important article on Aytoun. See also *The Times* (Oct. 2, 1858), pp. 10–11; *The Saturday Review, 6* (1858), 135–37; *The London Review, 11* (1858), 277–80; *The Gentleman's Magazine, 205* (1858), 171–72; *The Athenaeum, 31* (1858), 43–45; *The Spectator, 31* (1858), 843–44; and, for the minority opinion, *The Westminster Review, 70* (1858), 610–11.

2. *The Spectator, 31* (1858), 843.

3. *The Times* (Oct. 2, 1858), p. 10; *The London Review, 11* (1858), 280.

in his volumes a final work on the Ballads of Scotland," [4] a claim
which seems to have been justified.[5] Aytoun was "much gratified"
by the reception [6] but would probably have been most pleased
with the use Child was to make of his scholarship.[7]

Almost immediately after the publication of *The Ballads of
Scotland,* Aytoun renewed his literary partnership with Theodore
Martin in *Poems and Ballads of Goethe,*[8] a revision and expansion
of their earlier translations for *Blackwood's.* In the preface,
Aytoun announced their intention to fulfill the two major requirements of translations. On the one hand, their "ambition
and desire" was to lay before the public "such a selection from
the minor poems and ballads of the great German author, as
might tend to convey to an English reader something like an
adequate impression of his varied genius . . . they have spared
no pains to make their transcripts faithful in form as well as
spirit to the originals" (pp. v, vii). On the other hand, frequently
"they decided on adopting the metres which in their opinion
would best commend them to the taste of English readers. For,
after all, it is for them, and not for German scholars, that this
volume has been written" (p. ix).

Unfortunately, this attempt to be both faithful to the original
and pleasing to the audience was often split between the two
translators. Aytoun brought Goethe too far to the readers; Martin, not far enough. Aytoun wrote agreeable verse; Martin produced better cribs. Aytoun tended to add his own "beauties" and
moralisms to the condensed gems of Goethe. For example, a literal
rendition of "Exculpation" would read:

> You complain of the woman for changing
> from one to another:

4. *The Quarterly Review, 105* (1859), 336.

5. For Aytoun's place in the line of editors, see Sigurd Hustvedt, *Ballad Books
and Ballad Men* (Cambridge, Harvard University Press, 1930), p. 132.

6. The first edition of 2,098 copies sold quickly. The second and revised edition
of 1859 totaled 1,576 copies, and the third edition of 1870 was reduced to 776
copies.

7. F. J. Child, *The English and Scottish Popular Ballads,* eds. Helen C. Sargent
and George Lyman Kittredge (Boston and New York, Houghton Mifflin Co., 1904),
p. 683 and passim.

8. Aytoun and Martin, trans., *Poems and Ballads of Goethe* (Edinburgh and
London, William Blackwood and Sons, 1859).

> O do not blame her,—she seeks an
> unwavering man.

Aytoun offers:

> Wilt thou dare to blame the woman
> for her seeming sudden changes,
> Swaying east and swaying westward,
> as the breezes shake the tree?
> Fool! thy selfish thought misguides thee—
> find the *man* that never ranges;
> Woman wavers but to seek him—
> Is not then the fault in thee? (p. 18)

Occasionally, when the Victorian gentleman came up against the "Pagan tendencies" [9] of the German intellectual, he perverted the original. Rendered literally, "Holy Family" presents a sensuous picture with overtones of skepticism:

O the beautiful child, and O the fortunate mother!
How she is delighted in him, as he also in her!
What rapture might I feel at this splendid picture,
Were I not meanly condemned, like Joseph, to stand in a holy way!

Aytoun's translation produces an opposite effect:

O Child of beauty rare—
O mother chaste and fair—
How happy seem they both, so far beyond compare!
She, in her infant blest,
And he in conscious rest,
Nestling within the soft warm cradle of her breast!
What joy that sight might bear
To him who sees them there,
If, with a pure and guilt-untroubled eye,
He look'd upon the twain, like Joseph standing by. (p. 22)

The one masterpiece of the volume is "The Bride of Corinth." The two partners united their talents to produce a translation which is aesthetically satisfying in its own right and particularly

9. Aytoun's expression on p. 237 of the volume.

faithful to the original. It is the first English version to retain
Goethe's difficult meter. The reviews, mixed in their judgments
on the volume as a whole,[1] unanimously praised this major
effort. The *Saturday Review* called it "a miracle of imitative
art," [2] and the *Times* said, "one of the most extraordinary feats
in the way of translation that we know." [3]

Aytoun's quiet domestic life was shattered in 1859. His wife,
who for years had been "suffering from one of those occult
ailments which baffle medical skill," suddenly worsened.[4] Aytoun
wrote to his deputy sheriff at Orkney on April 6:

> Sooth to say, I am not in great spirits, for my poor dear
> wife has been very unwell of late, and I have been in the
> deepest anxiety about her.
>
> . . . she really seemed very ill, and she spoke and looked
> like an angel—was so sweet, kind, affectionate, and resigned,
> that I felt as if my heart would have burst; and the awful
> thought that I might soon be left alone in this world,
> without the companionship of one who for ten years has
> been dearer to me and more blessed to me than words can
> express, smote me with a sense of desolation. I have endeav-
> oured not to repine. I know that God sends his chastisements
> in mercy, not in wrath—that what He does for us is the best;
> but there is an awful significance in the lines—
>   "Sinful Macduff,
>   Not for their own offences, but for thine,
>   Fell slaughter on their souls!"
> I have prayed, and in praying have received that consolation

---

1. The most complete examination is in *The London Review, 12* (1859) , 121–45.
See also *The Times* (Jan. 15, 1859) , p. 12; *The Saturday Review, 7* (1859) , 187–88;
Fraser's, 59 (1859) , 710–17; *Bentley's Miscellany, 45* (1859) , 401–05; *The West-
minster Review, 71* (1859) , 624–25; *The North British Review, 30* (1859) , 207–72;
The Athenaeum, 32 (1859) , 215–17.

2. *The Saturday Review, 7* (1859) , 188.

3. *The Times* (Jan. 15, 1859) , p. 12. The first edition totaled 1,578 copies, and
the second edition, published the following year, had seven additional copies.
Both editions were completely sold out.

4. Martin, *Memoir,* p. 200.

that, in the event of the worst, I hope I shall be able to bend to the rod.[5]

Mrs. Aytoun died on April 15, 1859, four days after their tenth wedding anniversary, and Aytoun was left a childless, lonely man. He told Martin, "The great calamity of life has fallen upon me." [6]

Aggravating Aytoun's sorrow was his disappointment over public affairs. The Conservative ministry had recently been forced to resign, and the party was at low ebb. In his last article for *Blackwood's* before the death of his wife, Aytoun had pleaded for the return of his party to power: "It must be apparent even to the most superficial observer that the present crisis is a very serious one, quite unlike any which has occurred within the memory of the present generation." [7] He feared the consequences of an opposition victory or, worse yet, a weak coalition—appeasement of French aggression, a further reduction in voting requirements, and a general truckling to the "demands of the democrats." Should such a victory occur, "then we may indeed despair of the ultimate destinies of the country" (p. 642). A Whig-Liberal coalition took office in June 1859.

Aytoun wrote only one article in the last nine months of 1859.[8] It is on international affairs, but his personal grief hangs heavy over it. His new tone becomes evident in the first paragraph:

It is, we think, a belief very generally entertained even by men who are ready to acknowledge the working of God's providence upon earth, that war is a calamity which can be prevented or averted by the exercise of human will and prudence. . . . We have, all of us, become too much accustomed to rely upon human wisdom, prescience, and dexterity . . . the issues of life and death, are alone in the hands of the Almighty. (p. 765)

5. Ibid., p. 201.
6. Ibid.
7. *Blackwood's, 85* (1859), 626.
8. Ibid., pp. 765–80.

In the article he warns his countrymen of the old aggressiveness of France under the new Napoleon and, more importantly, vents his despair over the modern world:

In the councils of Europe at this moment there is so much moral obliquity, that we do not know in whom we can repose confidence, to whose honesty we may trust. The greed of empire, so long restrained, is now manifested and almost openly avowed by states of magnitude and power. Nation is arrayed against nation, and kingdom against kingdom, not, as of yore, for the sake of vindicating religious freedom, or of asserting claims of hereditary succession, but for a trial of brute strength, robbery being the object of one party, and dogged resistance the determination of the other. (p. 776)

Thus, 1859 was the unhappiest year of Aytoun's life. "Night after night," John Blackwood told Martin, "I used to call in upon him, and anything more melancholy than our old bright companion, sitting with his head leaning on his hands, cheerless and helpless, I never saw." Martin adds, "It was thus I found him one night I paid him an unexpected visit some time after Mrs. Aytoun's death. He was no longer the same man, and it seemed from his looks as if in a few months he had passed through years of suffering and illness." [9]

Aytoun lightened his gloom by writing *Norman Sinclair*. Thinly disguised as fiction, it is an objective review of his life, an attempt to distance and find pattern in the past. He began the autobiographical novel in July 1859 [1] and published it serially in *Blackwood's* from January 1860 to August 1861 and in its final three-volume form shortly thereafter. Norman Sinclair is a Scottish Episcopalian Tory who writes for a leading periodical. His two major experiences, the Reform election of 1832 and the railway mania of 1845, reproduce Aytoun's own, and his opinions on all subjects from politics to Spasmodic poets [2] also reflect the author's. Although *Norman Sinclair* as a novel will cause "a sen-

9. Martin, *Memoir,* pp. 203–04.
1. Letter of July 31, 1859, to Blackwood.
2. For his remarks on Spasmodic poets, see *Norman Sinclair,* 2, 185–6.

sation of absolute dismay"[3] to most readers because of its discursive plot, humorless caricatures, and prosaism, it is valuable as an index of its author's personality.[4]

Despite this nostalgic reminiscence of his earlier life and the healing power of time itself, Aytoun never completely recovered his genial spirits. The last four years of his life were neither pleasant nor productive and are best passed over rapidly. A stomach ailment, which he thought dyspepsia but which proved to be a more organic malady, made eating and sleeping difficult, sometimes impossible. The sedentary professor who had lived almost exclusively in one city was now forced to seek relief in the health resorts of France, Switzerland, and Germany. His literary output was curtailed: occasional articles for *Blackwood's* and a *Nuptial Ode on the Marriage of His Royal Highness The Prince of Wales* (1863).[5] In his loneliness, Aytoun married for the second time on Christmas Eve, 1863, the day on which his old friend Thackeray died. Indeed, Aytoun spent considerable time in his letters bewailing the recent deaths of men he had known—"the old men know when an old man dies." And he was old in body, if not in years. Although his mother and two sisters all lived to over ninety, Aytoun died on August 4, 1865, at the age of fifty-two.

3. *The Saturday Review*, *12* (1861), 670. The other important reviews are in *The Westminster Review*, 77 (1862), 599–600, and *The Spectator*, *34* (1861), 1403–04.

4. There have not been many readers. The first and only edition totaled 1,576 copies, all of which were not sold.

5. A surprisingly popular ode: 4,661 of its 5,280 copies were sold. One copy was sent to Victoria.

BIBLIOGRAPHY

PRIMARY SOURCES

UNPUBLISHED

Microfilms of the Aytoun letters in the National Library of Scotland

PUBLISHED

Books and Pamphlets by Aytoun

The Ballads of Scotland, ed. Aytoun, 2 vols. Edinburgh and London, William Blackwood and Sons, 1858.

The Book of Ballads, ed. Bon Gaultier, London, Orr, 1845.

The Book of Ballads, ed. Bon Gaultier, 5th ed. Edinburgh and London, William Blackwood and Sons, 1857. (The standard edition during Aytoun's lifetime.)

The Book of Ballads, ed. Bon Gaultier, 16th ed. Edinburgh and London, William Blackwood and Sons, 1903. (Important preface added by Theodore Martin.)

Bothwell—A Poem, Edinburgh and London, William Blackwood and Sons, 1856.

The Drummond Schism Examined and Exposed, By a Layman of the Church, Edinburgh, R. Grant and Son, 1842.

Firmilian: or The Student of Badajoz. A Spasmodic Tragedy By T. Percy Jones, Edinburgh and London, William Blackwood and Sons, 1854.

Inaugural Address to the Associated Societies of the University of Edinburgh, Edinburgh and London, William Blackwood and Sons, 1861.

Lays of the Scottish Cavaliers and Other Poems, Edinburgh and London, William Blackwood and Sons, 1849.

The Life and Times of Richard the First, London, T. Tegg, 1840.

"Memoir of Campbell, " *The Poetical Works of Thomas Campbell,* Boston, Little, Brown and Co., 1862.

Norman Sinclair, 3 vols. Edinburgh and London, William Blackwood and Sons, 1861.

Nuptial Ode on the Marriage of His Royal Highness The Prince of Wales, Edinburgh and London, William Blackwood and Sons, 1863.

Our Zion: or Presbyterian Popery, By Ane of that Ilk, Edinburgh, 1840.

Poems, ed. F. Page, London, Oxford University Press, 1921.

Poems and Ballads of Goethe, trans. Aytoun and Martin, Edinburgh and London, William Blackwood and Sons, 1859.

Poland, Homer, and Other Poems, London, Longman, Rees, Orme, Brown, Green, and Longman; and Edinburgh, Black, 1832.

W. E. Aytoun: Stories and Verse, ed. W. L. Renwick, Edinburgh, Edinburgh University Press, 1964.

Contributions to Blackwood's *by Aytoun*

"Ballads from Uhland," *39* (March 1836), 381–83.
"Ballads from Uhland," *39* (May 1836), 595–96.

"Twenty-second Book of *The Iliad* Translated," *45* (May 1839), 634–42.
"Hermotimus," *46* (November 1839), 592–96.

"Ballads from the Romaic," *47* (May 1840), 689–90.

"Blind Old Milton," *50* (December 1841), 811–13.

"The Martyr's Monument," *53* (January 1843), 125–27.
"The Burial March of Dundee," *53* (April 1843), 537–38.
"Charles Edward at Versailles," *54* (July 1843), 107–08.

"The Heart of the Bruce," *56* (July 1844), 15–19.
"Poems and Ballads of Goethe," *56* (July 1844), 54–68.
"The Old Scottish Cavalier," *56* (August 1844), 195.
"The Burns Festival with Speeches," *56* (September 1844), 370–98.
"The Execution of Montrose," *56* (September 1844), 289–96.
"Poems and Ballads of Goethe No. II," *56* (October 1844), 417–32.
"The Scottish Banking System," *56* (December 1844), 671–86.

"Poems and Ballads of Goethe No. III," *57* (February 1845), 165–80.
"Lord Malmesbury's Diaries," *57* (March 1845), 314–30.
"My First Spec in the Biggleswades," *57* (May 1845), 549–60.
"A Letter from London," *58* (August 1845), 173–84.
"How We Got up the Glenmutchkin Railway," *58* (October 1845), 453–66.
"The Railways," *58* (November 1845), 633–48.
"The Scottish Harvest," written in conjunction with H. Stephens, *58* (December 1845), 769–84.

"Ministerial Measures," *59* (March 1846), 373–84.
"The Surveyor's Tale," *59* (April 1846), 497–512.
"New Scottish Plays and Poems," *60* (July 1846), 62–82.

"Mesmeric Mountebanks," *60* (August 1846), 223–37.
"How I Became a Yeoman," *60* (September 1846), 358–75.
"Wild Sports and Natural History," *60* (October 1846), 389–410.
"Advice to an Intending Serialist," *60* (November 1846), 590–605.
"The Game Laws," *60* (December 1846), 754–72.

"Ancient and Modern Ballad Poetry," *61* (May 1847), 622–44.
"Constantin Kanaris, Epitaph," *61* (May 1847), 644.
"Hymn of King Olaf the Saint," *61* (June 1847), 682–83.
"Letter from a Railway Witness," *62* (July 1847), 68–82.
"Sir Robert Peel and the Currency," *62* (July 1847), 113–28.
"The Emerald Studs," *62* (August 1847), 214–35.
"How I Stood for the Dreepdaily Burghs," *62* (September 1847), 259–84.
"Magus Muir," *62* (November 1847), 614–18.
"The Widow of Glencoe," *62* (December 1847), 700–06.
"Our Currency, Our Trade, and Our Tariff," *62* (December 1847), 744–67.

"Edinburgh after Flodden," *63* (February 1848), 165–75.
"Our West Indian Colonies," *63* (February 1848), 219–38.
"Mr. Cobden on the National Defences," *63* (March 1848), 261–80.
"Greenwich Time," *63* (March 1848), 354–61.
"The Budget," *63* (March 1848), 383–92.
"How We Got Possession of the Tuilleries," *63* (April 1848), 484–512.
"The Inca and His Bride," *63* (June 1848), 750–66.
"The Scottish Deer Forests," *64* (July 1848), 92–107.
"The Buried Flower," *64* (July 1848), 108–12.
"A Review of the Last Session," *64* (September 1848), 261–90.
"Sonnet to Denmark," *64* (September 1848), 292.
"A Glimpse at Germany," *64* (November 1848), 515–42.
"Danube and Euxine," *64* (November 1848), 608–09.
"Conservative Union," *64* (November 1848), 632–40.

"Memoirs of Kirkcaldy," *65* (January 1849), 112–28.
"Modern Biography. Beattie's Life of Campbell," *65* (February 1849), 219–34.
"The Opening of the Session," *65* (March 1849), 357–82.
"The Scottish Marriage Bills," *66* (September 1849), 263–76.
"The Strayed Reveller," *66* (September 1849), 340–46.
"The Diary of Samuel Pepys," *66* (October 1849), 501–18.
"Peace and War Agitators," *66* (November 1849), 581–606.
"The National Debt and the Stock Exchange," *66* (December 1849), 655–78.

"British Agriculture and Foreign Competition," *67* (January 1850), 94–136.
"British Agriculture and Foreign Competition No. 2," *67* (February 1850), 222–48.
"Agriculture Commerce and Manufacturing," *67* (March 1850), 347–76.
"Britain's Prosperity—a New Song," *67* (April 1850), 389–92.

"The Dwarf and the Oak Tree," *67* (April 1850), 411–14.
"The Clearing of the Glens," *67* (April 1850), 475–80.
"Modern Argonauts," *67* (May 1850), 539–41.
"The Penitent Free-Trader," *67* (May 1850), 585–88.
"Alison's Political Essays," *67* (May 1850), 605–21.
"Ovid's Spring Time," *67* (May 1850), 621.
"Latter Day Pamphlets," *67* (June 1850), 641–58.
"The Hungarian Joseph," *67* (June 1850), 658–60.
"The Quaker's Lament," *67* (June 1850), 733–37.
"The Great Protection Meeting in London, Introductory Part," *67* (June 1850), 738–82.
"The Industry of the People," *68* (July 1850), 106–22.
"Free Trade and Our Cotton Manufactures," *68* (August 1850), 123–40.
"The Temple of Folly," *68* (August 1850), 229–30.
"African Sporting," *68* (August 1850), 231–46.
"The Proposed Exhibition of 1851," *68* (September 1850), 278–90.
"The Masquerade of Freedom," *68* (October 1850), 475–78.
"Alton Locke," *68* (November 1850), 592–610.
"The Renewal of the Income Tax," *68* (November 1850), 611–26.
"Who Rolled the Powder In," *68* (December 1850), 689–90.
"A Lecture on Journalism," *68* (December 1850), 691–97.
"The Defences of Britain," *68* (December 1850), 736–44.

"Additional Chapters for the History of John Bull," *69* (January 1851), 69–88.
"British Labour and Foreign Reciprocity," *69* (January 1851), 112–30.
"Ridley and Latimer," *69* (February 1851), 131–36.
"Additional Chapters for the History of John Bull," *69* (February 1851), 164–79.
"Lord Holland's Foreign Reminiscences," *69* (February 1851), 234–45.
"Lavengro," *69* (March 1851), 322–37.
"The Ministry and the Agricultural Interests," *69* (March 1851), 368–84.
"Latter Days of the Free Trade Ministry," *69* (April 1851), 491–512.
"Onward Tendencies," *69* (May 1851), 564–72.
"The Vision of Polyphemus," *69* (June 1851), 673–75.
"The Experiences of Free Trade," *69* (June 1851), 748–66.
"Downward Tendencies," *70* (July 1851), 106–21.
"The Raid of Arnaboll," *70* (August 1851), 220–44.
"The Scarborough Election," *70* (August 1851), 245–48.
"The Late D. M. Moir," *70* (August 1851), 249–50.
"Disfranchisement of the Boroughs," *70* (September 1851), 296–309.
"The Congress and the Agapedome," *70* (September 1851), 359–78.
"Autumn Politics," *70* (November 1851), 607–28.
"To the Shopkeepers of Great Britain," *70* (December 1851), 629–48.
"The Champions of the Rail," *70* (December 1851), 739–50.

"Lord George Bentinck," *71* (January 1852), 121–34.

"Longfellow's Golden Legend," *71* (February 1852), 212–25.
"Cupid on the Cabinet," *71* (February 1852), 231–35.
"Reform Measures of 1852," *71* (March 1852), 369–86.
"The Appeal to the Country," *71* (April 1852), 498–516.
"The Vineyards of Bordeaux," *71* (May 1852), 617–25.
"The Democratic Confederacy," *71* (May 1852), 626–44.
"Thoughts upon Dinners," *71* (June 1852), 734–49.
"The General Election," *72* (July 1852), 114–32.
"The Moor and the Loch," *72* (August 1852), 218–34.
"The Crusader's March," *72* (September 1852), 372.
"The Holidays," *72* (November 1852), 634–52.
"The Golden Age—A Poem," *72* (November 1852), 521–33.
"Sullivan's Rambles in North America," *72* (December 1852), 680–92.
"The Manchester Movement," *72* (December 1852), 759–70.
"Aiton's Travels in the East," *72* (December 1852), 745–57.

"Defeat of the Ministry," *73* (January 1853), 111–28.
"Supplementary Chapters for the History of John Bull," *73* (February 1853),
    166–84.
"Palissy and Potter," *73* (February 1853), 235–46.
"Clubs and Clubbists," *73* (March 1853), 265–77.
"Peace and War," *73* (March 1853), 364–78.
"The Malt Tax," *73* (March 1853), 379–86.
"Spiritual Manifestations," *73* (May 1853), 629–46.
"Minor Morals," *73* (June 1853), 745–59.
"A Chapter on Life Assurance," *74* (July 1853), 105–16.
"Scotland Since the Union," *74* (September 1853), 263–83.
"Haydon's Autobiography," *74* (November 1853), 519–38.
"Rapping the Question," *74* (December 1853), 711–25.

"The Aberdeen Cabinet," *75* (January 1854), 113–28.
"Macaulay's Speeches," *75* (February 1854), 193–203.
"Disraeli—A Biography," *75* (March 1854), 255–67.
"The Two Arnolds," *75* (March 1854), 303–14.
"The New Reform Bill," *75* (March 1854), 369–80.
"The Cost of the Coalition Ministry," *75* (April 1854), 492–506.
"Firmilian—A Tragedy," *75* (May 1854), 533–51.
"Ruskin on Architecture and Painting," *75* (June 1854), 740–56.
"The Glasgow Exhibitions to Oxford," *75* (June 1854), 757–62.
"Mrs. Stowe's Sunny Memories," *76* (September 1854), 301–17.
"The War and the Ministry," *76* (November 1854), 599–618.
"Prospects of the Modern Drama," *76* (December 1854), 689–713.

"The Conduct of the War," *77* (January 1855), 1–20.
"Revelations of a Showman," *77* (February 1855), 187–201.
"The Ministerial Changes," *77* (March 1855), 359–78.

"State of the Militia," *77* (April 1855), 467–80.
"The Royal Scottish Academy," *77* (May 1855), 582–97.
"The Reverend Charles Kingsley," *77* (June 1855), 625–43.
"The Palmerston Administration," *77* (June 1855), 724–39.
"Administrative Reform," *78* (July 1855), 116–34.
"Maud by Alfred Tennyson," *78* (September 1855), 311–21.
"Light Literature for the Holidays," *78* (September 1855), 362–74.
"Light Literature for the Holidays, No. II," *78* (October 1855), 463–77.

"The Wensleydale Creation," *79* (March 1856), 369–78.
"The Food of London," *80* (December 1856), 728–40.

"Mrs. Barrett Browning—Aurora Leigh," *81* (January 1857), 23–41.
"Letters from a Lighthouse, No. 1," *81* (February 1857), 227–42.
"Letters from a Lighthouse, No. 2," *81* (March 1857), 380–92.
"Barry Cornwall," *81* (March 1857), 356–65.
"All Fool's Day,—A Political Pantomime," *81* (April 1857), 393–415.
"Letters from a Lighthouse, No. 3," *81* (April 1857), 504–20.
"Lays of the Elections" (one-half written by Hamley), *81* (May 1857), 631–35.
"Letters from a Lighthouse, No. 4," *81* (May 1857), 636–48.
"American Explorations—China and Japan," *81* (June 1857), 702–18.
"Stewart's Practical Angler," *81* (June 1857), 748–57.
"Maga's Birth Day AEtatis D," *81* (June 1857), 777–78.
"Representation of the Colonies," *82* (July 1857), 110–28.

"The Scottish Universities," *83* (January 1858), 74–93.
"The Cost of Whig Government," *83* (June 1858), 733–44.
"The Great Imposture," *84* (July 1858), 111–22.

"Clothes and Scarecrows," *85* (March 1859), 274–91.
"Dasent's Tales from the Norse," *85* (March 1859), 366–75.
"The New Reform Bill," *85* (April 1859), 506–14.
"The Appeal to the Country," *85* (May 1859), 626–42.
"Our Relations with the Continent," *85* (June 1859), 765–80.

"Norman Sinclair Part I," *87* (January 1860), 14–20, and monthly thereafter until August 1861.
"Lord Dundonald's Memoirs," *87* (February 1860), 176–95.
"France and Central Italy," *87* (February 1860), 245–54.
"The Anglo-Gallican Budget," *87* (March 1860), 381–96.
"Poetic Aberrations," *87* (April 1860), 490–94.

"The Ministry and the Budget," *89* (May 1861), 517–36.
"Meditations on Dyspepsia No. 1, The Malady," *90* (September 1861), 302–22.

"Meditations on Dyspepsia No. 2, The Cure," *90* (October 1861), 406–19.
"The Late Earl of Eglinton," *90* (November 1861), 642–44.

"The Rights of Women," *92* (August 1862), 183–201.
"Watering Places," *92* (September 1862), 261–85.
"Germany and Her Prospects," *92* (October 1862), 413–39.

"Crinolineana," *93* (June 1863), 762–63.

"Banting on Corpulence," *96* (November 1864), 607–17.

"Modern Demonology," *97* (February 1865), 192–208.
"Sir E. Bulwer Lytton's Poems," *97* (March 1865), 330–41.
"Mr. Gladstone at Chester," *98* (July 1865), 107–20.

Bon Gaultier Papers to Which Aytoun Contributed

"Review of Unpublished Annuals. The Topaz, for 1842," *Tait's, 8* (1841), 749–56.
"The Poets of the Day. Edited by David Twaddle," *Tait's, 9* (1842), 237–45.
"Lays of the Would-Be Laureates," *Tait's, 10* (1843), 273–76.
"Puffs and Poetry," *Tait's, 10* (1843), 649–54.
"Young Scotland; or An Evening at Treport," *Tait's, 10* (1843), 686–92.
"A Night at Peleg Longfellow's," *Fraser's, 28* (1843), 160–68.
"My Wife's Album," *Tait's, 11* (1844), 49–55.
"Bon Gaultier and His Friends," *Tait's, 11* (1844), 119–31.
"Bon Gaultier and His Friends—No. II," *Tait's, 11* (1844), 341–48.
"Bon Gaultier and His Friends—No. III," *Tait's, 11* (1844), 477–87.

SECONDARY SOURCES

UNPUBLISHED

Adams, Norman Owens Whitehurst, "Byron and the Early Victorians—A Study of His Poetic Influence (1824–1855)," Doctoral Dissertation, University of Wisconsin, 1955.
Cunningham, James Vincent, "The Spasmodic School of Poetry," Doctoral Dissertation, St. John's (Brooklyn) University, 1941.
Gray, Donald Joseph, "Victorian Verse Humor: 1830–1870," Doctoral Dissertation, Ohio State University, 1956.
Henry, William Claude, "A Study of Alexander Smith and His Reputation as a Spasmodic Writer," Doctoral Dissertation, Northwestern University, 1942.
McKillop, Alan D., "The Spasmodic School in Victorian Poetry," Doctoral Dissertation, Harvard University, 1920.
Peckham, Morse, "Guilt and Glory—A Study of the 1839 Festus, a Nine-

teenth-Century Poem of Synthesis," Doctoral Dissertation, Princeton University, 1947.

Schweik, Robert C., "Selected Reviews of William Edmondstoune Aytoun," Doctoral Dissertation, Notre Dame University, 1957.

Thale, Jerome, "Sydney Dobell: A Spasmodic Poet," Doctoral Dissertation, Northwestern University, 1953.

PUBLISHED

Books

Arnold, Matthew, *Irish Essays and Others,* London, Smith, Elder and Co., 1882.

———, *Letters, 1848–1888,* ed. George W. E. Russell, 2 vols. New York, The Macmillan Co., 1896.

———, *Letters to Arthur Hugh Clough,* ed. H. F. Lowry, London, Oxford University Press, 1932.

Bailey, Philip James, *Festus: A Poem,* New York, Thomas R. Knox and Co., 1885. (From the second London edition.)

———, *Festus: A Poem,* New York, Worthington Co., 1889. (From the third London edition.)

———, *Festus: A Poem,* London, George Routledge and Sons Ltd., 1903. (Important preface added by Bailey.)

Baum, Paull F., *Tennyson, Sixty Years After,* Chapel Hill, University of North Carolina Press, 1948.

Beddoes, Thomas Lovell, *The Complete Works,* London, Fanfrolico Press, 1928.

Beerbohm, Max, *Seven Men and Two Others,* London, William Heinemann Ltd., 1950.

Bigg, J. Stanyan, *Night and the Soul,* London, Groombridge and Sons, 1854.

Brisbane, Rev. T., *The Early Years of Alexander Smith,* London, Hodder and Stoughton, 1869.

Browning, Elizabeth Barrett, *The Letters of Elizabeth Barrett Browning,* ed. F. G. Kenyon, 2 vols. New York, The Macmillan Co., 1897.

———, *Letters to Richard Hengist Horne,* ed. S. R. Townshend Mayer, New York, James Miller, 1877.

———, *The Poetical Works,* New York, The Macmillan Co., 1897.

Browning, Robert, *Men and Women,* New York, Doubleday and Co., Inc., n.d.

———, *The Shorter Poems,* ed. William Clyde DeVane, New York, F. S. Crofts and Co., 1934.

Bryant, Arthur, *Macaulay,* New York, D. Appleton and Co., 1933.

Buchanan, Robert, *The Fleshly School of Poetry,* London, Strahan and Co., 1872.

———, *A Look Round Literature,* London, Ward and Downey, 1887.

Buckley, Jerome Hamilton, *Tennyson—The Growth of a Poet,* Cambridge, Harvard University Press, 1961.

——, *The Victorian Temper,* Cambridge, Harvard University Press, 1951.

Bush, Douglas, *Mythology and the Romantic Tradition in English Poetry,* New York, Pageant Book Co., 1957.

Byron, Lord, *The Complete Poetical Works,* Boston, Houghton Mifflin Co., 1933.

Clough, Arthur Hugh, *The Poems,* eds. H. F. Lowry, A. L. P. Norrington, and F. L. Mulhauser, Oxford, Clarendon Press, 1951.

——, *Prose Remains,* London, Macmillan and Co., 1888.

DeVane, William Clyde, *A Browning Handbook,* New York, F. S. Crofts and Co., 1935.

Dobell, Sydney, *Poems,* Boston, Ticknor and Fields, 1860.

——, *Thoughts on Art, Philosophy, and Religion,* London, Smith, Elder, and Co., 1876.

Elton, Oliver, *A Survey of English Literature, 1830–1880,* 2 vols. London, Edward Arnold and Co., 1832.

Frykman, Erik, *W. E. Aytoun, Pioneer Professor of English at Edinburgh,* Goteborg, Almquist and Wiksell, 1963.

Gilfillan, George, *A Gallery of Literary Portraits,* Edinburgh, William Tait, 1845; ed. W. R. Nicoll, London and New York, Dutton and Dent, 1909.

——, *A Second Gallery of Literary Portraits,* Edinburgh, James Hogg, 1850.

——, *A Third Gallery of Portraits,* New York, Sheldon, Lamport, and Blakeman, 1855.

——, *The Martyrs and Heroes of the Scottish Covenant,* Edinburgh, Gall and Inglis, 1864.

Goethe, J. W. von, *Faust—Part I,* New York, New Directions, 1949.

Gosse, Sir Edmund, *The Life of Algernon Charles Swinburne,* London, William Heinemann Ltd., 1927.

——, *Portraits and Sketches,* New York, Charles Scribner's Sons, 1912.

——, *Silhouettes,* London, William Heinemann Ltd., 1925.

Graham, Walter, *English Literary Periodicals,* New York, T. Nelson and Sons, 1930.

Grant, Sir Alexander, *The Story of the University of Edinburgh During Its First Three Hundred Years,* 2 vols. London, Longmans, Green, and Co., 1884.

Hannay, James, *Satire and Satirists,* London, D. Bogue, 1854.

Horne, Richard Hengist, *A New Spirit of the Age,* New York, Harper and Brothers, 1844.

Jolly, E., *The Life and Letters of Sydney Dobell,* 2 vols. London, Smith, Elder, and Co., 1878.

Kellett, E. E., *Suggestions,* Cambridge, Cambridge University Press, 1923.

Kingsley, Charles, *Miscellanies,* London, John W. Parker and Son, 1859.

Kitchin, George, *A Survey of Burlesque and Parody in English,* Edinburgh and London, Oliver and Boyd, 1931.

Lorimer, James, *Studies—National and International*, Edinburgh, William Green and Sons, 1890.

Macaulay, Thomas Babington, *Critical, Historical and Miscellaneous Essays*, 6 vols. Boston, Houghton, Mifflin and Co., 1886.

———, *Lays of Ancient Rome and other Historical Poems*, ed. G. M. Trevelyan, London, Longmans, Green, and Co. Ltd., 1928.

Macdonald, Dwight, ed. *Parodies: An Anthology from Chaucer to Beerbohm —and After*, New York, Random House, 1960.

Mackenzie, Agnes Mure, *The Passing of the Stewarts*, New York, The Macmillan Co., 1937.

Mallock, W. H., *Every Man his own Poet; or the Inspired Singer's Recipe Book*, London, Whittaker and Co., 1873.

Marston, J. Westland, *The Dramatic and Poetical Works*, 2 vols. London, Chatto and Windus, 1876.

———, *Gerald; A Dramatic Poem: and Other Poems*, London, C. Mitchell, 1842.

Martin, Theodore, *Memoir of William Edmondstoune Aytoun*, Edinburgh and London, William Blackwood and Sons, 1867.

Massey, Gerald, *Poems*, Boston, Ticknor and Fields, 1864.

Masson, Rosaline, *Pollok and Aytoun*, Edinburgh and London, Oliphant Anderson and Ferrier, 1898.

Millar, J. H., *A Literary History of Scotland*, New York, Charles Scribner's Sons, 1903.

Moir, D. M., *Sketches of the Poetical Literature of the Past Half-Century*, Edinburgh and London, William Blackwood and Sons, 1852.

Mordell, Albert, ed. *Notorious Literary Attacks*, New York, Boni and Liveright, 1926.

Müller, Wilhelm, *Gedichte*, Berlin, B. Behr, 1906.

Nicoll, W. R., and Wise, Thomas J., eds., *Literary Anecdotes of the Nineteenth Century*, 2 vols. London, Hodder and Stoughton, 1896.

Oliphant, Mrs. (completed by Mrs. Gerald Porter), *William Blackwood and His Sons*, 3 vols. New York, Charles Scribner's Sons, 1897.

Riewald, J. G., *Sir Max Beerbohm—Man and Writer*, The Hague, Martinus Nijhoff, 1953.

Ruskin, John, *Selections*, ed. Chauncey B. Tinker, Boston, Houghton Mifflin Co., 1908.

Smith, Alexander, *Dreamthorp*, London, Oxford University Press, 1914.

———, *Last Leaves*, ed. Patrick Proctor Alexander, Edinburgh, William P. Nimmo, 1869.

———, *The Poetical Works of Alexander Smith*, ed. W. Sinclair, Edinburgh, W. P. Nimmo, Hay, and Mitchell, 1909.

Smith, James and Horace, *Rejected Addresses: or The New Theatrum Poetarum*, London, John Miller, 1812.

Snow, Royall H., *Thomas Lovell Beddoes—Eccentric and Poet*, New York, Corici and Friede, 1928.

Swinburne, Algernon Charles, *New Writings by Swinburne or Miscellanea Nova et Curiosa,* ed. Cecil Y. Lang, Syracuse, Syracuse University Press, 1964.

Taplin, Gardner B., *The Life of Elizabeth Barrett Browning,* New Haven, Yale University Press, 1957.

Taylor, Henry, *Philip van Artevelde,* Cambridge and Boston, J. Munroe and Co., 1835.

Tennyson, Alfred Lord, *Selections,* eds. William Clyde DeVane and Mabel Phillips DeVane, New York, F. S. Crofts and Co., 1940.

Tennyson, Charles, *Alfred Tennyson,* New York, The Macmillan Co., 1949.

Tennyson, Hallam, *Alfred Lord Tennyson, A Memoir,* 2 vols. London, Macmillan and Co., Ltd., 1897.

Thackeray, William Makepeace, *The Letters and Private Papers,* ed. Gordon N. Ray, 4 vols. Cambridge, Harvard University Press, 1945–46.

Thorp, Margaret Farrand, *Charles Kingsley, 1819–1875,* Princeton, Princeton University Press, 1937.

Tredrey, F. D., *The House of Blackwood, 1804–1954,* Edinburgh and London, William Blackwood and Sons Ltd., 1954.

Trevelyan, George Otto, *The Life and Letters of Lord Macaulay,* New York, Harper and Brothers, 1877.

Trilling, Lionel, *Matthew Arnold,* New York, Meridian Books, 1955.

Walker, Hugh, *The Literature of the Victorian Era,* Cambridge, Cambridge University Press, 1910.

Warren, Alba H., *English Poetic Theory, 1825–1865,* Princeton, Princeton University Press, 1950.

Watson, Robert A. and Elizabeth S., *George Gilfillan: Letters and Journals, with Memoir,* London, Hodder and Stoughton, 1892.

Selected Periodical Contributions

Bayne, Thomas, "Our Modern Poets: The Scotch Professors," *St. James's Magazine,* 2 (1876), 157–67, 270–80.

Blackwood, William, "The Death of William Aytoun," *Blackwood's,* 98 (1865), 384–88.

Clough, Arthur Hugh, "Recent English Poetry," *The North American Review,* 77 (1853), 1–30.

Cox, R. G., "The Great Reviews," *Scrutiny,* 6 (1937), 2–20, 155–75.

———, "Victorian Criticism of Poetry: The Minority Tradition," *Scrutiny,* 18 (1951), 2–17.

Garrod, H. W., "Matthew Arnold's 1853 Preface," *Review of English Studies,* 17 (1941), 310–21.

Gilfillan, George, "Recent Poetry," *The Eclectic Review,* N.S. 2 (1851), 447–62.

Hannay, James, "Recent Humorists: Aytoun, Peacock, Prout," *The North British Review,* 45 (1866), 75–104.

Kingsley, Charles, "Alexander Smith and Alexander Pope," *Fraser's, 48* (1853), 452–66.

———, "Thoughts on Shelley and Byron," *Fraser's, 48* (1853), 568–76.

Ludlow, J. M., "Theories of Poetry and a New Poet," *The North British Review, 19* (1853), 297–344.

Maurer, Oscar, "Anonymity vs. Signature in Victorian Reviewing," *University of Texas Studies in English, 27* (1948), 1–27.

McKillop, Alan D., "A Victorian Faust," *PMLA, 40* (1925), 743–68.

Millar, J. H., "William Edmondstoune Aytoun," *The New Review, 14* (1896), 103–12.

"The Minstrelsy of Scotland," *The Quarterly Review, 105* (1859), 305–41.

"Modern Light Literature—Poetry," *Blackwood's, 79* (1856), 125–38.

"Modern Poetry: its Genius and Tendencies," *The London Quarterly Review, 2* (1854), 238–57.

Patmore, Coventry, "New Poets," *The Edinburgh Review, 104* (1856), 337–62.

"Poetry—The Spasmodists," *The North British Review, 28* (1858), 231–50.

Shannon, Edgar F., "The Critical Reception of Tennyson's 'Maud,' " *PMLA, 68* (1953), 397–417.

Smith, Alexander, "Wardie—Spring-Time," *Good Words* (1862), pp. 272–73.

Somerville, D. C., "The Reputation of Robert Browning," *Essays and Studies, 15* (1929), 122–38.

Spencer, Herbert, "The Philosophy of Style," *The Westminster Review,* N.S. 2 (1852), 435–59.

Swinburne, Algernon Charles, "The Monomaniac's Tragedy, and Other Poems. By Ernest Wheldrake," *Undergraduate Papers,* No. 2, Pt. 3 (1858), pp. 97–102.

Thale, Jerome, "Browning's 'Popularity' and the Spasmodic Poets," *JEGP, 54* (1955), 348–54.

INDEX

Ainsworth, William Harrison, 74

Alison, Sir Archibald, 37

Aristotle, theory of poetry rejected by Spasmodics, 100-01, 127

Arnold, anonymous Spasmodic poem, 76

Arnold, Edwin, Aytoun's article "The Two Arnolds," 116-18

Arnold, Matthew, 45, 58, 99, 141 n., 180 n.; and Clough's review of Smith and Arnold, 102-04; criticism of Keats, Browning, and Shelley, 102-03; criticism of Smith, 102; 1853 Preface discussed, 104-07, 110, 118; Aytoun's article "The Two Arnolds," 116-18; contrasted favorably with Spasmodics in post-*Firmilian* criticism, 154-56

Athenaeum, The, 35 n., 76 n., 151 n., 183, 184 n., 185 n., 211 n., 214 n.; on Smith's *Edwin of Deira*, 169

Aytoun, Mrs. (mother), influence on Aytoun and friendship with Scott family, 4

Aytoun, Roger: and education of Aytoun, 4-5; and publication of *Poland, Homer, and Other Poems*, 8

Aytoun, William Edmondstoune

life: family and childhood influences, 3-5; education and early verses, 5-8; conservatism, 10-11, 17-18; law practice, 16-17, 20; studies in Germany, 18-19; religious beliefs, 21; as professor of Edinburgh University, 35-36, marriage, 41-42; termination of interest in politics, 109; death of wife, 214-15; disappointment over public

affairs, 215-16; sadness after wife's death and last years, 216-17

literary career and periodical writings: translation of *Faust*, 8, 19; early influence of Byron and Shelley, 11-12, 14-16; first contributions to *Blackwood's*, 20-21; prose pamphlets published, 21; Bon Gaultier parodies in periodicals, 27; prose parodies by Bon Gaultier, 34-35; as staff member of *Blackwood's*, 36-41; attacks on "railway mania," 38-39; attacks on Free Trade, 39; *Blackwood's* short stories, 39-41; translation of Müller, 44 n.; discussed as balladist in relation to Macaulay, 45-49; defense of ballad genre, 50-51; defense of Tory viewpoint of his ballads, 51-52; concept of balladist as minstrel, 56; development of position in controversy between "subjective" and "objective" poetry, 57-59; *Faust* criticized as model for Spasmodics, 63-64, 113; Byron criticized as model for Spasmodics, 65; ballads criticized by Gilfillan, 84; relative influence of *Firmilian* and Arnold's 1853 Preface, 106-07; origin of term "Spasmodic," 107; critical position, 108-12, 188-89; attack on Longfellow's *Golden Legend* and Bailey, 112-14; feud with Gilfillan before *Firmilian*, 114-18; praise of Edwin and Matthew Arnold, 116, 118; attack on Ruskin's *Lectures*, 144-45; denunciation of Catho-